Lecture Notes in Computer Science   14457

Founding Editors

Gerhard Goos
Juris Hartmanis

The series Lecture Notes in Computer Science (LNCS), including its subseries Lecture Notes in Artificial Intelligence (LNAI) and Lecture Notes in Bioinformatics (LNBI), has established itself as a medium for the publication of new developments in computer science and information technology research, teaching, and education.

LNCS enjoys close cooperation with the computer science R & D community, the series counts many renowned academics among its volume editors and paper authors, and collaborates with prestigious societies. Its mission is to serve this international community by providing an invaluable service, mainly focused on the publication of conference and workshop proceedings and postproceedings. LNCS commenced publication in 1973.

Dion H. Goh · Shu-Jiun Chen ·
Suppawong Tuarob
Editors

Leveraging Generative Intelligence in Digital Libraries: Towards Human-Machine Collaboration

25th International Conference on Asia-Pacific Digital Libraries, ICADL 2023
Taipei, Taiwan, December 4–7, 2023
Proceedings, Part I

 Springer

Editors
Dion H. Goh ⓘ
Nanyang Technological University
Singapore, Singapore

Shu-Jiun Chen ⓘ
Academia Sinica
Taipei, Taiwan

Suppawong Tuarob ⓘ
Mahidol University
Tambon Salaya, Amphoe Phutthamonthon,
Thailand

ISSN 0302-9743   ISSN 1611-3349 (electronic)
Lecture Notes in Computer Science
ISBN 978-981-99-8084-0   ISBN 978-981-99-8085-7 (eBook)
https://doi.org/10.1007/978-981-99-8085-7

This Springer imprint is published by the registered company Springer Nature Singapore Pte Ltd.
The registered company address is: 152 Beach Road, #21-01/04 Gateway East, Singapore 189721, Singapore

Paper in this product is recyclable.

Preface

Welcome to the proceedings of the of the 25th International Conference on Asia-Pacific Digital Libraries (ICADL 2023; https://icadl.net/icadl2023/). Since its inception in 1998 in Hong Kong, the ICADL series has become one of the major digital libraries conferences, along with the Joint Conference on Digital Libraries (JCDL) and the Theory and Practice of Digital Libraries (TPDL) conferences, where researchers and practitioners meet, network, and share knowledge and best practices.

This year's edition of the conference was held in Taipei, Taiwan from December 4 to December 7, 2023. As more countries around the world emerge from the COVID-19 pandemic, the conference was organized as an in-person event, but also featured online presentations for participants who were not able to travel to Taipei. ICADL 2023 was co-located with the 11th Asia-Pacific Conference on Library Information Education and Practice (A-LIEP 2023; https://a-liep.org/) as well as the annual meeting of the Asia-Pacific chapter of iSchools (AP iSchools; https://ischools.org/). These events were collectively known as the "2023 International Forum on Data, Information, and Knowledge for Resilient and Trustworthy Digital Societies" (https://ifdik2023.conf.tw/site/page.aspx?pid=901&sid=1521&lang=en).

In recognition of the growth and popularity of generative artificial intelligence (GAI), the theme of ICADL 2023 was "Leveraging Generative Intelligence in Digital Libraries: Towards Human-Machine Collaboration". In a relatively short span of time, GAI applications such as ChatGPT and Midjourney have captured the public's imagination with their potential for content generation. Being repositories of knowledge, digital libraries and their stakeholders may be positively or negatively impacted by GAI. Consequently, this conference aimed to explore the role of GAI in digital libraries and welcomed papers in this regard.

In response to the conference call, 85 papers from 21 countries were submitted to ICADL 2023. The review process was double-blind. Each submission was reviewed by at least three Program Committee (PC) members. Based on the reviews and recommendation from the PC, 15 full papers, 17 short papers, 2 practice papers and 12 poster papers were selected for inclusion in the proceedings. These papers covered a diverse range of topics, reflecting the interdisciplinary nature of the field of digital libraries. These topics include information retrieval, knowledge extraction and discovery, cultural and scholarly data, information seeking and use, digital archives and data management, design and evaluation of information environments, and applications of GAI in digital libraries.

We would like to thank all those who contributed to ICADL 2023. This conference would not have been possible without the effort and teamwork of many individuals across the globe. We thank the members of the Program Committee for their time, effort and expertise in reviewing the submissions. The Conference Chair, Hao-Ren Ke, worked tirelessly to bring this conference to fruition. Thanks also to the Publicity Chairs, Songphan Choemprayong, Adam Jatowt, Chern Li Liew, Akira Maeda, Maciej Ogrodniczuk and Sue Yeon Syn, as well as the Web Chair, Shun-Hong Sie. In addition, we are grateful to Adam Jatowt, Emi Ishita and Shigeo Sugimoto who have provided leadership and support during the planning and implementation phases of this conference.

Finally, we would like to thank all the authors, presenters, and participants of ICADL 2023. This conference is made possible by your support and contributions.

December 2023

Dion H. Goh
Shu-Jiun Chen
Suppawong Tuarob

Organization

Conference Co-chairs

Shu-Hsien Tseng National Central Library, Taiwan
Hao-Ren Ke National Taiwan Normal University, Taiwan

Program Committee Co-chairs

Dion H. Goh Nanyang Technological University, Singapore
Shu-Jiun Chen Academia Sinica, Taiwan
Suppawong Tuarob Mahidol University, Thailand

Publicity Co-chairs

Songphan Choemprayong Chulalongkorn University, Thailand
Adam Jatowt University of Innsbruck, Austria
Chern Li Liew Victoria University of Wellington, New Zealand
Akira Maeda Ritsumeikan University, Japan
Maciej Ogrodniczuk Institute of Computer Science, Polish Academy of
Sciences, Poland
Sue Yeon Syn Catholic University of America, USA

Web Chair

Shun-Hong Sie National Taiwan Normal University, Taiwan

Program Committee

Trond Aalberg Norwegian University of Science and Technology,
Norway
Biligsaikhan Batjargal Ritsumeikan University, Japan
Chih-Ming Chen National Chengchi University, Taiwan
Kun-Hung Cheng National Chung Hsing University, Taiwan
Songphan Choemprayong Chulalongkorn University, Thailand

Chiawei Chu	City University of Macau, China
Mickaël Coustaty	La Rochelle Université, France
Fabio Crestani	Università della Svizzera Italiana, Switzerland
Edward Fox	Virginia Tech, USA
Liangcai Gao	Peking University, China
Jen Jou Hung	Dharma Drum Institute of Liberal Arts, Taiwan
Emi Ishita	Kyushu University, Japan
Hiroyoshi Ito	University of Tsukuba, Japan
Adam Jatowt	University of Innsbruck, Austria
Makoto P. Kato	University of Tsukuba, Japan
Marie Katsurai	Doshisha University, Japan
Yukiko Kawai	Kyoto Sangyo University, Japan
Hao-Ren Ke	National Taiwan Normal University, Taiwan
Mat Kelly	Drexel University, USA
Christopher S. G. Khoo	Nanyang Technological University, Singapore
Yunhyong Kim	University of Glasgow, UK
Chei Sian Lee	Nanyang Technological University, Singapore
Shaobo Liang	Wuhan University, China
Chern Li Liew	Victoria University of Wellington, New Zealand
Chung-Ming Lo	National Chengchi University, Taiwan
Akira Maeda	Ritsumeikan University, Japan
Muhammad Syafiq Mohd Pozi	Universiti Utara Malaysia, Malaysia
Atsuyuki Morishima	University of Tsukuba, Japan
Jin-Cheon Na	Nanyang Technological University, Singapore
David Nichols	University of Waikato, New Zealand
Chifumi Nishioka	National Institute of Informatics, Japan
Maciej Ogrodniczuk	Institute of Computer Science, Polish Academy of Sciences, Poland
Hiroaki Ohshima	University of Hyogo, Japan
Gillian Oliver	Monash University, Australia
Christos Papatheodorou	National and Kapodistrian University of Athens, Greece
Magnus Pfeffer	Stuttgart Media University, Germany
Yohei Seki	University of Tsukuba, Japan
Shigeo Sugimoto	University of Tsukuba, Japan
Kazunari Sugiyama	Osaka Seikei University, Japan
Yasunobu Sumikawa	Takushoku University, Japan
Sue Yeon Syn	Catholic University of America, USA
Masao Takaku	University of Tsukuba, Japan
Diane Velasquez	University of South Australia, Australia
Shoko Wakamiya	Nara Institute of Science and Technology, Japan
Di Wang	Renmin University of China, China

Chiranthi Wijesundara	University of Colombo, Sri Lanka
Dan Wu	Wuhan University, China
Zhiwu Xie	University of California, Riverside, USA
Marcia Zeng	Kent State University, USA
Maja Žumer	University of Ljubljana, Slovenia

Additional Reviewers

Banerjee, Bipasha
Bernard, Guillaume
Day, Min-Yuh
Husnain, Mujtaba
Iqbal Kajla, Nadeem
Kahu, Sampanna

Li, Da
Mibayashi, Ryota
Mohd Pozi, Muhammad Syafiq
Wang, Yuanyuan
Wu, Qian

Contents – Part I

Social Media Analytics

Information Retrieval

Information Seeking and Use

Contents – Part II

Scholarly Information Processing

Knowledge Extraction

GAI and Digital Libraries

Enhancing the Learning of Chinese Poem Creation Through an Auto-Generation and Evaluation System

Yan Cong[1]([⊠]) [iD] and Masao Takaku[2] [iD]

[1] Graduate School of Library, Information and Media Studies, University of Tsukuba, Tsukuba, Japan
cong.y@slis.tsukuba.ac.jp
[2] Institute of Library, Information and Media Science, University of Tsukuba, Tsukuba, Japan
masao@slis.tsukuba.ac.jp

Abstract. Creating and evaluating Chinese poems is challenging for learners. To address this, we propose an auto-generation model and evaluation system to assist learners in poem creation and provide feedback on constraint adherence. We conducted a user experiment with 16 participants and generated up to 100 poems per keyword using 29 random keywords. The proposed system significantly improved poem completeness and usability, but did not enhance creation satisfaction. Users found it easy to confirm adherence to poem rules, but that verifying rhymes presented difficulties. The participants expressed overall satisfaction with the process, and the poems created were perceived as fluent and thematically consistent. However, limitations in keyword usage hinder emotional expression. This study highlights the need to overcome these challenges in order to facilitate learners' creation and evaluation of Chinese poems.

Keywords: Generation · Evaluation · GPT-2 model · User Interface · Constraints of Tang poems

1 Introduction

Tang poems are indispensable resources in Chinese classical literature and culture. Written during the Tang Dynasty of China from (7th - 10th centuries CE), they are known for their unique styles and strict constraints, such as rhyme and tone patterns, which help readers understand the meanings, thoughts, and intentions of the poems.

The 2018 edition of the Upper Secondary School Curriculum Guidelines in Japan [5] introduced a language activity that encouraged students to create Chinese poems while checking their styles and rhythmic rules. However, the implementation of such activities has been limited because of the lack of relevant case studies and resources [16,17]. Additionally, instructors need a greater understanding of and interest in Chinese poem creation, which further hinders the promotion of such activities.

© The Author(s), under exclusive license to Springer Nature Singapore Pte Ltd. 2023
D. H. Goh et al. (Eds.): ICADL 2023, LNCS 14457, pp. 3–17, 2023.
https://doi.org/10.1007/978-981-99-8085-7_1

The traditional method of creating a poem [6,14] involves comprehending word meanings, understanding styles and rhyming rules, and reference to a poetry dictionary [7]. However, this process can be challenging because it requires a deep understanding of the meanings of words and an adherence to the rules of Tang poems [15]. Consequently, beginners often struggle to select poetic words and adhere to certain constraints when creating Chinese poems.

To facilitate the process of poem creation, we utilized an automatic generation model that simplifies the task compared to traditional methods. Automatic generation of poems allows beginners to experience the process of writing high-quality poems that conform to the styles and constraints without a deep understanding of words and rules. By providing an engaging experience, this approach not only promotes the study of Chinese classical literature but also garners interest in poem creation.

We addressed the challenge of evaluating the created poems, by implementing an evaluation system consisting of rule judgment and scoring subsystems. The rule judgment subsystem determines rule compliance, whereas the scoring subsystem assigns scores based on rule adherence. By combining an auto-generation system with an evaluation system, our approach simplifies the poem creation process and enhances the learning of beginners.

In summary, our research makes the following contributions:

(1) We propose a method to assist beginners in overcoming the challenges of creating poems by utilizing automated generation models and an evaluation system to score poems created according to the rules of Chinese poems.
(2) The proposed system supports beginners to experience the process of creating poems without requiring an in-depth understanding of methods of poem creation. It provides hints and feedback on the adherence to the constraints after poem creation.

Additionally, our research aims to address the following research questions (RQs).

RQ1. Can the proposed system enhance poem creation in terms of (a) poem completeness; (b) creation satisfaction; and (c) usability (ease of use)?
RQ2. Can the proposed system facilitate user adherence to the constraints of poem creations?
RQ3. How do users perceive the created poems in terms of the expressive power of the content?

2   Related Work

In our review of related works in the fields of auto-generation systems and learning support systems for Chinese poetry, we compared these studies with our research to identify differences.

Automatic Generation of Chinese Poems. Several recent studies have explored different methods for generating Chinese poetry using various language models. For instance, Wang et al. [21] proposed a method for poem generation using a recurrent neural network (RNN) Encoder-Decoder model to ensure coherence and meaning in the generated poems based on the user's intention. Evaluation of their research indicated the effectiveness of their approach to poem generation based on manual assessments of the quality of the generated poems. Yi et al. [22] proposed the generation of Chinese poetry and developed a system for automatically generating quatrains using an RNN Encoder-Decoder model. While their automatically generated poems received high ratings, they had issues adhering to the basic rhymes and structural rules of Chinese poetry. These methods primarily focus on the approach to poem generation based on the intentions of users and aim to create poems of the highest quality.

Hirata et al. [10] proposed an approach for automatically generating Japanese haiku using the GPT-2 language model. They evaluated the effectiveness of the language model in haiku generation by using their own evaluation metrics for adherence to the constraints of haiku.

Wang et al. [21] and Yi et al. [22] primarily focused on automatic generation, examining the relationships between poetic phrases, coherence, and meaning in a poem.

By contrast, our approach combines a pre-trained GPT-2 automatic generation model with an evaluation system for constraint-adherence feedback.

Support Systems for Learning Chinese Poems. Qiu et al. [18,19] developed a support system for the creation of Chinese poetry by users in Japan by selecting options for poems. They constructed a database of Chinese poetic words categorized by tone patterns and used it to create poems from the last line of poetry. Ishida et al. [12,13] designed a website for beginners to correct Chinese poetry by adhering to the constraints of a poem.

Unlike existing research, our study focuses on both the automatic generation of Chinese poetry and support for adherence to the constraints of poems, while covering comprehensive aspects such as tone patterns, fluency, and coherence in poem creation. Furthermore, previous evaluation systems focused mainly on combining poetic phrases to generate poems. Our approach allows the simultaneous generation of individual keywords and characters. In our research, the poems are automatically generated by a language model, followed by an integration system that verifies the generated poems to provide a score ranking using the proposed system and visualizes the verified results through a user interface.

3   Methodology

The proposed system comprises the following three mechanisms: an automatic generation system, and an evaluation system that includes rule judgment and scoring subsystems.

As shown in Fig. 1, the system operates as follows: (1) A user inputs a keyword into the system, and the automatic generation system utilizes a pre-trained GPT-2 model [9] to generate poems based on the keyword. (2) All generated poems are passed on to the rule judgment subsystem. The subsystem judges the poems based on adherence to styles, rhymes, and tone-pattern rules. It then provides the judgment results of the structural constraints, referred to as Result 1. (3) Result 1 is passed through the scoring subsystem, which assigns scores to poems based on their adherence to rules. Poems scoring over 500 points are delivered to users, as shown in Results 2.

This chapter explains our system and the characteristics of Tang poems, including their styles, rhymes, and tone patterns. We introduce how we incorporated them into our generation and evaluation of poems.

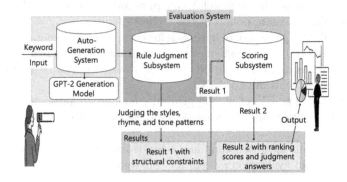

Fig. 1. The Overview of the Proposed System

3.1   Automatic Generation System

Several GPT-2 Chinese language models have been trained on Chinese, such as gpt2-chinese-cluecorpussmall [4]. We used a pre-trained GPT-2 poetry model [20] to automatically generate poems. This GPT-2 model was pre-trained on over 800,000 Chinese poems supplied by GPT2-Chinese [9].

3.2   Rule Judgment Subsystem

The evaluation system determines whether the created poems match the rules of (a) style, (b) rhyme, and (c) tone patterns using the rule judgment subsystem, and ranks the results for presentation to users via the scoring subsystem. In this section, we introduce the rules for poems and how they work within the rule judgment subsystem.

When the rule judgment subsystem deals with the judgment results, the matched results are judged as "True" and are further assigned 1 or 0.5 points. The mismatched results are represented as "False" and are assigned a value of 0 for the scoring subsystem.

Styles. Tang poems are famous for their unique styles, which include five-syllable, seven-syllable, quatrain (絕句, jueju) and regulated verse (律詩, lushi)

[6,15]. These styles are characterized by specific rules regarding the number of characters in each line and the number of lines in a poem.

The system checks the styles of all the generated poems. If a poem satisfies a particular style, the system will continue checking further constraints. If the poem does not adhere to the style rules, the scoring subsystem assigns a score of -1.

Rhyme [8,11]. Rhyme in Tang poems refers to the repetition of the same vowel at the end of specific lines. Specifically, in a quatrain, the 1st, 2nd, and 4th lines or the 2nd and 4th lines rhyme. Characters with the same vowel are regarded as rhyming characters. In terms of tone, it is preferred for these characters to have a level rather than oblique tone.

We used the simplified table of the 14 New Chinese Rhymes [2] by the Chinese Poetry and Verse Society to judge rhyming characters. This table, which consists of a brief list of 14 rhymes, was compiled based on standard Chinese pinyin.

The rule judgment subsystem checks rhymes as shown in Table 1: (1) When the same rhyme is used in the 1st, 2nd and 4th lines, 1 point is assigned. (2) When a rhyme is used in the 2nd, and 4th lines, 0.5 points are assigned. (3) When the rhyme character has a level tone, the result is judged as 1 point. Results that do not match these rules are assigned a score of 0.

Table 1. Rhyme Rules and Judgment Results

Rhyme Rules	Judgment Results
(1) Whether the 1st, 2nd, and 4th lines rhyme	1 point
(2) When the 2nd and 4th lines rhyme	0.5 points
(3) Level tone or oblique tone on rhyme character	Level - tone (平): 1

Tone pattern [8,11]. Tone patterns consist of level tone (平 by character), marked as ○, and oblique tone (仄 by character), marked as ●. This indicates tonal variation in the characters.

We use the Ping Shui Rhyme table [3] and Chinese Pin Yin Library in Python [1] to determine the character tones. The system checks the following six constraints and returns the judgment results, as presented in Table 2.

(1) 2–4 Different (二四不同): This means the 2nd character needs to differ from the 4th character in tone in each line of a quatrain. The rule judgment subsystem checks whether the tones of the 2nd and 4th characters differ in a line for the fourth time during the quatrain. If the tones differ, 1 point is assigned. and 0 points otherwise.

(2) 2–6 Same (二六对): This constraint is specific to 7-syllable quatrains. The tone of the 2nd character in each line of the 7-syllable quatrain should be the same as that of the 6th character. In the case of a 7-syllable poem, the rule judgment subsystem checks whether the tone of the 2nd character is the same as that of the 6th. If so, 1 point is assigned, and 0 points otherwise.

Table 2. Tone Pattern Rules and Judgment Results

Tone Pattern Rules	Judgment Results
Tone patterns of characters	Level (平), Oblique (仄)
(1) 2–4 Different (二四不同)	Different : 1
(2) 2–6 Same (二六対)	Same : 1
(3) Fan Bo (反包)	Different : 1
(4) Nian Fa (粘法)	Same : 1
(5) No same tones at last 3 characters	No same tones : 1
(6) Without using the same characters	Without same characters : 1

(3) Fan Bao (反包): In a 5-syllable quatrain, the tones of the 2nd character differ in the 1st and 2nd lines, and between the 3rd and 4th lines. In addition, the tone of the 4th character should differ. The rule judgment subsystem checks whether the tones of the characters between lines differ in a quatrain. In a 7-syllable quatrain, the 6th characters should differ between lines. The system checks each character between lines four times in a 5-syllable quatrain, and six times in a 7-syllable quatrain. If the tones of the characters are different, 1 point is assigned and otherwise, 0 points. The system records the results of the checks.

(4) Nian Fa (粘法): In a 5-syllable quatrain, the tones of the 2nd characters should be the same in the 2nd and 3rd lines. Similarly, the tones of the 4th character should be the same. In a 7-syllable quatrain, the 6th character tones should be the same as well. The rule judgment subsystem checks whether character tones are the same between pairs of lines. If the tones of the characters are the same, 1 point, and 0 points otherwise. When a judgment result is received, the system records the results for the number of checks.

(5) Without using the same tones for the last 3 characters: The last 3 characters should not all use the same tones, whether level (marked "○○○") or oblique (marked "●●●"). The rule judgment subsystem checks whether the last three characters of each line of a poem have different tones. If there are no same tones for the last characters at the end of each line, 1 point is assigned, and 0 points otherwise. Subsequently, the results are recoded for the number of checks.

(6) The same character should not be used twice in a poem, except for reduplicated characters pairs. The rule judgment subsystem determines whether a poem has been written without the same characters. If no duplicate characters are found, the system judges the result as 1 point and otherwise, 0 points. The results are recoded for the number of checks.

3.3 Scoring Subsystem

The scoring subsystem calculates the scores for all constraints of the rhyme and tone patterns based on the points recorded by the rule judgment subsystem. The scoring subsystem then ranks and presents the poems based on the scores. This section introduces the metrics used in the scoring subsystem.

Rhyme constraints calculate scores based on the three rules of rhyme in Table 1. Formula (1) shows the scoring metric, where $RhymeScore$ is the total score of the rhymes, and R_1, R_2, and R_3 are the results of the three rhyme rules. The $RhymeScore$ is determined as follows: If R_1 is greater than zero, the $RhymeScore$ is calculated as the sum of R_1 multiplied by 100 and R_3 multiplied by 100; if R_2 is greater than zero, $RhymeScore$ is R_2 multiplied by 100, and plus R_3 multiplied by 100.

$$RhymeScore = \begin{cases} R_1 \times 100 + R_3 \times 100 & \text{if } R_1 > 0 \\ R_2 \times 100 + R_3 \times 100 & \text{if } R_2 > 0 \end{cases} \tag{1}$$

The tone pattern constraints are calculated as the sum of the scores under the six rules defined in Table 2. The scoring metric is calculated using Formula (2), where $TonePatternScore$ is the total score for the tone patterns, IP is the ideal point, and P_i is the i-th number of points. $TonePatternScore$ is calculated as the ratio of the sum of points achieved for each rule to the sum of the ideal points for each rule. This ratio is then multiplied by 100. It represents a score that reflects adherence to the tone-pattern constraints.

$$TonePatternScore = \frac{\sum_{i=1}^{6} P_i}{\sum_{i=1}^{6} IP_i} \times 100 \tag{2}$$

The total scores for the rhyme and tone patterns are calculated using Formula (3). In this formula, $TotalScore$ is obtained by adding the $RhymeScore$ and $TonePatternScore$. After calculating the $TotalScore$, poems can be ranked based on their overall adherence to rhyme and tone pattern constraints.

$$TotalScore = RhymeScore + TonePatternScore \tag{3}$$

4 User Experiment

We conducted an experiment to assess the usefulness of the proposed system from the user's perspective. In the experiment, the proposed system was evaluated with the created poems to demonstrate the completion of the poem creation process, verify whether the created poems were aligned with constraints, and assess user satisfaction.

The user experiment was conducted between April 18 and 27, 2023. We recruited 16 native Japanese speakers for the experiments, from universities and technical schools who were beginners in Chinese poetry. Of the 16 participants, 13 were majoring in informatics, 2 in life sciences, and 1 in dental hygiene.

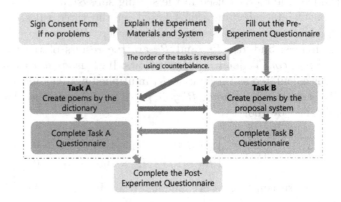

Fig. 2. Procedures of User Experiment

4.1 Experimental Design

Experimental Procedures. Figure 2 shows the user experiment procedures. First, the participants read and signed consent forms without any issues. The experimental materials and the system were then explained to the participants. Before starting the tasks, participants completed pre-experiment questionnaires that included demographic information and prior knowledge of Tang poems. Next, the participants were asked to create poems in both Tasks A and B. In Tasks A and B, the participants were instructed to create poems using a poem dictionary [7] and the proposed system within 25 min, respectively. After creating poems for each task, participants completed post-task questionnaires. Finally, participants provided feedback by completing the post-experiment questionnaire.

We reversed the order of Tasks A and B with random assignment to ensure counter-balanced and fair results between the participant groups.

User Interface. We developed the user interface used in Task B, as illustrated in Fig. 3. Once a participant selects a keyword on Page A interface presents the contents of the auto-generated poems along with the ranking scores on Page B. When a participant clicks to a poem linked on Page B, the tone patterns of the characters and rule judgment results are shown on the next Page C. The results consist of two components on Page C: One is the content of the created poems with the characteristics of tone patterns, and the other is the rule judgment results in a separate table below the created poems.

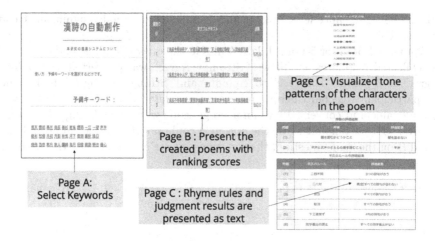

Fig. 3. User Interface

Experimental Keywords. We selected a set of keywords for poem creation. These keywords were intended to be attached to the beginning of the poem to be created.

The keywords were selected from a poem dictionary, "Chinese poetry creation documents" [7] with a random function. After randomly selecting keywords individually from the 34 chapters containing approximately 13,750 words, duplicates and keywords that did not return results were removed, resulting in 29 keywords.

Experimental Parameters. In our experimental setting, we employed a pre-trained GPT-2 poetry model to generate up to 100 poems based on a given keyword. In this study, we only focused on generating 7-syllable quatrains with four lines. Using the pre-trained GPT-2 model, the keyword was attached to the beginning of the first line of the poem.

Experimental Questionnaires. Four questionnaires were designed for the experiment. They were the pre- and post-experiment questionnaires and two post-task questionnaires, Task A and B questionnaires. The Task A and B questionnaires were designed using the same questions to compare the results obtained from the two methods. The pre-questionnaire was administered before the participants began the experiment to gather relevant information. The post-questionnaire was administered after completion of the experiment to collect feedback and insights from participants regarding their overall experience.

4.2 Analysis Methods and Results

Analysis Method. We focused on analyzing responses to the post-task and post-experiment questionnaires, and employed significance testing to compare the results between Tasks A and B in the post-task questionnaires using the t-test. The significance level was set at 5%, and the marginally significant trend level at 10%.

We used 4-point or 5-point Likert scales in the questionnaires, and converted the collected responses as follows: "Strongly Agree" was converted to 4 points, "Agree" to 3 points, "Disagree" to 2 points, and "Strongly Disagree" to 1 point. If a participant selected the option "I could not determine," it was treated as a missing value and converted into an average value when calculating the t-value. However, if a participant chose the option "I could not determine" in both Tasks A and B on the same question, these responses were excluded from the analysis.

Table 3. Results of the Post-task Questionnaires; Note: **($p < 0.1$), *($p < 0.5$), +($p < .10$)

No.	Questions	Task A Mean (SD)	Task B Mean (SD)	t - value
Q1	Poem Completeness	1.31 (1.21)	3.44 (1.06)	$t(16) = 6.07$ **
Q2	Creation Satisfaction	3.00 (0.87)	3.19 (0.39)	$t(15) = 0.84$
Q3	Poem Styles Confirmation	3.06 (0.83)	3.75 (0.56)	$t(15) = 2.57$ *
Q4	Rhyme Confirmation	2.20 (0.81)	2.80 (0.95)	$t(15) = 1.61$
Q5	Rhyme Character Confirmation	2.87 (0.70)	3.31 (0.77)	$t(15) = 2.00$ +
Q6	Tone Patterns Confirmation	2.81 (0.81)	3.38 (0.70)	$t(15) = 2.05$ +
Q7	Fluency Satisfaction	2.14 (0.45)	3.25 (0.55)	$t(13) = 5.34$ **
Q8	Is the poem written on the same theme?	2.54 (0.81)	3.44 (0.40)	$t(13) = 3.77$ **
Q9	Does the poem express feelings?	2.21 (0.94)	2.27 (0.85)	$t(13) = 0.27$

Results of Post-Task Questionnaires. Table 3 presents the analysis of the results of questions Q1 to Q9 in the post-task questionnaires. The table includes the following information: the mean and standard deviation (SD) for both tasks, t-values, and significance levels (p).

Q1, regarding Poem Completeness, showed that the mean of Task A was 1.31 (SD=1.21), while the mean of Task B was 3.44 (SD=1.06). The t-value indicates a statistically significant difference between Tasks A and B. The results for Task B were more complete than those for Task A ($p < .01$; $t(16) = 6.07$).

Q2, regarding Creation Satisfaction, showed that the mean of Task A was 3.00 (SD=0.87), while the mean of Task B was 3.19 (SD=0.39). The t-value showed that there was no significant difference between Tasks A and B ($p > .10$; $t(15) = 0.84$).

Q3, regarding Poem Style Confirmation, showed that the mean of Task A was 3.06 (SD=0.83), while the mean of Task B was 3.75 (SD=0.56). The t-value showed a significant difference between Tasks A and B ($p < .05$; $t(15) = 2.57$).

Q4, regarding Rhyme Confirmation, showed that the mean of Task A was 2.20 (SD=0.81), while the mean of Task B was 2.80 (SD=0.95). The t-value showed no significant difference between Tasks A and B ($p > .10$; $t(15) = 1.61$).

Q5, regarding Rhyme Character Confirmation, showed the mean of Task A was 2.87 (SD=0.7), while the mean of Task B was 3.31 (SD=0.77). The t-value showed that a significant trend with a significance greater than 0.05 and less than 0.10 ($0.05 < p < 0.10$; $t(15) = 2.00$).

Q6, regarding Tone Patterns Confirmation, showed that the mean of Task A was 2.81 (SD=0.81), while the mean of Task B was 3.38 (SD=0.70). The t-value indicated a significant trend with the significance greater than 0.05 and less than 0.10 ($0.05 < p < 0.10$; $t(15) = 2.05$).

Q7, regarding Fluency Satisfaction, showed that the mean of Task A was 2.14 (SD=0.45), while the mean of Task B was 3.25 (SD=0.55). The t-value indicated that there was a statistically significant difference ($p < 0.01$; $t(13) = 5.34$). Task B received significantly higher ratings than did Task A.

Q8, regarding Whether a poem, is written on the same theme indicated the mean of Task A was 2.54 (SD=0.81), while the mean of Task B was 3.44 (SD=0.4). The t-values differed a significantly ($p < 0.01$; $t(13) = 3.77$). Task B received significantly higher ratings than did Task A.

Q9, regarding Does the poem express feelings, showed the mean of Task A was 2.21 (SD=0.94), while the mean of Task B was 2.27 (SD=0.85). Based on the t-values, we found no significant difference ($p > 0.10$; $t(13) = 0.27$).

Results of Post-Experiment Questionnaire. Table 4 demonstrates the distribution of questions from Q1 to Q6 of the post-experiment questionnaire. In addition, the participants provided free comments regarding their overall impressions of the proposed system.

Table 4. Results of the Post-experiment Questionnaire

No.	Post-experiment Questionnaire Questions	Strongly Agree	Agree	Disagree	Strongly Disagree
Q1	Was the system able to create the poems?	12	4	0	0
Q2	Was the system able to confirm the rhyme?	4	9	2	1
Q3	Was the system able confirm the tone patterns?	12	4	0	0
Q4	Do you think using the proposed system made it easier to confirm the rhyme?	10	2	4	0
Q5	Do you think using the proposed system made it easier to confirm the tone patterns?	10	6	0	0
Q6	Do you think the proposed system was easy to use?	9	7	0	0

For Q1, 12 participants strongly agreed, and 4 agreed that they could complete poems using the proposed system. For Q2, 13 participants agreed, while 3 disagreed, on confirming the rhyme smoothly. For Q3, 12 participants strongly agreed, and 4 agreed that the proposed system confirmed the tone patterns. For Q4, 12 participants agreed, and 4 disagreed that the system helped to confirm the rhymes. For Q5, all participants expressed positive agreement, that it was easier to confirm the tone patterns presented by the proposed system. In Q6, all the participants agreed that the proposed system was easy to use.

These results indicate that most participants found the proposed system helpful in creating poems smoothly and confirming tone patterns, and that it displayed the ease of use. However, some participants expressed difficulties in confirming the rhymes using the system.

5   Discussion

In this section, we answer the research questions (RQs) based on the results of the post-task questionnaires (P-TQ), post-experiment questionnaires (P-EQ), and free descriptions of the P-EQ. We also discuss the limitations of our study.

RQ1. Can the proposed system enhance poem creation in terms of (a) poem completeness, (b) creation satisfaction, and (c) usability? For (a) poem completeness, based on the statistically significant difference for Q1 (Poem Completeness) in the P-TQ and the unanimous agreement among participants to Q1 (Was the system able to create the poems?) in the P-EQ, we believe that the proposed system helps users create a quatrain with four lines. For (b) creation satisfaction, the result of Q2 (Creation Satisfaction) in the P-TQ showed no significant difference between tasks, suggesting that the proposed method did not effectively assist participants in creating poems. Participants mentioned by free description that the created poems were sometimes difficult to read because of a lack of annotations. This could be a factor contributing to dissatisfaction. For (c) usability, based on the results of responses from Q4 ("Do you think using the proposed system made it easier to confirm the rhyme?"), Q5 ("Do you think using the proposed system made it easier to confirm the tone patterns?"), and Q6 ("Do you think the proposed system was easy to use?") in the P-EQ, all participants expressed that the system was easier to use, and that the tone patterns were easier to confirm using the system. However, for rhyme confirmation, only 12 participants agreed with its usability, whereas 4 disagreed. This discrepancy may be attributed to the UI functions of the user interface. The system visualizes the answers of the tone patterns using the content of the created poems, making it easy for participants to check. However, the participants had to refer to a different part of the website to find rhyme information, which resulted in a less user-friendly experience.

RQ2. Can the proposed system facilitate users in confirming the created poems' adherence to the constraints? We answered RQ2 by analyzing the responses regarding the confirmations of Q3 (styles), Q4 (rhyme), Q5 (rhyme characters), and Q6 (tone patterns) in P-TQ and Q2 ("Was the system able to confirm the rhyme?"), and Q3 ("Was the system able confirm the tone patterns?") in the P-EQ. We found that there was a significant difference regarding styles, no significant difference regarding rhymes, and a significant trend in rhyme characters and tone patterns. This means that the proposed system can help users verify styles, rhyme characters, and tone patterns smoothly, but not in confirming the rhyme. Additionally, in the P-EQ, participants stated that the system was useful for confirming tone patterns, but not rhyme. Although there was no significant difference between tasks, these findings aligned with the analysis in RQ1, where participants faced challenges in confirming the rhyme owing to limitations in the user interface.

RQ3. How do users perceive the created poems in terms of the expressive power of the content? We answered RQ3 by analyzing the responses regarding the Q7 (Fluency Satisfaction), Q8 ("Is the poem written on the same theme?"), and Q9 ("Does the poem express feelings?") in the P-TQ. We found that there were significant differences regarding fluency satisfaction and the response of Is the poem written on the same theme, thus, we thought the system helped users create poems smoothly. However, there was no significant difference when asked Does the poem express feelings. This can be attributed to the use of pre-defined keywords. The lack of a significant difference suggests that the auto-generated poems sometimes needed help to convey the users' feelings.

Limitation. This study used the pre-trained GPT-2 model to generate poems owing to its provision of a Chinese poetry model. However, an additional measure that would improve the user's satisfaction with the model would be to fine-tune the model to follow more Chinese-poem-specific requirements. In addition, it is worth noting that as of June 2023, OpenAI and other enterprises have introduced newer language models, such as GPT-3 and ChatGPT. The use of those new models remains future research, potentially leading to improved poem generation results.

The proposed system presented the created poems with the results of the tone patterns of characters in a poem, however, the rule judgment results of rhyme and tone patterns were only shown for individual characters, making it inconvenient for users to check rhyme answers. We will consider developing a function that where by all the results of the rules can be visualized in a poem.

Our user experiment used a limited set of 29 pre-defined keywords, involved only 16 participants, and set the limit for generating up to 100 poems per keyword. The small sample size and limited data collection may raise concerns about the reliability and generalizability of the findings. To address these issues, future studies should increase the amount of data and expand the pool of participants for the user experiment.

6   Conclusions and Future Work

In this study, we propose an automatic generation system comprising an evaluation system for creating poems. The auto-generation system could create poems that follow the constraints of Tang poems and the evaluation system helped the user check the styles, rhyme, and tone patterns, then provided a scoring rank of poems and rule judgment results through a user interface. Our goal was to assist beginners in creating poems without extensive knowledge of the creative process. Following the poem's creation, hints and feedback were provided on adherence to the constraint results.

We recruited 16 native Japanese speakers for the experiments. The results show that the proposed system improved significantly in terms of poem completeness and usability, but not in terms of creation satisfaction. The proposed system effectively confirmed adherence to the constraints of the styles, rhyme characters, and tone patterns of the created poems, but there were some difficulties when confirming the rhyme. The users expressed satisfaction with the fluency and thematic consistency of the poems. However, they felt that the system had limitations in expressing feelings due to the constraints of the chosen keywords.

In future work, we plan to develop user interface functions to help users learn poems easily by hinting at rhymes and adding word annotations. The goal is to increase both the ease of reading poems and beginners' interest in creating them.

Acknowledgment. This work was supported by JSPS KAKENHI, Grant Numbers JP20K12543 and JP23K11761.

References

1. Chinese converter (Python). https://pypinyin.readthedocs.io/zh_CN/master/
2. Chinese new rhyme. https://en.wikipedia.org/wiki/Middle_Chinese
3. Ping Shui Rhyme (in Chinese). Baidu Baike. https://baike.baidu.com/item/%E5 %B9%B3%E6%B0%B4%E9%9F%B5/2271158
4. uer/gpt2-chinese-cluecorpussmall.   https://huggingface.co/uer/gpt2-chinese-cluecorpussmall/tree/main
5. Upper secondary school curriculum guideline 2018–03 notification (in Japanese) (2022).   https://www.mext.go.jp/content/20230120-mxt_kyoiku02-100002604_03.pdf
6. Ariga, Y.: Sorin Chinese Poetry Composition Lecture Introductory Edition (in Japanese). Kokusho Publishing Association (1995)
7. Ariga, Y.: Sorin Chinese Poetry Composition Lecture Vocabulary (in Japanese). Kokusho Publishing Association (1995)
8. Attridge, D.: Poetic Rhythm: An Introduction. Cambridge University Press, Cambridge (1977)
9. Du, Z.: GPT2-Chinese: tools for training GPT2 model in Chinese language. GitHub (2019). https://github.com/Morizeyao/GPT2-Chinese
10. Hirata, K., Yokoyama, S., Yamashita, T., Kawamura, H.: Haiku generation using language model by transformer and its evaluation (in Japanese). Information Processing Society of Japan/Information Fundamentals and Access Technologies **2021-IFAT-143**(2), 1–6 (2021)
11. Iritani, S.: Introduction to Chinese Poetry (in Japanese). Chunichi Publishing Company (1979)
12. Ishida, K.: On the knowledge obtain method of Chinese poem by its correcton software (in Japanese). Jpn. Soc. Artif. Intell. JSAI05, 104–104 (2005). https://doi.org/10.11517/pjsai.JSAI05.0.104.0
13. Ishida, K.: On a web service site for the correction of Chinese poems (in Japanese). Jpn. Soc. Artif. Intell. JSAI06, 157–157 (2006). https://doi.org/10.11517/pjsai.JSAI06.0.157.0

14. Kawada, M.: Collection of poetry (in Japanese). Reproduction of Ritsumeikan Publishing 1928 issued (1980)
15. Nitta, D.: Manners Series How to Make Chinese Poetry New Edition (in Japanese). Meiji Shoin (2003)
16. Okamoto, T.: Guidance on creating Chinese poetry at the secondary education level (in Japanese). Research Bulletin: Collection of Essays from Kobe University Secondary School **4**, 9–14 (2020)
17. Onuki, M.: Lesson practice to provide "enrichment learning" in the unit of Chinese poetry in Japanese language course at senior high school: using a mock class for university students on creating rhyming poems in translation as a guide (in Japanese). J. Stud. Educ. Pract. **25**, 12–22 (2022). https://doi.org/10.50841/kyoikujissen.25.0_12
18. Qiu, F., Nakamura, K., Komiya, S.: A proposal of a system to support the versification of a Chinese poem: constraints on versification and support for versification by utilizing a database of poetic dictionary (in Japanese). IEICE Tech. Rep. **111**(211), 37–42 (2011)
19. Qiu, F., Nakamura, K., Komiya, S.: A proposal of system to support the versification of a Chinese poem?: Constraints on versification and support for versification by utilizing a database of poetic diction (in Japanese). IEICE Tech. Rep. **112**(300), 31–36 (2012)
20. Radford, A., Wu, J., Child, R., Luan, D., Amodei, D., Sutskever, I.: Language models are unsupervised multitask learners. OpenAI Blog (2019). https://openai.com/blog/better-language-models/
21. Wang, Z., et al.: Chinese poetry generation with planning based neural network. Proc of COLING **2016**, 1051–1060 (2016)
22. Yi, X., Li, R., Sun, M.: Generating Chinese classical poems with RNN encoder-decoder. In: Chinese Computational Linguistics and Natural Language Processing Based on Naturally Annotated Big Data, pp. 211–223 (2017)

Evaluating the Use of Generative LLMs for Intralingual Diachronic Translation of Middle-Polish Texts into Contemporary Polish

Cezary Klamra[1], Katarzyna Kryńska[2], and Maciej Ogrodniczuk[1](✉)

[1] Institute of Computer Science, Polish Academy of Sciences, Jana Kazimierza 5, 01-248 Warszawa, Poland
maciej.ogrodniczuk@ipipan.waw.pl
[2] Institute of Polish Language, Polish Academy of Sciences, al. Mickiewicza 31, 31-120 Kraków, Poland
katarzyna.krynska@ijp.pan.pl

Abstract. This paper presents efforts towards creating a tool for translating texts from Middle Polish into modern Polish. Archaic texts sourced from the CBDU digital library were translated into modern language using ChatGPT and the resulting parallel corpus was used to train a neural text-to-text model. We assessed the results using automatic metrics and performed human evaluation of translations of the best-performing model and ChatGPT. Even though the performance of the trained models was far from perfect, the quality of translations produced with Chat-GPT was good in most cases. Although caution should be exercised, we believe that LLMs have a high potential for text-to-text annotation applications.

Keywords: Intralingual diachronic translation · Automatic annotation · Large Language Models

1 Introduction

Numerous archaic Polish texts have been made available as part of historical corpora or digital libraries [6,7,14]. However, comprehension of these texts may be challenging due to the far-reaching linguistic differences between archaic Polish and its modern counterpart. In this paper, we present our recent efforts towards using generative intelligence to create a tool for converting Middle-Polish texts into modern language — a task often referred to as intralingual diachronic translation.

For this purpose, a set of parallel corpora of archaic and modern texts should be used. Yet, scarcity of such resources is an obstacle that hinders the development of diachronic normalization or translation methods based on machine learning [28] and their development would require labour-intensive and time-consuming annotation.

© The Author(s), under exclusive license to Springer Nature Singapore Pte Ltd. 2023
D. H. Goh et al. (Eds.): ICADL 2023, LNCS 14457, pp. 18–27, 2023.
https://doi.org/10.1007/978-981-99-8085-7_2

The ongoing development of large language models (henceforth: LLMs) may soon overcome this difficulty. In our solution, we leverage ChatGPT to translate Middle-Polish texts into modern Polish and use the resulting parallel corpus to train a neural text-to-text model. The main source of such texts is the Digital Library of Polish and Poland-Related News Pamphlets from the 16th to the 18th Century[1] (CBDU, from Polish *Cyfrowa Biblioteka Druków Ulotnych Polskich i Polski Dotyczących z XVI, XVII i XVIII Wieku*) [7,21].

Although the purpose of this work is rather exploratory, several possible practical applications of a diachronic machine translation tool in the digital library can be proposed. Apart from the most obvious improvements in the comprehensibility of the presented artefacts, the translation model could also be used in the indexing engine, allowing the library to be searched using a modern language query.

The paper is structured as follows. Section 2 provides an overview of the relevant literature. The process of creating a parallel corpus of archaic and modern Polish sentences is outlined in Sect. 3. The development of the tool, based on the aforementioned corpus, is described in Sect. 4. Automatic and human-based evaluation of the obtained results is presented in Sect. 5. Finally, Sect. 6 contains concluding remarks for the paper.

2   Related Work

Most prior research on intralingual diachronic machine translation has focused on East Asian languages. Various studies have discussed machine translation from ancient to modern Chinese, along with creating relevant language resources for this task [19,32,33]. Similarly, [22] describes machine translation from ancient to modern Korean. The work focusing on Indo-European languages is mainly limited to methods of diachronic normalization of spelling [2,16]. Such methods have also been developed for Polish [11,28], however, they focused on language from the 18th and 19th centuries, much closer to modern Polish than the language of earlier centuries, represented in CBDU.

Using LLMs to perform linguistic annotation has already been proposed (see e.g. [4,30]), however, the idea has been gaining more attention as the capabilities of the models continued to rapidly improve. Some of the recently published language resources annotated with LLMs include [8,18]. It has been argued that the quality of LLM-annotated data may surpass that of data annotated by humans, including experts [5,10,29]. At the same time, LLMs significantly reduce the cost of annotation and speed up the process.

Most of the work on LLM-based linguistic data annotation has focused on the classification task performed in English. LLM-based annotation in English and Slovenian has been examined in [17]. However, several studies have evaluated the quality of translations generated using LLMs. [12] assessed the quality and robustness of the translations produced with LLMs and found that using

---

[1] https://cbdu.ijp.pan.pl/.

GPT-4 as the engine significantly boosts the performance over ChatGPT-3.5. [9] conducted a human evaluation and analysis of the quality of translation performed with three GPT-based models and compared the results with the highest ranked systems in WMT22. [13] demonstrates that LLMs may leverage paragraph-level context to produce more coherent translations compared to a sentence-to-sentence setting.

As [26] points out, using ChatGPT for text annotation has its drawbacks. ChatGPT is nondeterministic (i.e., identical inputs might lead to different outputs) and vulnerable to adversarial examples, and hence the consistency of the predictions is limited. In some cases, changing even a single character can have a negative impact on the reliability of the outputs [27]. Although these studies examined the classification task, these concerns are valid for text-to-text tasks as well: according to [23], ChatGPT tends to hallucinate when performing a non-English-centric translation.

3   Annotation with ChatGPT

Documents from CBDU (see Sect. 1) were exported from the original TEI P5 XML format. In total, 258 transcribed documents were used, jointly consisting of over 380,000 segments. During export, the paragraphs were extracted and unnecessary tags were removed – specifically `<gap>` (used to mark a gap in the text, for example, when the original text was unreadable), `<foreign>` tag (used to mark foreign words) and `<pb>` tag (used to mark page breaks). Some words were available in two variants: original and regularized (variants were labelled with `<orig>` and `<reg>` tags and placed inside a `<choice>` tag). In such cases, the latter version was preferred. Furthermore, in some of the documents, certain words were suffixed with the slash symbol ("/") which, if present, was also removed.

The texts were then annotated using ChatGPT (model: `gpt-3.5-turbo`). The paragraphs were split into sentences using Wtpsplit[2] [20] — we decided to use a language-agnostic tool, as punctuation rules in archaic and modern Polish are not the same and applying Polish-specific solutions yielded unsatisfactory results. The translation was performed in batches of sentences; the sentences within each batch originated from the same paragraph, maintaining their original order to ensure coherence. Only the longest paragraphs were split into several batches.

The model was instructed to provide the results in JSON format, which facilitated the parsing of the results. Preliminary experiments have shown that the model occasionally transfers the textual structure (e.g. enumerations) onto the JSON format, resulting in inconsistent key usage. Providing the model with a set of examples successfully prevented that in most cases, hence we decided to use a few-shot prompt. Sporadically, some of the translations were missing from the response. In such cases, the translation was repeated until a correct response was obtained. Some of the texts contained Latin interjections or even consisted

---

[2] We used the model `wtp-canine-s-121` and set the threshold parameter at 0.05.

solely of Latin text. Most of the translations of such sentences were accurate, nonetheless.

The prompt used consisted of five conversation turns and included two sets of example sentences (same for all examples):[3]

> **User:** Przetłumacz poniższe zdania na współczesny język polski. Podaj odpowiedź w formacie JSON (pod kluczem „translations"). Zdania: *[Translate the below sentences into modern Polish. Provide the answer in JSON format (with the "translations" key). Sentences:]* „*example source sentence A1*" „*example source sentence A2*" . . .

```
Assistant: {
         "translations": [
           "example target sentence A1",
           "example target sentence A2",
            . . .
         ]
       }
```

> **User:** Zdania: *[Sentences:]* „*example source sentence B1*" „*example source sentence B2*" . . .

```
Assistant: {
         "translations": [
           "example target sentence B1",
           "example target sentence B2",
            . . .
         ]
       }
```

> **User:** Zdania: *[Sentences:]* „*sentence to translate 1*" „*sentence to translate 2*" . . .

The desired model response had the following form:

```
Assistant: {
    "translations": [
      "translated sentence 1",
      "translated sentence 2",

       . . .
    ]
  }
```

---

[3] The example translations included in the prompt can be accessed at https://github.com/ipipan/cbdu-idt.

Finally, the translations were parsed. The resulting corpus consists of 12043 pairs of archaic and modern Polish sentences. The corpus was divided into training, development, and test subsets (using an 80:10:10 proportion). The cost of annotation was USD 11.25.

4   Experiments

As the scope of the problem addressed is limited to a single language, we decided to focus on models pre-trained on Polish texts. We tuned plT5-base, plT5-large[4] [3] and plBART[5] for 10 epochs. In all experiments, we held the learning rate at 10^{-4} and used AdamW optimizer ($\varepsilon = 10^{-8}$, $\beta_1 = 0.9$, $\beta_2 = 0.999$) with linear scheduler (with 500 warm-up steps). The batch size was 2 for plT5-large and 8 for other models. The models were evaluated on the validation subset of the corpus every epoch; we report results on the checkpoint corresponding to the highest BLEU score (i.e. the checkpoint after the last epoch for plT5-base and plBART and after the sixth epoch for plT5-large).

5   Evaluation

5.1   Automatic Evaluation

We assessed the performance of the trained models on the test subset of the corpus. Standard reference-based machine translation evaluation metrics, BLEU, ChrF and TER, were computed using the SacreBLEU library [24] (default parameter values were used). Additionally, we report the values of a recall-oriented metric Rouge-L and a neural-based metric COMET[6] [25]. We also calculated perplexity as a measure of the fluency of the generated text.[7] Note that all the above metrics, except perplexity, require a list of human-produced translations as references, whereas we use sentences translated with ChatGPT. Therefore, it is not possible to compare the performance of ChatGPT and the trained models, and the reliability of the metrics may be limited.

The results of the evaluation are presented in Table 1. Clearly, plT5-large is the best-performing model. Although all models were trained on texts translated using ChatGPT, it is not ChatGPT but plT5-large that produces the most fluent text. This can be explained by the fact that plT5 is a monolingual model trained on a large Polish corpus. Translations produced with ChatGPT tend to contain paraphrases. The translations produced with the trained models are more similar to the original.

---

[4] https://huggingface.co/allegro/plt5-base, https://huggingface.co/allegro/plt5-large.

[5] https://huggingface.co/sdadas/polish-bart-base.

[6] Model used: `Unbabel/wmt22-comet-da`. The metric is based on the XLM-R model, which only supports modern Polish, hence the performance of the metric may be constrained.

[7] Perplexity was computed using the Polish GPT-2 XL model (https://huggingface.co/sdadas/polish-gpt2-xl).

Table 1. Automatic evaluation results.

Model	BLEU	ChrF	TER	Rouge-L	COMET	Perplexity
Source sentences	—	—	—	—	—	556.06
ChatGPT-3.5	—	—	—	—	—	297.82
plBART-base	15.96	44.25	76.16	0.44	0.65	383.53
plT5-base	18.41	46.20	74.47	0.47	0.66	310.65
plT5-large	**19.55**	**48.18**	**72.04**	**0.49**	**0.70**	**290.50**

5.2 Human Evaluation

To compare the performance of ChatGPT and the trained models and to over-come the shortcomings of the reference-based machine translation metrics, we performed a human evaluation of the translations performed with ChatGPT and the best-performing model, plT5-large. A random sample of 100 texts has been selected, each of which has been assessed in two dimensions, adequacy and fluency. Adequacy refers to how accurately the translated sentence conveys the intended meaning of the original sentence; an accurate translation should preserve the core meaning of the original sentence. Fluency assesses how well the translated sentence reads to a native speaker of the target language, i.e. whether it is natural and linguistically correct.

Table 2. Human evaluation: 5-point scale.

Score	Adequacy	Fluency
5	all meaning	flawless Polish
4	most meaning	good Polish
3	much meaning	non-native Polish
2	some meaning	disfluent Polish
1	no meaning	incomprehensible

Following the approach described in [31], a 5-point scale has been used (see Table 2). All texts were evaluated by a single annotator familiar with the Middle-Polish language. Five texts were incomprehensible for the annotator without their context; we decided to replace them with other texts randomly sampled from the test subset of the corpus.

The results of the human-based evaluation are presented in Table 3. Although automatic evaluation suggests that plT5-large produces more fluent translations, here ChatGPT outperforms plT5-large in both adequacy and fluency, the difference in performance is particularly strong for the latter. In Table 4 it can be clearly seen that the language quality of ChatGPT is very good or good in 92% of the cases, compared to 76% for sentences translated with plT5-large.

Table 3. Human evaluation results: average scores.

Model	Adequacy	Fluency
ChatGPT	**3.78**	**4.48**
plT5-large	3.54	4.07

Table 4. Human evaluation results: score frequencies.

Score	Adequacy (%)		Fluency (%)	
	ChatGPT	plT5-large	ChatGPT	plT5-large
5	24	17	57	36
4	38	37	35	40
3	30	31	7	21
2	8	13	1	1
1	0	2	0	2

Some additional remarks can be drawn from the annotator's notes, which were collected during the manual evaluation process. plT5-large could not successfully translate some of the short sentences, even if ChatGPT handled them correctly. For some medium-length sentences, which scored very high (5) in fluency for ChatGPT, the translation generated with plT5-large was of poor quality (2). In the case of very long sentences, plt5-large tends to generate much shorter translations, omitting some parts of the original sentence, resulting in a lower adequacy score. Some of the plT5 translations contained repetitions of words or longer phrases, having a negative impact on the fluency score. The sample contained a sentence consisting solely of Latin words, which plT5 failed to correctly translate: not only did it not translate the sentence into Polish, but the output contained Latin words mixed with words of neither Polish nor Latin origin; at the same time, ChatGPT achieved a fair translation quality.

It is possible that the low performance of plT5-large results from insufficient size of the training corpus or over-training — the best checkpoint was selected based on the BLEU score, however it has been shown that the metric has flaws and using it for model selection might lead to suboptimal decisions [15].

6   Conclusions

This paper addresses the problem of intralingual diachronic translation for Polish. Archaic texts from the CBDU digital library were translated into contemporary Polish using ChatGPT. The resulting parallel corpus was used to train neural text-to-text models. The results of the automatic evaluation indicate that tuned models may produce translations more fluent than ChatGPT (on which they were trained). However, human-based evaluation has shown that ChatGPT translations are better than the translations of the best-performing trained model in terms of both adequacy and fluency. While the performance of the trained models is far from perfect, the quality of ChatGPT-produced translations was rated as good or very good in most cases. Although caution should be exercised, we believe that LLMs have a high potential for text-to-text annotation applications. The annotated corpus and the predictions of the models are available at https://github.com/ipipan/cbdu-idt.

Possible reproducibility issues are a major limitation of this work: as Chat-GPT is nondeterministic, repeating the procedure described would likely yield different translations, even if the same prompt was used. Training may not have been conducted optimally due to reliance on BLEU values for model selection (see Sect. 5). Furthermore, The prompt used to translate the texts included the same set of examples for all cases; using an example selection technique could improve the quality of the translation [1, 9].

References

1. Agrawal, S., Zhou, C., Lewis, M., Zettlemoyer, L., Ghazvininejad, M.: In-context examples selection for machine translation. In: Findings of the Association for Computational Linguistics: ACL 2023, pp. 8857–8873. Association for Computational Linguistics, Toronto, Canada (2023). https://doi.org/10.18653/v1/2023.findings-acl.564
2. Bawden, R., Poinhos, J., Kogkitsidou, E., Gambette, P., Sagot, B., Gabay, S.: Automatic normalisation of early Modern French. In: Proceedings of the Thirteenth Language Resources and Evaluation Conference, pp. 3354–3366. European Language Resources Association, Marseille, France (2022). https://aclanthology.org/2022.lrec-1.358/
3. Chrabrowa, A., et al.: Evaluation of transfer learning for Polish with a text-to-text model. In: Proceedings of the Thirteenth Language Resources and Evaluation Conference, pp. 4374–4394. European Language Resources Association, Marseille, France (2022). https://aclanthology.org/2022.lrec-1.466
4. Ding, B., et al.: Is GPT-3 a good data annotator? In: Proceedings of the 61st Annual Meeting of the Association for Computational Linguistics (Volume 1: Long Papers), pp. 11173–11195. Association for Computational Linguistics, Toronto, Canada (2023). https://doi.org/10.18653/v1/2023.acl-long.626
5. Gilardi, F., Alizadeh, M., Kubli, M.: ChatGPT outperforms crowd-workers for text-annotation tasks. arXiv:2303.15056 (2023)
6. Gruszczyński, W., et al.: The electronic corpus of 17th-and 18th-century polish texts. Lang. Resour. Eval. 56(1), 309–332 (2022)
7. Gruszczyński, W., Ogrodniczuk, M.: Cyfrowa Biblioteka Druków Ulotnych Polskich i Polski dotyczących z XVI, XVII i XVIII w. w nauce i dydaktyce. In: Materiały konferencji Polskie Biblioteki Cyfrowe 2010, pp. 23–27. Poznań, Poland (2010)
8. Hartvigsen, T., Gabriel, S., Palangi, H., Sap, M., Ray, D., Kamar, E.: ToxiGen: a large-scale machine-generated dataset for adversarial and implicit hate speech detection. In: Proceedings of the 60th Annual Meeting of the Association for Computational Linguistics (Volume 1: Long Papers), pp. 3309–3326. Association for Computational Linguistics, Dublin, Ireland (2022). https://doi.org/10.18653/v1/2022.acl-long.234

9. Hendy, A., et al.: How good are GPT models at machine translation? A comprehensive evaluation. arXiv:2302.09210 (2023)
10. Huang, F., Kwak, H., An, J.: Is ChatGPT better than human annotators? potential and limitations of ChatGPT in explaining implicit hate speech. In: Companion Proceedings of the ACM Web Conference 2023. ACM (2023). https://doi.org/10.1145/3543873.3587368
11. Jassem, K., Graliński, F., Obrębski, T., Wierzchoń, P.: Automatic Diachronic Normalization of Polish Texts. Investig. Linguist. **37**, 17–33 (2018). https://doi.org/10.14746/il.2017.37.2
12. Jiao, W., Wang, W., Huang, J., Wang, X., Tu, Z.: Is ChatGPT a good translator? Yes with GPT-4 as the engine. arXiv:2301.08745 (2023)
13. Karpinska, M., Iyyer, M.: Large language models effectively leverage document-level context for literary translation, but critical errors persist. arXiv:2304.03245 (2023)
14. Kieraś, W., Woliński, M.: Manually annotated corpus of Polish texts published between 1830 and 1918. In: Proceedings of the Eleventh International Conference on Language Resources and Evaluation (LREC 2018). European Language Resources Association (ELRA), Miyazaki, Japan (2018). https://aclanthology.org/L18-1609
15. Kocmi, T., Federmann, C., Grundkiewicz, R., Junczys-Dowmunt, M., Matsushita, H., Menezes, A.: To ship or not to ship: an extensive evaluation of automatic metrics for machine translation. In: Proceedings of the Sixth Conference on Machine Translation, pp. 478–494. Association for Computational Linguistics (2021). https://aclanthology.org/2021.wmt-1.57
16. Korchagina, N.: Normalizing medieval german texts: from rules to deep learning. In: Proceedings of the NoDaLiDa 2017 Workshop on Processing Historical Language, pp. 12–17. Linköping University Electronic Press, Gothenburg (2017). https://aclanthology.org/W17-0504
17. Kuzman, T., Mozetic, I., Ljubešic, N.: ChatGPT: beginning of an end of manual linguistic data annotation? Use case of automatic genre identification. arXiv:2303.03953 (2023)
18. Laskar, M.T.R., Rahman, M., Jahan, I., Hoque, E., Huang, J.: CQSumDP: a ChatGPT-annotated resource for query-focused abstractive summarization based on debatepedia. arXiv:2305.06147 (2023)
19. Liu, D., Yang, K., Qu, Q., Lv, J.: Ancient-modern chinese translation with a new large training dataset. ACM Trans. Asian Low-Resource Lang. Inf. Process. **19**(1), 3325887 (2019). https://doi.org/10.1145/3325887
20. Minixhofer, B., Pfeiffer, J., Vulić, I.: Where's the point? Self-supervised multilingual punctuation-agnostic sentence segmentation. arXiv:2305.18893 (2023)
21. Ogrodniczuk, M., Kryńska, K.: Evaluating machine translation of Latin interjections in the digital library of polish and Poland-related news pamphlets. In: Tseng, Y.H., Katsurai, M., Nguyen, H.N. (eds.) From Born-Physical to Born-Virtual: Augmenting Intelligence in Digital Libraries. ICADL 2022. LNCS, vol. 13636. Springer, Cham (2022). https://doi.org/10.1007/978-3-031-21756-2_34
22. Park, C., Lee, C., Yang, Y., Lim, H.: Ancient Korean neural machine translation. IEEE Access **8**, 116617–116625 (2020). https://doi.org/10.1109/ACCESS.2020.3004879
23. Peng, K., et al.: Towards making the most of ChatGPT for machine translation. arXiv:2303.13780 (2023)

24. Post, M.: A call for clarity in reporting BLEU scores. In: Proceedings of the Third Conference on Machine Translation: Research Papers, pp. 186–191. Association for Computational Linguistics, Belgium, Brussels (2018). https://www.aclweb.org/anthology/W18-6319

25. Rei, R., Stewart, C., Farinha, A.C., Lavie, A.: COMET: a neural framework for MT evaluation. In: Proceedings of the 2020 Conference on Empirical Methods in Natural Language Processing (EMNLP), pp. 2685–2702. Association for Computational Linguistics (2020). https://www.aclweb.org/anthology/2020.emnlp-main.213

26. Reiss, M.V.: Testing the reliability of ChatGPT for text annotation and classification: a cautionary remark. arXiv:2304.11085 (2023)

27. Shen, X., Chen, Z., Backes, M., Zhang, Y.. In ChatGPT we trust? Measuring and characterizing the reliability of ChatGPT. arXiv:2304.08979 (2023)

28. Skórzewski, P., Jassem, K., Graliński, F.: Automated normalization and analysis of historical texts. In: Vetulani, Z., Paroubek, P., Kubis, M. (eds.) LTC 2017. LNCS (LNAI), vol. 12598, pp. 73–86. Springer, Cham (2020). https://doi.org/10.1007/978-3-030-66527-2_6

29. Törnberg, P.: ChatGPT-4 outperforms experts and crowd workers in annotating political twitter messages with zero-shot learning. arXiv:2304.06588 (2023)

30. Wang, S., Liu, Y., Xu, Y., Zhu, C., Zeng, M.: Want to reduce labeling cost? GPT-3 can help. In: Findings of the Association for Computational Linguistics: EMNLP 2021, pp. 4195–4205. Association for Computational Linguistics, Punta Cana, Dominican Republic (2021). https://doi.org/10.18653/v1/2021.findings-emnlp.354

31. White, J.S., O'Connell, T.A., O'Mara, F.E.: The ARPA MT evaluation methodologies: evolution, lessons, and future approaches. In: Proceedings of the First Conference of the Association for Machine Translation in the Americas. Columbia, Maryland, USA (1994). https://aclanthology.org/1994.amta-1.25

32. Yang, Z., Chen, K., Chen, J.: Guwen-UNILM: machine translation between ancient and modern Chinese based on pre-trained models. In: Wang, L., Feng, Y., Hong, Yu., He, R. (eds.) NLPCC 2021. LNCS (LNAI), vol. 13028, pp. 116–128. Springer, Cham (2021). https://doi.org/10.1007/978-3-030-88480-2_10

33. Zhang, Z., Li, W., Su, Q.: Automatic translating between ancient Chinese and contemporary Chinese with limited aligned corpora. In: Tang, J., Kan, M.-Y., Zhao, D., Li, S., Zan, H. (eds.) NLPCC 2019. LNCS (LNAI), vol. 11839, pp. 157–167. Springer, Cham (2019). https://doi.org/10.1007/978-3-030-32236-6_13

HistoChatbot: Educating History by Generating Quizzes in Social Network Services

Yasunobu Sumikawa[1(✉)] and Adam Jatowt[2]

[1] Department of Computer Science, Takushoku University, Tokyo, Japan
`ysumikaw@cs.takushoku-u.ac.jp`
[2] Department of Computer Science, University of Innsbruck, Innsbruck, Austria
`adam.jatowt@uibk.ac.at`

Abstract. Microblogging platforms can provide novel, attractive opportunities for communicating and disseminating content about important events from the past. We propose a novel framework for building interactive chatbot systems that post history-related content including automatic quizzes related to current temporal context and that take and assess user responses. The chatbot is currently available on Twitter sharing history-related quizzes in English (The code, quiz data and evaluation results are available at https://github.com/sumilab/programs/tree/master/histo_chatbot_quiz.). We are the first to propose guidelines for designing history-focused chatbot systems that aim at fulfilling educational and entertaining objectives in microblogging platforms.

Keywords: social media analysis · public history · collective memory

1 Introduction

History is commonly believed to play a significant role in our society letting us understand the processes which shape the present and giving meaning and orientation with regard to the past. Education of history starts from elementary schools onwards. Many initiatives aim however at educating and sharing historical knowledge in parallel to the traditional framework of schooling in order to provide complementary information and to raise our interest in history. Public history in particular is a research area defined as communication between history and ordinary users or "non-researchers" [2] that aims to let historical knowledge reach the wide public. Social media in particular can serve as a convenient and effective venue for disseminating historical knowledge. Previous studies have already shed light on such sharing activities taking place on Twitter in the context of commemorating World War I [5], or based on the categorization of history-related tweets into 6 fundamental categories of commemoration [17].

In this paper, we propose several retrieval and recommendation models of extracting and sharing history-related content. Based on our findings we report design guidelines for developing effective chatbots to provide quizzes that attract and encourage users to learn more about history. We also showcase a working

D. H. Goh et al. (Eds.): ICADL 2023, LNCS 14457, pp. 28–35, 2023.
https://doi.org/10.1007/978-981-99-8085-7_3

prototype that we implemented based on our framework called `HistoChatbot` which periodically communicates history-related content. The purpose of the proposed chatbot system is to discover, collect and process historical content accumulated in Wikipedia and one that is circulating on Twitter, and then to communicate such content in the form of quizzes, either automatically or in response to user tweets, for actively disseminating historical knowledge. In order to realize this objective, we propose the following work modes:

– Providing quizzes on past events that occurred on the same calendar day as the interaction time
– Providing quizzes on past events related to the current news
– Providing quizzes on past events related to the current trending topics
– Providing quizzes on past events related to entities specified by users (i.e., events, people and organizations)

The proposed chatbot is an effective tool to actively share content related to history in a rather novel fashion - within online social networks and using automatically generated questions. As mentioned above, it generates and provides quizzes as well as evaluates answers as correct/incorrect based on different types of prompts which are either implicit (based on calendar, recent news, or trending topics) or explicit (based on user input). Note that while at present the chatbot is designed to work with historical event synapses contained in Wikipedia and with history-related tweets, it can be adapted for sharing short heritage content from collections maintained by memory institutions (archives, libraries, or museums). This could present an interesting opportunity for GLAM institutions (Galleries, Libraries, Archives, and Museums) to appeal to the wider public, especially to younger users.

Related work. Our proposal is to use chatbots for automatizing the effective dissemination of historical content in online social networks. Chatbots used for education started also to appear recently. The common application is the study of foreign languages [9,11] under the assumption that learning languages need to be done in an interactive manner. For details, readers can refer to a general survey of chatbot technologies [1]. The chatbot designed in this study is oriented towards learning guidance and aims to provide education. It tweets past events collected from Wikipedia and Twitter [18], yet it can be flexibly extended to other content (even one from other domains like biology or chemistry). Question answering on historical document collections [19] or on history-related content [4,6] as well as temporal information retrieval [12,13] have been recently actively researched, and we believe it is good time now to employ such technologies for educating history in social networks.

2   History-Related Data Collection

To populate the historical event database that underlies our chatbot system we need to find short descriptions of a large number of important historical events. As automatically extracting such event synopses from open text collections (e.g.,

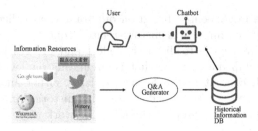

Fig. 1. High-level overview of the proposed chatbot system.

Web or historical textbooks) is rather still error-prone, we harvested the data on important past events from dedicated list pages in Wikipedia. Wikipedia describes important events for each date in the dedicated year and month-day articles. We used year pages[1], as well as day pages[2] (i.e., each day from January 1 to December 31). In total, the dataset we compiled contains the descriptions of 71,374 events from all years spanning from 1AD to 2019AD.

To generate history-related quizzes, we apply a question generation method [3] based on the recurrent BERT model to the collected Wikipedia data. This method takes a pre-selected answer and the text passage containing it as input to generate a matching question for the chosen answer by considering its passage context. This is done with pre-trained transformers (seq-2-seq models) using a straight-forward end-to-end method.

Before generating questions, we first extracted all named entities to be used as answers. For simplicity, we considered as the named entities any linked texts pointing to other Wikipedia articles. Finally, we input the prepared answers and their passages into the question generation method. In total, we have generated in this way 22,883 history-related questions from events that were previously collected from Wikipedia.

3   History-Focused Quiz Posting

Figure 1 shows the conceptual diagram of `HistoChatbot`. The current chatbot posts quizzes on Twitter from our Historical Information DB according to server-side settings that run the program; in the current implementation the quizzes are posted periodically and users can provide answers whenever they notice the questions. The chatbot evaluates tweets as correct or wrong according to the lexical match between the gold answer and the user tweet that provides an answer. The user then receives a feedback tweet informing whether the answer was correct or not. In this section, we describe the key work modes of the proposed chatbot and the way in which it selects and recommends history-related content.

In all the modes, we need to apply ranking since several event (question) candidates could be used by the chatbot. We rank candidates according to their

---

[1] E.g., https://en.wikipedia.org/wiki/1998.

[2] E.g., https://en.wikipedia.org/wiki/February_25.

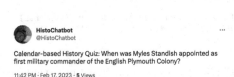

Fig. 2. Calendar-based quiz mode's example.

Fig. 3. Example of user–chatbot interaction being a response to the question shown in Fig. 2.

importance based on the assumption that Wikipedia articles which are often linked by many other articles are important. We use the following approach to rank events, and indirectly, the questions that were generated from them.

$$Importance(evt) = \sum_{ett \in Entity(evt)} Link(ett) \tag{1}$$

$$result(E) = \arg\max_{evt \in E} Importance(evt) \tag{2}$$

where E is a set of events. The above equations count the numbers of Wikipedia articles linking to the entities mentioned in the description of a given event as a way to approximate the event's importance. The function $Link(ett)$ counts the number of Wikipedia articles linking to a given entity, while evt and ett denote events and entities, respectively. $Entity(evt)$ denotes the set of entities extracted from the content of event description evt.

Calendar-based Quiz Mode. In the most basic mode, calendar-based mode, the chatbot posts quizzes about past events that occurred on the same calendar day in the past. This is in the same spirit as some newspapers which report (often at the end of the printed volume) important events that happened in the past on the same day, or ones that were reported by the same newspaper on that particular day. Figure 2 shows an example of results generated through the application of this mode. According to Wikipedia, Myles Standish was elected as the first commander of the Plymouth Colony militia in 1621. Our chatbot posted this quiz on Feb 17, 2023, which is exactly the same day as the date of that event. Figure 3 shows how the chatbot evaluates the user's answer[3].

With the calendar-based mode, the chatbot can actually provide several updates to its followers at regular times of the day, since there were usually multiple events that occurred on a particular calendar day in the past, throughout human history. The selection of an event to be tweeted is done as follows:

$$result(d, E) = \arg\max_{evt \in E}\{Importance(evt) \mid date(evt) == d\} \tag{3}$$

---

[3] We assume here that the HistoChatbot Developer denotes a real user.

HistoChatbot
@HistoChatbot

Current-News-related History Quiz: When was the Sagarmatha National Park created?

6:00 PM · Oct 17, 2021 · HistoChat

HistoChatbot
@HistoChatbot   ...

Trending-related History Quiz: When did King Charles I of England marries Catholic princess Henrietta Maria?

4:42 PM · Oct 17, 2021 · HistoChat

Fig. 4. Current-news-based quiz mode example.

Fig. 5. Trending-words-based quiz mode example.

where d is the current date (represented by day and month information) and $date(evt)$ is the date when the event evt, which was not yet shared, occurred.

Current-news-based Quiz Mode. This mode outputs content about past events which are similar to the current events. To collect data on the current events, we created a list that includes Twitter official accounts of multiple news companies including CNN, BBC, NYT, and others[4]. Figure 4 shows an example of the chatbot's output in this work mode. This quiz asks about the year when a particular national park was created because its trigger was the recent CBC British Columbia's tweet[5] about the latest event that happened in a park.

Generating quizzes in this mode is executed each time there is news shared from one of the above-mentioned Twitter accounts of news companies. The chatbot first collects a newly issued tweet from the media companies. It then extracts nouns from the tweet's text to be used for extracting relevant event descriptions from our database. We use logical OR search based on the extracted nouns to find events most similar to the target utilized tweet. Next, the chatbot creates bag-of-words feature vectors for representing the selected event descriptions and the news company's tweet text. It then applies cosine similarity to these feature vectors and calculates the events' ranking scores considering both the cosine similarity and event importance scores. The calculation is as follows:

$$Impr(evt, E) = \frac{\sum_{ett \in Entity(evt)} Link(ett)}{Max(\{\sum_{ett \in Entity(evt')} Link(ett)) \mid evt' \in E\})}$$

$$score(txt, evt, E) = \alpha CosSim(txt, evt) + (1 - \alpha)Impr(evt, E) \quad (4)$$

$$result(txt, E) = \arg\max_{evt \in E} score(txt, evt, E) \quad (5)$$

where txt is the text of a news and α is a hyper-parameter to adjust the scores of $CosSim$ and $Impr$. In this mode, we use a news event description as a text. We set 0.5 as a default score to α. As the range of values of the cosine similarity in our case is $[0, 1]$, the function $Impr$ used in this equation returns the normalized value of importance, so that the importance of the entities has also the same range of values. The normalization is done by dividing the importance score of each event by the maximum value of the importance scores of all the events in our database.

---

[4] https://mobile.twitter.com/i/lists/1256794745512185857.
[5] https://mobile.twitter.com/cbcnewsbc/status/1449609372296953859.

Trending-words-based Quiz Mode. Twitter lists words that many users were recently interested in by indicating them as trending. We use the trending contents to post quizzes that users may be potentially interested in. Figure 5 shows an example of the output in this work mode. Since the word "maria" was included in the New Zealand's[6] trending word list on 17 October 2021, the chatbot generated the quiz that includes this word.

The procedure for generating a quiz in this mode is as follows. The chatbot first collects the trending words through the Twitter trends/place API. After removing # to extract text from hashtags, the chatbot loads event descriptions from our database. If there is at least one event description that includes this trending text, it is used for quiz selection. The chatbot then creates feature vectors for both the found event descriptions and for the collected trending words. Next, it applies cosine similarity using the feature vectors, and calculates the ranking score by combining the cosine similarity and importance scores. This algorithm uses the same equations as the current-news-based work mode.

Entity-based Quiz Mode. We describe now our last work mode. Its idea is to post quizzes corresponding to users' requests. If a user wants to receive questions about particular entity, she can request a related quiz about that entity. For example, if a user requested a quiz about Japan by sending the tweet "Give me a quiz about japan" to the chatbot, the chatbot extracts the word "japan" from the text, loads events related to Japan, and outputs a top-scored quiz based on the result of applying Eq. 5.

For simplicity, we currently apply the template-based entity detection in this mode[7]. In particular, we utilize a template "Give me a quiz about". The chatbot then extracts all the words following this template. Next, the historical information database is searched for events that involve all the detected entities to be used as candidate events for constructing chatbot's reply. If none such event exists, the events that include at least one entity are considered as candidates.

4 Conclusions and Future Work

In this paper we have described a framework for designing responsive chatbot systems that post history-related quizzes in SNSs. We proposed several work modes for recommending the events relevant to users or to the current context (same day, popular news, trending words). The proposed framework can serve as initial step for designing similar chatbot systems to actively disseminate knowledge from other domains besides history for educational purposes.

In future, we will measure event popularity (e.g., with statistical approaches similar to [21]) to better select content for dissemination. Estimating educational value (e.g., [8]), interestingness degree [10], bias degree [15] or contemporary relevance [14,16] of historical events will be further investigated for increasing the attractiveness and credibility of shared content. Finally, we will experiment

---

[6] Assuming for this example that the user lives in New Zealand.

[7] In the future, we plan to apply named entity recognition tools to allow users to write arbitrary texts.

with incorporating large language models [20, 22] (e.g., ChatGPT) to provide more human-like conversational capabilities and commonsense reasoning [7] and by this to increase responsiveness and believably of the chatbot.

References

1. Adamopoulou, E., Moussiades, L.: An overview of chatbot technology. In: Maglogiannis, I., Iliadis, L., Pimenidis, E. (eds.) AIAI 2020. IAICT, vol. 584, pp. 373–383. Springer, Cham (2020). https://doi.org/10.1007/978-3-030-49186-4_31
2. Cauvin, T.: The rise of public history: an international perspective. Historia Crítica No. 40 **68**, 3–26 (2018)
3. Chan, Y.H., Fan, Y.C.: A recurrent BERT-based model for question generation. In: Proceedings of the 2nd Workshop on Machine Reading for Question Answering, pp. 154–162. ACL, Hong Kong, China (2019)
4. Chen, W., Wang, X., Wang, W.Y.: A dataset for answering time-sensitive questions (2021)
5. Clavert, F., Majerus, B., Beaupré, N.: #ww1. twitter, the centenary of the first world war and the historian. Twitter for Research 2015
6. Cole, J.R., Chaudhary, A., Dhingra, B., Talukdar, P.: Salient span masking for temporal understanding. arXiv preprint arXiv:2303.12860 (2023)
7. Davis, E.: Benchmarks for automated commonsense reasoning: a survey. arXiv preprint arXiv:2302.04752 (2023)
8. Hong, J.C., Cheng, C.L., Hwang, M.Y., Lee, C.K., Chang, H.Y.: Assessing the educational values of digital games. J. Comput. Assist. Learn. **25**(5), 423–437 (2009)
9. Huang, W., Hew, K.F., Fryer, L.K.: Chatbots for language learning-are they really useful? a systematic review of chatbot-supported language learning. J. Comput. Assist. Learn. **38**(1), 237–257 (2022)
10. Jatowt, A., Hung, I.-C., Färber, M., Campos, R., Yoshikawa, M.: Exploding TV sets and disappointing laptops: suggesting interesting content in news archives based on surprise estimation. In: Hiemstra, D., Moens, M.-F., Mothe, J., Perego, R., Potthast, M., Sebastiani, F. (eds.) ECIR 2021. LNCS, vol. 12656, pp. 254–269. Springer, Cham (2021). https://doi.org/10.1007/978-3-030-72113-8_17
11. Jia, J.: CSIEC: a computer assisted English learning chatbot based on textual knowledge and reasoning. Knowl.-Based Syst. **22**(4), 249–255 (2009)
12. Joho, H., Jatowt, A., Roi, B.: A survey of temporal web search experience. In: Proceedings of the 22nd International Conference on World Wide Web, pp. 1101–1108 (2013)
13. Kanhabua, N., Nguyen, T.N., Niederée, C.: What triggers human remembering of events?: a large-scale analysis of catalysts for collective memory in Wikipedia, pp. 341–350. JCDL '14, London, United Kingdom (2014)
14. Kanhabua, N., Niederée, C., Siberski, W.: Towards concise preservation by managed forgetting: research issues and case study. iPres'13, Lisbon, Portugal (2013)
15. Lim, S., Jatowt, A., Färber, M., Yoshikawa, M.: Annotating and analyzing biased sentences in news articles using crowdsourcing. In: Proceedings of the Twelfth Language Resources and Evaluation Conference, pp. 1478–1484 (2020)
16. Sato, M., Jatowt, A., Duan, Y., Campos, R., Yoshikawa, M.: Estimating contemporary relevance of past news. In: ACM/IEEE, JCDL 2021, pp. 70–79. IEEE (2021)
17. Sumikawa, Y., Jatowt, A.: Analyzing history-related posts in twitter. Int. J. Digit. Libr. **22**(1), 105–134 (2021)

18. Sumikawa, Y., Jatowt, A.: Designing chatbot systems for disseminating history-focused content in online social networks. D - IEICE TRANSACTIONS on Information and Systems (Japanese Edition) J104-D(5), 486–497 (2021), (in Japanese)
19. Wang, J., Jatowt, A., Yoshikawa, M.: ArchivalQA: a large-scale benchmark dataset for open-domain question answering over historical news collections. In: Proceedings of the 45th International ACM SIGIR Conference on Research and Development in Information Retrieval, pp. 3025–3035 (2022)
20. Wang, L., et al.: A survey on large language model based autonomous agents. arXiv preprint arXiv:2308.11432 (2023)
21. Yamamoto, Y., Tezuka, T., Jatowt, A., Tanaka, K.: Supporting judgment of fact trustworthiness considering temporal and sentimental aspects. In: Bailey, J., Maier, D., Schewe, K.-D., Thalheim, B., Wang, X.S. (eds.) WISE 2008. LNCS, vol. 5175, pp. 206–220. Springer, Heidelberg (2008). https://doi.org/10.1007/978-3-540-85481-4_17
22. Zhao, W.X., et al.: A survey of large language models (2023)

Investigation of ChatGPT Use in Research Data Retrieval

Motokazu Yamasaki, Yoichi Tomiura, and Toshiyuki Shimizu(✉) ⓘ

Kyushu University, Fukuoka 819-0395, Japan

yamasaki.motokazu.491@s.kyushu-u.ac.jp, {tomiura.yoichi.802,
shimizu.toshiyuki.457}@m.kyushu-u.ac.jp

Abstract. In recent years, huge amounts of research data have been generated, and it has become important to search them efficiently and accurately in order to make use of research data. Existing search engines and keyword-based search methods require users to enter appropriate keywords or phrases, and it is difficult to obtain satisfactory results if users do not have detailed information about the desired data. In this study, we investigated whether ChatGPT could be used to reach the desired research data by users who are not familiar with them. Specifically, we investigated whether users could find the research data cited in a research paper by entering the abstract of the paper into ChatGPT and then asking for the data necessary to write the research paper. The results showed that research data could be found in 65% of the cases, confirming that the use of ChatGPT increases the discoverability of research data.

Keywords: Dataset search · Research data · ChatGPT

1 Introduction

In recent years, there has been a trend toward publishing research papers and research data on the Internet, and it is expected that new research will be conducted using open data. In line with this trend, research has also been conducted on research data retrieval [1]. While full-text search is possible for research papers, full-text search is not possible for research data because research data is often a set of numerical values or images. When searching research data, it is common to perform keyword searches using Google Dataset Search [2] or other search engines through metadata assigned to the research data. However, researchers are not always familiar with the field of research data they want, and it is often difficult to use appropriate keywords when searching. In addition, research data are not always given sufficient metadata, and it is sometimes difficult to obtain appropriate search results using keyword searches [1]. Therefore, we examined the use of ChatGPT to find the research data that researchers want even if it is difficult for a user to specify keywords when searching for research data.

ChatGPT enables searches using natural language sentences. In fact, a study has been conducted on the use of ChatGPT to search the literature [3,4]. It is thought that by

D. H. Goh et al. (Eds.): ICADL 2023, LNCS 14457, pp. 36–40, 2023.
https://doi.org/10.1007/978-981-99-8085-7_4

expressing the research that a researcher wants to conduct in text and giving it to Chat-GPT, the researcher can search for research data available for conducting that research. Though responses by ChatGPT are not always correct, and some non-existent research data or incorrect descriptions of research data may be found but can be verified using the name of the data, the URL, or the DOI.

Consider a situation in which a researcher uses ChatGPT to search for research data needed to conduct certain research. The researcher can describe his/her research in a compact text, such as an abstract of a paper. Therefore, we examined the use of ChatGPT by entering this text into ChatGPT and asking it to suggest research data that would be useful in conducting the research. As an experiment to reproduce such a situation, we have considered the following simulation: We input the abstract of a research paper that has already been published (but is a recent article that we believe ChatGPT is not using for training) and ask ChatGPT to suggest useful research data.

2 Method

We conducted an experiment using ChatGPT to search for research data used in a research paper from the abstract of the research paper. For this experiment, we collected 50 research data available on the Internet, and also collected two papers citing the data for each research data, making a total of 100 pairs of research paper and research data.[1] The papers citing the research data were obtained by focusing on the data papers accompanying the research data and collecting the research papers citing the data papers.

In this study, we assume a situation in which we ask ChatGPT to suggest useful research data for a research paper he or she would like to write. Since ChatGPT has learned information until September 2021, we collected research data that was created before 2020. We also collected research papers written after 2022.

We examined whether ChatGPT seemed to have learned about the data when collecting research data. We asked ChatGPT, "Are you familiar with [Dataset Name]?" and we excluded the data if ChatGPT responded, for example, "I apologize, but as of my last knowledge update in September 2021, I am not familiar with [Dataset Name]." because they were judged to be impossible for ChatGPT to retrieve such research data.

We entered the abstract of the paper and the phrase "Give me 10 datasets to help me write this paper." into ChatGPT, and we were answered with 10 research datasets from the abstract of the paper that would be useful for writing that paper. We investigated whether any of the 10 included the research data that the paper cited. When the output did not contain the desired research data, we additionally entered "Give me 10 more." and were answered with a maximum of 30 datasets. Using the above methods, we investigated whether the desired research data were included in up to 30 data answered for each of the 100 research papers.

In the process of the preliminary experiment, we tried using behavioral prompts such as "You are an excellent searcher." and entering supplementary explanations such as "I would like to conduct research on the following." However, since no significant difference was observed in the responses compared to when only the simple question

---

[1] The list of research data and research papers used in this study is available at https://doi.org/10.48708/6796400.

"Give me 10 datasets to help me write this paper." were entered, the experiment was conducted by entering only simple questions.

3 Results

Responses including the correct dataset were obtained for 65 pairs of abstract and dataset by ChatGPT. In this experiment with 100 pairs, 50 research data and 2 research papers per research data, 23 of these 50 research data were not found.

ChatGPT responded with the following information when answering the results.

- Summary of the research
- Characteristics of datasets useful for research content
- Name of each dataset
- Brief description of each dataset and its use

In addition, the URL to access the dataset as well as the name of the dataset was sometimes answered.

4 Discussion

4.1 Comparison with Keyword Search

To compare the data retrieval with that proposed by ChatGPT, a keyword search was performed using Google Dataset Search. We used keywords suggested by ChatGPT in this comparison. We entered the abstract of the research paper and the sentence "I would like to find datasets that will help me write this paper. Please suggest keywords that I could use in my search." into ChatGPT, and the first one of the suggested keywords (key phrases) was used for the search. For example, when we entered the abstract of a research paper written about a technique to create a video of a talking face from audio and facial images into ChatGPT, we were answered with keywords such as "Audio-visual dataset" and "Face keypoints dataset". We conducted an experiment on the top 30 results of Google Dataset Search, and found 7 (14%) of the 50 research paper/research data pairs. Table 1 provides a summary of the research results obtained using ChatGPT and Keyword Search methods. When ChatGPT answered research data, 65% of all pairs were able to find research data, suggesting that ChatGPT's suggestion of research data may be useful for research data retrieval. The reason for this is thought to be ChatGPT's ability to perform associations. While ChatGPT uses a language model to probabilistically generate the words that follow sentences when responding, keyword searches are based on whether or not the entered keywords match the metadata description.

In this study, we compared two types of searches: keyword searches and searches by interacting with ChatGPT. In addition, we plan to further examine the comparison method, since we only used the first one of the suggested keywords (key phrases) in this comparison, although we are likely to try multiple keywords when conducting keyword searches.

Table 1. Comparison between ChatGPT and keyword search.

	Success	Failure
ChatGPT	65	35
Keyword Search	7	43

4.2 Characteristics of Research Data to Be Answered by ChatGPT

In conducting the experiments in this study, ChatGPT tended to propose dataset names that contain abbreviations or proper nouns. Examples include "The KITTI Dataset (Karlsruhe Institute of Technology and Toyota Technological Institute)" [5] and "The UK-DALE dataset" [6].

4.3 Devising Inputs to ChatGPT

In some cases, when the desired research data could not be found by ChatGPT, it was possible to find the data by giving ChatGPT the features of the desired research data. For example, when a video dataset called "UCF101" [7] was cited in a paper in the field of Computer Vision and Pattern Recognition, and when we asked ChatGPT to answer the research data, it answered mainly image format datasets. Then, if we asked for the answer of the dataset in video format, the video dataset was answered mainly, and we were able to find the desired dataset "UCF101".

Thus, it is possible that more research data can be discovered by devising inputs to ChatGPT. However, since the characteristics were described by the author (who knows the answers) in this case, there is a challenge whether the author of the paper can ask ChatGPT for valid characteristics.

4.4 About the Papers We Used

In the 100 research papers we used in our experiment, we found that some papers, precisely 16 papers out of the 100 papers, explicitly mentioned the dataset names within their abstracts. Notably, all experiments conducted on these papers, where dataset names were explicitly referenced in the abstract, resulted in successful data retrieval through the utilization of ChatGPT.

In order to better simulate the situation of research data retrieval, we plan to refine the experimental process and focus on papers that do not include dataset names within their abstracts.

4.5 About the LLM Used

Since we used the free version of ChatGPT, the results may differ from those obtained using the paid version of ChatGPT. The free version is GPT-3.5, while the paid version is GPT-4.0 [8], a newer version. We intend to experiment with the paid version in the future.

5 Conclusion

In this study, we investigated the effectiveness of research data retrieval using ChatGPT, and were able to find research data cited in 65 out of 100 research papers. Since it is often difficult to find appropriate data when searching for research data using keywords, we believe that ChatGPT has a potential to assist in the search process. In the future, we plan to further investigate ways to make it easier to reach the desired data by devising input into ChatGPT.

References

1. Chapman, A., et al.: Dataset search: a survey. VLDB J. **29**, 251–272 (2020)
2. Brickley, D., Burgess, M., Noy, N.: Google dataset search: building a search engine for datasets in an open web ecosystem. In: The World Wide Web Conference (WWW 2019), pp. 1365–1375 (2019)
3. Haman, M., Školník, M.: Using ChatGPT to conduct a literature review. Account. Res. **6**, 1–3 (2023)
4. McGowan, A., et al.: ChatGPT and Bard exhibit spontaneous citation fabrication during psychiatry literature search. Psych. Res. **326**, 115334 (2023)
5. Kelly, J., Knottenbelt, W.: The UK-DALE dataset, domestic appliance-level electricity demand and whole-house demand from five UK homes. Sci Data **2**, 150007 (2015)
6. Geiger, A., Lenz, P., Stiller, C., Urtasun, R.: Vision meets robotics: the KITTI dataset. Int. J. Robot. Res. **32**(11), 1231–1237 (2013)
7. Soomro, K., Zamir, A.R., Shah, M.: UCF101: a dataset of 101 human actions classes from videos in the wild. arXiv:1212.0402 (2012)
8. OpenAI.: GPT-4 Technical Report. arXiv:2303.08774 (2023)

Aspect-Based Sentiment Analysis of Racial Issues in Singapore: Enhancing Model Performance Using ChatGPT

Manoj Reddy Tudi[(✉)], Jin-Cheon Na, Meky Liu, Hongjin Chen, Yiqing Dai, and Li Yang

Wee Kim Wee School of Communication and Information, Nanyang Technological University, Singapore 637718, Singapore

{manojred001,tjcna,meky001,chen1576,daiy0017, yang0666}@ntu.edu.sg

Abstract. This study employs Aspect-Based Sentiment Analysis (ABSA) and advanced AI methodologies to analyze public sentiment on racial issues in Singapore from 2018–2023. By utilizing synthetic data generation and In-Context Learning with ChatGPT API, we enhanced the performance of our ABSA model. Our findings highlight the utility of these methods in overcoming data imbalance and providing a comprehensive understanding of sentiment polarity associated with racially related aspect terms. Despite the higher cost of using sophisticated language models, the study underscores the potential of these techniques in offering nuanced insights into complex societal dynamics, illuminating a promising path for future research in sentiment analysis.

Keywords: Aspect-Based Sentiment Analysis (ABSA) · Social Media Analysis · Racial Issues · Synthetic Data Generation · In-Context Learning · ChatGPT API

1 Introduction

In the rapidly evolving digital landscape, social media platforms serve as vital arenas for public discourse on complex societal issues, including race and ethnicity. Harnessing the wealth of data these platforms provide is at the forefront of this study. By employing Aspect-Based Sentiment Analysis (ABSA), our focus rests on assessing public sentiment surrounding racial issues in the diverse society of Singapore.

The research aims to utilize text mining and deep learning techniques to evaluate real-world social challenges and uncover trends in public attitudes toward racial issues. Specifically, we will use data sourced from the Hardware Zone forum and Reddit to train ABSA models. These models will then predict sentiment polarity linked to racially related aspect terms. This nuanced methodology allows for an in-depth examination of sentiments regarding various facets of racial issues, thus highlighting the utility of ABSA in social media data analysis. The objectives of this study include:

© The Author(s), under exclusive license to Springer Nature Singapore Pte Ltd. 2023
D. H. Goh et al. (Eds.): ICADL 2023, LNCS 14457, pp. 41–55, 2023.
https://doi.org/10.1007/978-981-99-8085-7_5

- Implementing ABSA models to evaluate racial issues as depicted on Singapore's social platforms.
- Utilizing Open AI's ChatGPT API to address issues of data imbalance in sentiment analysis.
- Applying Advanced In-Context Learning (ICL) for ABSA to improve the model's performance.

To enhance the accuracy of the ABSA model and address data imbalance, we incorporate ChatGPT, a state-of-the-art language model, for data augmentation. By enriching minority categories (i.e., positive category) with synthetic data, ChatGPT allows for a more representative and balanced dataset for sentiment analysis. To further enhance the ABSA model's predictive capabilities, this study leverages a novel learning paradigm known as SuperICL [1]. With SuperICL, we aim to improve the model's ability to identify and understand a variety of racially related aspect terms, ensuring a comprehensive analysis of public sentiment towards racial issues.

The significance of this study lies in two primary areas:

- The application of ABSA to racial data offers a novel perspective in understanding public sentiment and its impact on social dynamics in a racially diverse society like Singapore.
- The integration of ChatGPT, synthetic data, and SuperICL to improve fine-tuned ABSA model performance.

Through these contributions, this study provides invaluable insights into the complex nature of racial issues in digital discourse, contributing substantially to the field of sentiment analysis in social science research.

2   Literature Review

2.1   Introduction to Aspect-Based Sentiment Analysis (ABSA)

Sentiment analysis aims to discern and categorize user opinions into document-level, sentence-level, and aspect-level [2–4]. Document level assumes a single opinion per document, sentence-level analyzes sentiments in sentences, while aspect-level, the most detailed, determines sentiments associated with specific aspects within content [5]. Aspect-Based Sentiment Analysis (ABSA) is a branch of aspect-level analysis and is primarily concerned with identifying sentiment polarities related to particular aspects within a sentence, which may have multiple aspects with varying sentiments [6, 7]. In this study, ABSA will be used to glean insights from race-related social media data in Singapore.

2.2   Review of Race-Related Studies in Singapore

Previous research on Singapore's racial issues has predominantly adopted qualitative methods or narrative reviews. For instance, studies by Lim et al. [8] and Chua [9] utilized the Critical Junctures Theory (CTS) to explore the impact of government policies on ethnic inequalities. Other researchers, like Velayutham [10], used case studies to investigate the attitudes of Chinese Singaporeans toward Malays and Indians. However, these traditional methodologies, often manual and labor-intensive, may yield inconsistent findings, and their scope and depth are inherently limited due to the challenges of manually analyzing large data sets. Furthermore, while questionnaire-based studies [11, 12] have attempted to quantify public sentiment towards racial harmony in Singapore, they do not fully capture the complexity and diversity of public opinion, nor the nuances of discrimination, as highlighted by Chew et al. [13].

Addressing these limitations, our study introduces an automated approach using Aspect-Based Sentiment Analysis (ABSA), which is underpinned by text mining and deep learning techniques. Although the precision of ABSA might differ slightly from manual methods, it can handle large-scale data, extract relevant features automatically, and quantify public sentiment effectively. More importantly, ABSA is a learning model that can adapt to new aspects and sentiments, ensuring its performance remains robust and up-to-date as social discourse evolves. This ABSA approach provides a more comprehensive, nuanced, and quantitatively reliable understanding of racial issues in Singapore. By shifting from manual to automated data analysis, our study not only adds depth to the existing literature but also introduces an innovative method for exploring complex societal issues.

2.3 Existing Approaches to Address Data Imbalance

Imbalanced datasets are a common challenge in machine learning, where the distribution of classes is not equal. This can lead to biased models that favor the majority class and perform poorly on the minority class. Several techniques have been proposed to address this issue, including oversampling, undersampling, and synthetic data generation [14]. Oversampling involves duplicating instances of the minority class to balance the dataset, while undersampling involves removing instances of the majority class. Synthetic data generation involves creating new instances of the minority class using techniques such as SMOTE [15]. Data augmentation is another technique used to address imbalanced datasets by generating new instances of the minority class. ChatGPT, an OpenAI's large language model, has shown promise in this area [16]. ChatGPT can be used to generate synthetic text data that is similar to human-written text, making it a useful tool for data augmentation in natural language processing tasks. Zero-shot prompting with ChatGPT emerged as a robust solution for augmenting training data, particularly in low-resource settings for NLP tasks [16]. The method not only surpassed most traditional approaches but also displayed less dependence on the quality of the original training dataset. In line with these capabilities, our study also leverages ChatGPT for aspect-based sentiment analysis. Specifically, the model excels at generating text that includes given aspect terms while also reflecting targeted sentiment polarities.

2.4 In-Context Learning

In-context learning (ICL) has emerged as a novel paradigm in language models, garnering significant attention from recent studies [17, 18]. This approach has proven to be effective in various NLP tasks [18–20]. The core feature of ICL lies in its ability to learn from a limited set of examples and then make predictions based on the acquired knowledge, resembling human learning patterns. Unlike traditional machine learning, ICL does not require fine-tuning, resulting in significant time and resource savings, while still achieving improved performance. Numerous researchers have already demonstrated the benefits of implementing ICL in different tasks, for example, Min et al. [20] conducted comprehensive experiments, covering sentiment analysis, paraphrase detection, natural language inference, and so forth, resulting in noticeable performance improvements. Therefore, motivated by the proven effectiveness of ICL in various NLP tasks, this study also employed SuperICL with ABSA, an enhanced version of ICL, to investigate potential enhancements in ABSA. SuperICL is an advanced approach where a fine-tuned model's prediction labels are used as input to ICL, augmenting the learning process by combining the strengths of both fine-tuning and ICL [1]. Building on the advancements in ICL, SuperICL presents an innovative approach that merges fine-tuned smaller models with larger language models. This dual-model architecture allows for the smaller models to contribute task-specific knowledge, while the larger models maintain a broad understanding of language. The result is an enhanced performance across a range of tasks [1]. Motivated by these advantages, our study explores the potential application of SuperICL to ABSA.

3   Methodology: ABSA for Social Media Analysis

3.1   Data Preparation

Data Collection. This project collected data on racial issues from two social platforms: the HardwareZone (HWZ) forum, a Singapore-based IT-oriented portal, and the Singapore subreddit (r/Singapore) on Reddit. For HWZ, a two-step scraping process was utilized, which involved using a keyword list to retrieve search terms and scrape thread URLs, followed by scraping posts within these threads. Posts from the most recent 5 years were collected (until April 2023). This resulted in a raw data set of 457,728 posts from HWZ awaiting further filtering for relevance to racial issues. Data from the Singapore subreddit on Reddit was scraped using an API and filtered based on the specified keywords. This process yielded a collection of 321,866 posts.

In the early stages of our study, several challenges were encountered in determining the initial aspect terms and categories for ABSA. Issues arose due to the non-exclusivity of terms, variability in term format, and some terms lacking the necessary specificity to accurately represent racial topics. To mitigate these issues and improve the granularity of our aspect identification, we utilized fuzzy search methods, relying on the Python library FuzzyWuzzy [21], to handle term inconsistencies and concept variations. These aspect terms, representing various facets of racial discourse in Singapore, were then grouped into nine categories to allow for a more comprehensive and nuanced ABSA.

Data Selection. The data selection process aimed to minimize noise and ensure the inclusion of a broad spectrum of data related to racial issues from HWZ and Reddit. Initial text pre-processing steps consisted of sentence segmentation, deduplication, and the exclusion of sentences with fewer than three words. To enhance the relevance of selected data, we used FuzzyWuzzy, a Python library [21], to implement a fuzzy search method. This technique calculates a similarity score for each sentence in the dataset,

Table 1. Aspect Categories and Aspect Terms

Aspect Category	Aspect Term
Racial Privilege	Chinese privilege, Malay privilege, Indian privilege, majority privilege, sinkie privilege, Chinese right, Singaporean privilege, India right, minority privilege, merlion privilege, racial privilege, AMDK privilege
Education	subsidy, Mendaki, CDAC, SINDA
Employment	CECA, Indian IT, anti-ceca, thick accent, poor English, speak Chinese, speak Malay, speak Indian, speak Tamil, speak mandarin, racial accent
Housing	hdb quota, EIP, racial quota, Indian landlord, Chinese landlord, Malay landlord
Physical Appearance	skin color, yellow skin, dark skin, brown skin, colored, tanned skin
Discrimination	racial victim, race discrimination, racism, balik cina, racial slur, racial attack, racial insult, racial hatred, racial segregation, racial riot, racial bias, racial profiling, racist, racial tension, race card, racial stereotype
Wealth	poor Chinese, rich Chinese, poor Malay, rich Indian, rich Asian, poor sinkie, rich sinkie, rich Malay
CMIO (Chinese, Malay, Indian, and others)	CMIO, CMIO Model, Chinese race, Indian race, Malay race, other race, AMDK, majority race, minority race, Chinese majority, sinkie Chinese, local Chinese
General	racial harmony, racial tolerance, racial equality, racial balance, racial feeling, multi-racial society, inter-racial relationship, racial difference, racial pillar, racial issue, racial identity, racial policy, racial group, Racial Harmony Day

comparing it to our predefined aspect terms. The 'fuzzy matched count' refers to the number of aspect terms within a text body that meet or exceed a given similarity score threshold, as determined by FuzzyWuzzy. Initially, we selected posts with similarity scores above 50 and a fuzzy-matched count of more than 5; these initial parameters were empirically chosen to balance data relevance and noise reduction. Subsequently, after additional text preprocessing, we applied more stringent criteria, elevating the similarity score threshold to 54 and requiring a fuzzy-matched count of at least 12. These revised parameters were chosen to further refine the dataset by reducing noise while retaining posts of high relevance.

Data Labelling. The whole dataset for aspect-based sentiment analysis consists of 9,743 records. In this project, 2,751 out of 9,743 records were manually labeled as the training set, utilizing the ChatGPT API to expedite the annotation process. The ChatGPT API, which offers advanced NLP capabilities, was employed to initially indicate the sentiments of specific aspect terms. These preliminary annotations were subsequently verified and corrected by human annotators. The sentiments of aspect terms were labeled by three individuals, and the inter-annotator agreement was assessed using Cohen's Kappa coefficient, calculated from 1,000 sentences labeled by all three annotators. An average Cohen's Kappa value of 0.7136 verified the consistency and efficacy of the manual annotation.

Dataset Partitioning. The dataset, comprising 2,751 labeled data points, was constructed for model training and testing and was partitioned in an 80:20 ratio. The 80:20 split was chosen to maximize the training set size, given the limited available data, while still providing a sufficient test set for model evaluation. The labeled dataset exhibits an imbalance in the distribution of the target sentiment, with data labeled as having a negative sentiment substantially outnumbering that labeled with a positive sentiment. The overall composition of the training, validation, and testing sets is presented in Table 2. The imbalance in the dataset, particularly the scarcity of 'Positive' instances, is expected given that the aspect terms are specifically related to racially sensitive topics, which are often accompanied by neutral or negative sentiments in discussions.

Table 2. Training & Validation and Test Datasets

Negative			Neutral			Positive		
Train	Valid	Test	Train	Valid	Test	Train	Valid	Test
810	266	248	665	215	249	175	69	54
1324			1129			298		

Based on the 2,751 labeled data points mentioned above, a term list was extracted directly from the sentences and aligned with predefined aspect terms. By integrating this term list with the final aspect term list, a comprehensive new term list was generated. To construct the dataset for prediction with unlabeled data, an exact string match was performed between a composite list of the term list and defined aspect terms and the unlabeled data that met the matched count threshold of 12. Ultimately, a total of 16,208 data points were obtained from which 6,992 were selected for prediction.

3.2   Method 1 – A Fine-Tuned ABSA Model

The traditional approach to ABSA involves a direct and uncomplicated process of training the model solely on the original, human-annotated dataset. In this method, the ABSA model is trained for 6 epochs. After each epoch, the model's performance is evaluated on a validation set, and the model's state - that is, the specific configuration of its internal parameters that achieved the highest accuracy on the validation set is saved. This app-roach serves as the standard method, which will be compared with the iterative training approach involving both original and synthetically generated datasets (i.e., Method 2). For both traditional and iterative training approaches, the ABSA model employed is LCF-BERT [22], sourced from the PyABSA library [23]. The employed model uses the transformer model "bert-base-cased" [24].

3.3   Method 2 – Enhancing the Fine-Tuned ABSA Model Using ChatGPT: Addressing Data Imbalance

Implementation of ChatGPT for Synthetic Data Generation. For enhancing the overall ABSA model accuracy, OpenAI's GPT-3.5 Turbo model was employed to gen-erate synthetic sentences. The focus was primarily on augmenting the minority class, which was the positive sentiment sentences. The GPT-3.5 Turbo model received a list of context-related aspect terms. For each term, a prompt (see Table 3) was prepared, requesting the model to generate 20 sentences reflecting positive sentiment. The aspect term in focus was embedded into each sentence in a contextually coherent manner. The resultant sentences were reminiscent of comments found on Reddit, accurately embody-ing the desired sentiment, and containing the given aspect term. Using this approach, 780 positive sentences were generated. Table 3 shows the prompt used to generate 20 positive sentences for the aspect term "subsidy", within the aspect category "housing".

Table 3. ChatGPT API prompt used to generate synthetic data.

I'm developing an Aspect-Based sentiment classifier, which assigns a positive, negative, or neutral tag to text based on its aspect. I need you to generate sample positive data resembling Reddit posts or comments
Generate the data in JSON format with no extra objects
Generate 20 sentences. Aspect term: **subsidy** (**Housing** in Singapore context)

Iterative Training Algorithm to Improve Model Accuracy. Building on the use of OpenAI's GPT-3.5 Turbo to generate synthetic training data, an innovative training algorithm has been devised that strategically alternates between original and synthetic data across multiple iterations. This approach not only enriches the diversity and volume of the training data but also capitalizes on the distinctive properties of both datasets. By alternating between original human-annotated sentences and synthetically generated sentences, the training of the model is tailored to leverage the strengths of each data set. The following section delineates the specifics of this iterative training process for ABSA.

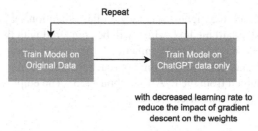

with decreased learning rate to
reduce the impact of gradient
descent on the weights

Fig. 1. Schematic representation of the iterative training process alternating between original and synthetic datasets.

Algorithm 1 Iterative Training using Original and Synthetic Datasets for ABSA

Input: original dataset D_o, synthetic dataset D_s, and number of iterations I
Initialize: Pre-trained ABSA model
for each iteration I **do**
    if the best model from the previous iteration exists **then**
        load the best model
    end if
    if the current iteration is even **then**
        dataset = D_o
        set model hyperparameters for D_o
    else
        dataset = D_s
        adjust model hyperparameters for D_s
    end if
    for each epoch **do**
        train (model, dataset)
    end for
    save the model with the best validation set accuracy
end for

The algorithm illustrated in Fig. 1 and Algorithm 1 presents an elegant solution to enhance ABSA training. It begins with the initialization of the ABSA model. The core of the algorithm is in its iterative process where it alternates between the original and synthetic datasets. For even-numbered iterations, the algorithm selects the original dataset and configures the ABSA model with hyperparameters that are attuned to this dataset (i.e., epochs = 3, learning rate = 2e-05, dropout = 0.3). Conversely, for odd-numbered iterations, the synthetic dataset, generated by ChatGPT, is selected with the model hyperparameters tailored specifically to this data (i.e., epochs = 1, learning rate = 9e-07, dropout = 0.1). Each iteration includes a training phase over a predetermined number of epochs. The model state at the end of each iteration is saved, serving as a checkpoint for the next iteration. This iterative training method, coupled with the usage of both original and synthetic data, ensures a robust ABSA model that can accurately handle a diverse set of sentiment scenarios.

3.4   Method 3 – Improving the Fine-Tuned ABSA Model via In-context Learning

Method 3 employs an advanced technique known as In-Context Learning (ICL) for sentiment prediction within ABSA. The inspiration for this method draws from a concept called SuperICL, previously used in a different context, not directly related to ABSA [1]. The SuperICL approach was leveraged and adapted to the requirements of ABSA, intending to refine the ABSA model's predictions. The process of implementing Advanced In-Context Learning (ICL) for ABSA proceeds as follows:

1. For each test example in the dataset, the algorithm attempts to find similar examples in the training dataset. To accomplish this, it first computes the BERT embeddings of the test input.
2. Subsequently, it calculates the cosine similarity between the embeddings of the test text and the embeddings of all training examples, resulting in a similarity score.
3. Based on the similarity score, it sorts the training examples and selects the top 'N' training examples that are most like the test example for each sentiment polarity.
4. The sentiment polarity predictions for the training examples are generated using a fine-tuned ABSA model, either via Method 1 or Method 2, as outlined in this study. These predictions are incorporated alongside all the training examples and the test input to provide an additional contextual layer, enriching the data that will be fed to OpenAI's text-davinci-003 model.
5. This curated set of similar examples, along with the test example, is then formatted into a specific context format as shown in Table 4.
6. This contextual information is passed to OpenAI's model (text-davinci-003) as a prompt, with an expectation for the model to predict the sentiment polarity of the test example.

In the proposed approach, the selection of similar training examples based on the cosine similarity of BERT embeddings serves multiple objectives. First, it helps in contextualizing the sentiment of the test example. By identifying semantically close training samples, the algorithm implicitly captures the nuanced usage of words and phrases specific to the sentiment class, thereby offering a richer contextual background for the test data. Second, this selection acts as a form of data augmentation. The training examples provide diverse yet relevant instances that the model can reference, which enhances its ability to generalize. Finally, the use of relevant examples fine-tunes the model's predictive capabilities in a way that is contextually anchored. When these curated examples are fed into a sophisticated model like text-davinci-003, they provide a targeted context that helps the model zero in on the specific features that are most indicative of sentiment in the test example. This is particularly important for models like ChatGPT, which are trained on vast and diverse datasets; they benefit from narrowed, context-specific information to make more accurate and nuanced predictions. In other words, the provision of relevant training examples effectively serves as a guiding framework that helps the ChatGPT model better understand the specific sentiment context it is asked to evaluate, thereby increasing the confidence and accuracy of its sentiment classification.

Table 4 shows a prompt using ICL examples, aimed at acquiring the label for the test input "Racial harmony is a common goal for all Singaporeans", where "Racial harmony" is the aspect term and the transformer model's prediction is also given.

Table 4. Prompt used for ABSA using SuperICL (i.e., Method 3)

Similar Examples:
Text: Fortunately, most Singaporeans understand the importance of racial harmony
Aspect Term: racial harmony
Transformer Model Prediction: Positive
Label: Positive

....

Test Input:
Text: Racial harmony is a common goal for all Singaporeans
Aspect Term: Racial harmony
Transformer Model Prediction: Positive
Label:

By utilizing the principles of SuperICL in the realm of ABSA, this method offers a unique approach that harnesses the power of transformers to provide a more context-aware sentiment prediction mechanism.

3.5 Performance Comparison

To examine the efficacy of the methodologies, we have subjected each method to an extensive evaluation process and compared the performance based on the calculated F1 scores for each sentiment class, as well as an overall F1 score. In the nomenclature used to designate each method variant, 'I' denotes iterations for Method 2, 'N' stands for the number of ICL examples per class in Method 3, and 'Method 2 + 3' implies an amalgamation of Methods 2 and 3, with the specified number of ICL examples per class.

Table 5. Performance comparison of various methodologies in ABSA.

Method used	F1 Score	F1 Negative	F1 Neutral	F1 Positive
Method 1	0.7731	0.8008	0.7731	0.6422
Method 2 – 3I	0.7786	0.8069	0.7790	0.6557
Method 2 – 5I	0.7840	0.8105	0.7785	0.6731
Method 2 – 7I	0.7659	0.7874	0.7722	0.6500
Method 2 – 9I	0.7822	0.8117	0.7703	0.6847
Method 2 – 11I	0.7858	0.8084	0.7839	0.6852
Method 3 – 3N	0.8094	0.8478	0.7916	0.7037
Method 2 + 3 – 3N	0.8131	0.8403	0.8000	0.7358
Method 2 + 3 – 5N	0.8276	0.8506	0.8125	0.7800
Method 2 + 3 – 10N	0.8240	0.8538	0.8142	0.7273

Performance Analysis. The results outlined in Table 5 demonstrate that both Method 2 and Method 3 contribute positively to the ABSA performance, as seen through the increase in corresponding F1 scores. Each method was successful in boosting the model's sentiment classification ability, with varying degrees of enhancement. Method 1 served as the foundational benchmark, posting an overall F1 score of 0.7731. The F1 scores for negative, neutral, and positive sentiments were 0.8008, 0.7731, and 0.6422, respectively. The relatively lower F1 score for positive sentiment analysis suggests the model's difficulty in accurately identifying positive sentiments using conventional training methodologies.

In Method 2, the performance improved with an increase in iterations. From 3 to 11 iterations ('3I' to '11I'), the overall F1 score saw a steady rise, from 0.7786 to 0.7858. The F1 score for the positive sentiment category also witnessed a significant improvement, indicating that the iterative training approach utilizing synthetic data has mitigated the data imbalance problem, thereby improving the model's precision in identifying positive sentiments.

Method 3 illustrated its proficiency in capturing sentiment with greater accuracy. Even with just 3 examples per class ('3N'), it achieved an F1 score of 0.8094, outperforming both Method 1 and Method 2 at 11 iterations. The F1 scores across all sentiment categories were enhanced, underlining the effectiveness of employing Advanced ICL to strengthen the ABSA model's sentiment analysis capability.

The integration of Method 2's fine-tuned ABSA model as an input layer for Method 3's SuperICL approach significantly enhances the overall performance of the ABSA model. When these methods were combined (Method 2 + 3), impressive results were observed across all sentiment categories. With just 3 examples per class ('3N'), the overall F1 score climbed to 0.8131. As the number of examples increased to 5 ('5N'), an outstanding F1 score of 0.8276 was achieved, marking the best performance among all the evaluated methods.

The consistent increase in F1 scores from Method 1 to Method 2 + 3 signifies the benefits of synthetic data and innovative training strategies in overcoming data imbalance and bolstering ABSA performance. Method 3, employing SuperICL, excels in accuracy by leveraging both the fine-tuned ABSA model and additional context-aware insights, effectively capturing intricate sentiment nuances that other methods may overlook. However, the relative advantage of each method might vary depending on the specifics of the task at hand and data availability.

The bar graph in Fig. 2 complements Table 5 by illustrating the weighted average precision and recall scores for each method, in addition to the F1 scores already covered. These measures provide a more nuanced understanding of the model's performance in different scenarios. Method 1 sets a baseline with a precision and recall of 0.775 and 0.7731, respectively. Method 2 displays increased precision and recall as the iterations progress, culminating at 0.7887 and 0.7858, respectively, in the eleventh iteration. The most effective methods are Method 3 and the hybrid of Methods 2 and 3, which consistently achieve the highest precision and recall scores. For instance, with 3 examples per class, the combined method (Method 2 + 3) attains a precision of 0.8103 and a recall of 0.8094. As the number of examples per class grows, so do these scores, reaching 0.8292 and 0.8276 respectively with 5 examples, demonstrating the combined method's superior performance.

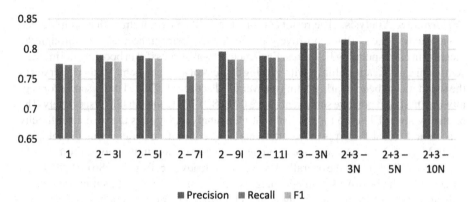

Fig. 2. A comparative evaluation of Precision, Recall, and F1 scores.

4 Analysis of Racial Issues in Singapore

After constructing the model using the labeled dataset, it was employed to predict sentiments for the remaining 6,992 records. The labeled dataset was then integrated with the predicted dataset to conduct an aspect-based sentiment analysis. The following sections delve into various aspects of sentiment analysis. Notably, we used the model from Method 2 with 11 iterations (11*I*) rather than the optimal model from Method 3. This decision was made primarily due to economic considerations; while Method 3 and Method 2 + 3 offer slightly superior performance, the cost of using the ChatGPT API makes it financially less feasible to process such a large number of records.

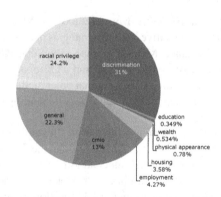

Fig. 3. Breakdown of data based on Aspect Categories

Aspect Categories Breakdown. Figure 3 provides a breakdown of the dataset based on the nine aspect categories outlined in Table 1. The top four aspect categories in our dataset, namely discrimination (31%), racial privilege (24.2%), general (22.3%), and CMIO (13%) account for a considerable portion of the dataset, while the remaining categories comprise less than 10% of the dataset.

ROI Score. To compare the sentiments of public opinions on various race-related topics, we developed the Racial Opinion Index (ROI) based on Kim's methodology for measuring public opinion on Twitter regarding nuclear power [25]. ROI is determined by quantifying the number of positive, neutral, and negative sentiment data of a particular aspect term, the calculating formula is shown below. Using ROIs, we can ascertain the overall public opinion on specific topics, such as identifying the issues that tend to elicit negative sentiment from the public or the race-related policies that are favored by the majority. Based on the formula of ROI, a score greater than 100 suggests a predominantly negative public opinion towards a particular topic or aspect term. Conversely, a score less than 100 indicates generally positive public sentiment. An ROI score of 100 implies an equal number of positive and negative opinions regarding the given aspect term.

$$Racial\ Opinion\ Index\ (ROI)$$
$$= \frac{N(Negative\_sentences(m)) - N(Positive\_sentences(m))}{N(Total\_sentences(m))} * 100 + 100$$

Analyzing the trends in ROI for various race-related topics reveals that certain topics, such as "discrimination" and "employment," have fluctuated in public sentiment. While some topics have maintained high ROI scores, indicating their prominence, others have experienced notable spikes or declines. Topics with consistently low ROI scores, like "physical appearance," indicate decreasing negativity over time. This data suggests a dynamic and evolving landscape of public sentiment on race-related issues.

5   Discussion

5.1   Limitations and Challenges

Our study encountered several limitations and challenges. One significant challenge is the financial aspect associated with the use of OpenAI's text-davinci-003 engine, as used in Method 3. This model's effectiveness in generating synthetic data and refining predictions comes at a higher cost, which may limit its applicability for resource-strapped projects. Furthermore, our dependence on LCF-BERT as the ABSA model could constrain the generalizability and effectiveness of our approaches. Although LCF-BERT has demonstrated strong performance, it is an older model, and there are more advanced and sophisticated ABSA models available that could potentially yield improved results.

5.2   Implications for Future Research

Future research could focus on evaluating the effectiveness of our proposed methods with newer, more sophisticated ABSA models, which could lead to performance and generalizability improvements. Additionally, it would be a worthwhile endeavor to explore strategies for reducing the financial implications of using powerful language models by considering the use of open-sourced large language models as an alternative to ChatGPT.

6 Conclusion

This study, centered on racial issues within Singapore, signifies a step forward in understanding complex societal dynamics using advanced AI and NLP tools. By employing ABSA and leveraging synthetic data generation and in-context learning through the ChatGPT API, we managed to enhance the performance of sentiment analysis models. Method 2, which involves iterative training using synthetic data, showed an improved ABSA model's ability to understand and categorize sentiments, while Method 3 further enhanced the model's performance through targeted in-context learning. These methodologies, despite their costs, can be invaluable for projects where high precision in sentiment analysis is required, illuminating a path for more effective ABSA application in future research.

Acknowledgment. This work is supported by DSO National Laboratories in Singapore (No. DSOCL21092). Any opinions, findings, and conclusions, or recommendations expressed in this material are those of the author(s) and do not necessarily reflect the views of the DSO National Laboratories.

References

1. Xu, C., Xu, Y., Wang, S., Liu, Y., Zhu, C., McAuley, J.: Small models are valuable plugins for large language models. arXiv preprint arXiv:2305.08848 (2023)
2. Zhang, C., Li, Q., Song, D.: Aspect-based sentiment classification with aspect-specific graph convolutional networks. arXiv preprint arXiv:1909.03477 (2019)
3. Do, H.H., Prasad, P.W.C., Maag, A., Alsadoon, A.: Deep learning for aspect-based sentiment analysis: a comparative review. Expert Syst. Appl. **118**, 272–299 (2019)
4. Schouten, K., Frasincar, F.: Survey on aspect-level sentiment analysis. IEEE Trans. Knowl. Data Eng. **28**(3), 813–830 (2015)
5. Tan, X., Cai, Y., Xu, J., Leung, H.-F., Chen, W., Li, Q.: Improving aspect-based sentiment analysis via aligning aspect embedding. Neurocomputing **383**, 336–347 (2020)
6. Fei, H., Chua, T.-S., Li, C., Ji, D., Zhang, M., Ren, Y.: On the robustness of aspect-based sentiment analysis: rethinking model, data, and training. ACM Trans. Inf. Syst. **41**(2), 1–32 (2022)
7. Yang, J., Yang, J.: Aspect based sentiment analysis with self-attention and gated convolutional networks. In: 2020 IEEE 11th International Conference on Software Engineering and Service Science (ICSESS), pp. 146–149. IEEE (2020)
8. Lim, S., Yang, W.W., Leong, C.-H., Hong, J.: Reconfiguring the Singapore identity space: beyond racial harmony and survivalism. Int. J. Intercult. Relat. **43**, 13–21 (2014)
9. Huat, C.B.: Multiculturalism in Singapore: an instrument of social control. Race & Class **44**(3), 58–77 (2003)
10. Velayutham, S.: Races without racism?: Everyday race relations in Singapore. Identities **24**(4), 455–473 (2017)
11. Chew, P.K.H.: Racism in Singapore: a review and recommendations for future research. J. Pac. Rim Psychol. **12**, e5 (2018)
12. Ling Ooi, G.: The role of the developmental state and interethnic relations in Singapore. Asian Ethnicity **6**(2), 109–120 (2005)
13. Chew, P.K.H., Young, J.L., Tan, G.P.K.: Racism and the Pinkerton syndrome in Singapore: effects of race on hiring decisions. J. Pac. Rim Psychol. **13**, e16 (2019)

14. Brownlee, J.: Imbalanced classification with Python: better metrics, balance skewed classes, cost-sensitive learning. Mach. Learn. Mastery (2020)
15. Chawla, N.V., Bowyer, K.W., Hall, L.O., Philip Kegelmeyer, W.: SMOTE: synthetic minority over-sampling technique. J. Artif. Intell. Res. **16**, 321–357 (2002)
16. Ubani, S., Polat, S.O., Nielsen, R.: ZeroShotDataAug: generating and augmenting training data with ChatGPT. arXiv preprint arXiv:2304.14334 (2023)
17. Li, X., Qiu, X.: Finding supporting examples for in-context learning. arXiv preprint arXiv: 2302.13539 (2023)
18. Dong, Q., et al.: A survey for in-context learning. arXiv preprint arXiv:2301.00234 (2022)
19. Brown, T., et al.: Language models are few-shot learners. Adv. Neural. Inf. Process. Syst. **33**, 1877–1901 (2020)
20. Min, S., et al.: Rethinking the role of demonstrations: what makes in-context learning work? arXiv preprint arXiv:2202.12837 (2022)
21. SeatGeek, FuzzyWuzzy, GitHub Repository (2020). https://github.com/seatgeek/fuzzywuzzy
22. Zeng, B., Yang, H., Xu, R., Zhou, W., Han, X.: LCF: a local context focus mechanism for aspect-based sentiment classification. Appl. Sci. **9**(16), 3389 (2019)
23. Heng, Y.: PyABSA: A Modularized Framework for Reproducible Aspect-Based Sentiment Analysis [Computer software] (2023)
24. Devlin, J., Chang, M.-W., Lee, K., Toutanova, K.: Bert: pre-training of deep bidirectional transformers for language understanding. arXiv preprint arXiv:1810.04805 (2018)
25. Kim, D.S., Kim, J.W.: Public opinion sensing and trend analysis on social media: a study on nuclear power on Twitter. Int. J. Multim. Ubiquit. Eng. **9**(11), 373–384 (2014)

Cultural Data Analysis

Text Line Detection in Historical Index Tables: Evaluations on a New French PArish REcord Survey Dataset (PARES)

Guillaume Bernard[1]([✉]) [iD], Casey Wall[1], Mélodie Boillet[2] [iD],
Mickaël Coustaty[1] [iD], Christopher Kermorvant[2] [iD], and Antoine Doucet[1] [iD]

[1] Laboratoire L3i – Université de La Rochelle, La Rochelle, France
{guillaume.bernard,casey.wall,mickael.coustaty,antoine.doucet}@univ-lr.fr
[2] TEKLIA, Paris, France
{boillet,kermorvant}@teklia.com

Abstract. In this paper, we address the challenge of document image analysis for historical index table documents with handwritten records. Demographic studies can gain insight from the use of automatic document analysis in such documents through the study of population movements. To evaluate the efficacy of automatic layout analysis tools, we release the PARES dataset [6], which contains 250 labeled index table images originating from French archives. Also, we run state-of-the-art algorithms (U-FCN, R-CNN and Transformers) in order to detect the lines within index tables, a common prerequisite for handwritten text recognition (HTR). Our results indicate that text line extraction works well with the U-FCN model, while also indicating that Transformer architectures show promise for accurate text line detection in such historical documents with great efficiency. This is a encouraging step towards a Transformer-based architecture for both layout and content detection. This process and dataset represent a first step to automatically analyze handwritten and historical index tables. In addition to this paper and the PARES [6] dataset of historical index tables of 250 images, we release segmentation masks, the code we used to train and test the models, and the models themselves.

Keywords: Dataset · Historical Documents · Document Image Analysis · Document Segmentation · Deep Learning

1 Introduction

National archives around the world hold historical documents of various kinds. These include handwritten archives, such as census tables, that may record births, deaths or marriages, to name but a few. As with other types of documents of interest in digital humanities, such as newspapers or photographs, the indexing of such documents in digital libraries is intended to facilitate scholarly analysis in a controlled environment and to avoid potential damage to the original material.

D. H. Goh et al. (Eds.): ICADL 2023, LNCS 14457, pp. 59–75, 2023.
https://doi.org/10.1007/978-981-99-8085-7_6

The analysis of these documents can provide insights into demographic studies. For instance, understanding the diffusion of family names could provide valuable insights when put into the context of relevant historical events. This could also help us to understand patterns of population displacements across specific territories. However, the lack of publicly available historical census table datasets is a challenge. In a broad sense, our methodology of extracting valuable information from historical documents, such as named entities and dates, is not a novel concept within digital libraries. Nonetheless, it appears that only a limited number of researchers specifically focus on historical index or census tables [12,18], as a result of these challenges in analyzing such data. Therefore, tools developed for tables analysis and handwritten text recognition (HTR) shall be useful for the communities interested in historical documents.

The automatic analysis of historical documents, such as books or newspapers, has been widely explored, mainly due to the wide availability of high-quality digitized images. Given the advances in automated processing techniques applied to historical documents, it is now possible to handle more novel and intricate data types, such as tabular data. Therefore, state-of-the-art approaches should be evaluated on this kind of documents.

The contributions of this work are of twofold.

1. We present a novel dataset of historical index tables from the French National Archives: PARES, which stands for PArish REcord Survey [6]. This dataset contains annotated images specifically designed for document layout analysis (DLA). Both the original images and the segmentation annotations are made publicly available on Zenodo.
2. As the aim of processing these documents is to recognize and analyze the handwritten text, in this paper we focus on the preliminary step of text line detection. Hence, we compare multiple state-of-the-art document image analysis deep neural networks on the table text line detection task. We also share the implementations and source codes on Zenodo [5] and Software Heritage [2–4].

The paper is organized as follows. In Sect. 2, we introduce the Historical Index Table dataset. In Sect. 3, we present the state-of-the-art models for text line detection, including document image segmentation and instance segmentation models. Finally, in Sect. 4, we train and compare baseline models on the introduced dataset in order to extract the text records from our index tables.

2   Historical Index Table Dataset: PARES

Several recent projects have contributed to the release of handwriting table datasets. The READ ABP Tables is a collection of German handwritten records of Diocese Of Passau collected from 1847 to 1878 with more than 200 images [18]. The PoPP dataset [12] contains early 20th century historical census tables for the city of Paris, France. Similarly, the French Socface project also aims at contributing to the research for demographic studies. The collection includes census tables that were written over a span of a century, beginning in 1836. The research primarily emphasizes handwriting text recognition, and the datasets are soon to be made available in open access[1]. HisClima [29] is another partially handwritten set of historical tables of naval weather logbooks from the United States. Last, the Lectaurep project [21] provides French handwritten tables recording French notary deeds. The aforementioned datasets and their corresponding projects center around two primary challenges: analysing document layout and recognizing handwritten text. On another hand, while not being a table dataset, SIMARA [33] is a dataset of handwritten archive finding aids, comprised of metadata describing historical archives. Finding aids are handwritten and feature the same scientific challenges regarding handwritten text recognition. As an index, each finding aids contains expected data, such as the title of a document, its classification number, location, etc., just as in our index dataset.

Within this context, and alongside this paper, we release the PARES dataset consisting of 250 digitised index tables from the French National Archives, together with ground truth layout annotations. Based on visual observation, we employed heuristic methods to identify and label the table headers, table lines, page headers, and footers to create segmentation masks. This is a first step towards handwritten text recognition. Indeed, in this historical research context, we want to localize the text first, then apply HTR tools to make the most of the records. Finally, the extraction of named entities, which represent highly valuable content within these records, plays a crucial role in contextualizing and facilitating a comprehensive understanding of the dataset for demographic studies.

In the following sections, we describe the PARES dataset and the corresponding annotations in detail.

2.1 PARES Dataset Description

The dataset contains 250 images of handwritten index tables from about 1670 A.D. to 1862 A.D. They come from two French cities, Vic-sur-Seille (French department of Moselle) and Echevronne (French department of Côte d'Or). While they relate to the distant past, the documents are quite recent as they are handwritten transcriptions of older parish registers, the original index tables written from the period mentioned. Our index tables were copied during the 1960's and 1970's by only a few different writers for two different studies led by *INED* (*Institut National des études Démographiques* − 'French National Institute for Demographic Studies'), one for each location [7,15,31]. As can be seen in Fig. 1, two different and normalized paper templates were used, whose size ranges between A3 and A4 format (ISO 216). These historical tables were previously analyzed for a project managed by INED studying the French population movements before 1830 [15]. The 250 images we mention in this paper are part of a wider set of 537 images that are fully transcribed. Every token of each line is

---

[1] https://socface.site.ined.fr/ (in French).

semantically described (name, surname, father of/mother of, profession...). We intend to release these transcriptions when we will study the handwritten text recognition on these tables.

In 2015, these documents were digitised using two industrial devices. For highly damaged documents, the *Mamiya 645 DF +* digital back captured documents with 60 Mpx and output documents in TIFF format. Digitised documents were rescaled down to 300 DPI and the acquisition tool was regularly recalibrated to maintain color consistency across documents. The other tables that were not damaged were digitised with a *Fujitsu FI 6800* scanner, which outputs 300 DPI images in TIFF format. These digitisations respect the Metamorfoze Preservation Imaging Guidelines [34].

In this publication, we study a subset of this corpus (250 randomly selected images among the 537 images), to identify both research questions and issues for the humanities and social sciences. The high annotation cost led us to annotate 250 images for a first, early release of documents that will be useful for the community. For convenience, we converted the TIFF images to PNG images, a format that compresses images without degrading them.

Fig. 1. The different types of documents of the *Historical Index Table Dataset*. From left to right, we will reference these types as 'Category n°1' or 'C1' up to 'C7'. Categories shown are C1, C4, C6 and C7. Details are given in Table 1.

We have categorized the pages into seven distinct groups based on their particularities, which encompass color shifts, layouts, and degradations. An example image for some of these categories is presented in Fig. 1, and we report the category statistics in Table 1. C1 and C3 are, for the most part, high quality documents without serious damage, and account for 90% of the dataset. Other document categories include highly damaged pages or pages with unique characteristics.

A notable aspect of this dataset is that the records are written using only two different physical paper templates. Pages in categories 1, 2, 3, 6 and 7 have 25 recordings while those of categories 4 and 5 are larger and can record up to 35 items. In Table 1, C4 and C5 images have higher resolutions and a different aspect ratio as compared to the other documents. They represent less than 8% of the dataset, which is hence homogeneous.

Table 1. Distribution of the document categories over the 250 images of the dataset. It contains information on the image resolutions (in pixels) and the aspect ratio.

Category	Description	Count	Image Height Mean (Std)	Image Width Mean (Std)	Aspect ratio
1	Clean image with no visible damage	149	4007 (11.29)	3191 (14.05)	≈4:5
2	Higly damaged documents	2	3980 (1.41)	3204 (19.09)	
3	Color-shifted variants of C1	74	3986 (9.80)	3199 (11.25)	
4	Different layout with very light background	9	4956 (8.41)	3192 (3.00)	≈2:3
5	Yellow-hued variants of C4	9	4968 (7.62)	3194 (1.86)	
6	Table headers differing from those in C1 to C5	1	3976 (NaN)	3181 (NaN)	≈4:5
7	Incompliant of pre-defined layout	6	4015 (0.00)	3197 (0.00)	

2.2 Document Layout and Annotations

Layout analysis is an important step prior to document understanding. With this dataset, we wish to retrieve the different components of the image – primarily the text lines which are the handwritten records. The tables have a very clear and organized structure because they are based on very simple templates. We identify four different regions in each document.

- **Page header** : the name of the French department, the city, and the year. Some documents have extra annotations written by a pencil or a black pen. The headers occasionally add context, help to understand the documents, or are used for internal referencing. According to the paper templates, four instances are expected.
- **Page footer** : boolean information (full register or not) and sometimes pencil annotated page numbers. One instance is expected in the paper template document.
- **Table header** : labels on columns indicating the expected content. 19 instances are expected, except for categories n°4 to 6 where there are 23 instances expected.
- **Text line** : the recording itself. From the left boundary of the table to the right, the annotations span across all the columns. Occasionally, corrections were written above or below the main lines within the documents. In such cases, we consider this added information as an independent line unit. Depending on the templates, 25 or 35 text lines are expected.

For each image in the given set, we created segmentation masks in accordance with the aforementioned classes. An example of an annotation is shown in Fig. 2. The four classes (page header, page footer, table header and text line) are described with four colors and extra page headers & line units are visible. The annotations are bounding polygons as the objects boundaries (such as text lines) are not as clear and precise as they could be in real world – street like – scene images.

Table 2. Statistics of the components annotated in the whole dataset of 250 images.

Component	Count	Mean	Std	Q1	Median	Q3	Min	Max
Page header	1,451	5.80	1.57	5.00	5	7	3	10
Page footer	475	1.90	0.54	2.00	2	2	1	4
Table header	4,799	19.20	1.60	19.00	19	19	18	23
Text line	5,560	22.24	8.31	18.25	25	26	2	63

The scientific problem one aims to solve with such a dataset is the automatic detection of the element instances within the given documents, in this case, focusing on text lines. These documents are mainly handwritten, leading to inconsistent use of the template: some text is written out of the cells, overlaps with other text or lines, is crossed out, etc. Our aim is to identify the region of information to perform handwritten text recognition (HTR), not to extract the complex details of the layout of each table, such as columns or cells, with the intention of converting the table into something that looks like a CSV file, for example. We aim at localizing text regions to perform text extraction and named entity recognition before indexing them. This is where the added value resides for archives and digital libraries [33], as it can potentially serve as finding aids for census tables and directly contribute to demographic studies. As a result, the detection of text lines is the baseline task we perform on this dataset.

To annotate the images, we used the open-source Callico[2] platform. The annotations for all the 250 images were exclusively created by a small group, comprising solely the authors of this paper. This approach ensured consistency and adherence to the same annotation rules across the entire dataset. All selected images include each of the four classes just mentioned. In addition to the images, we provide the annotations as segmentation masks, as depicted in Fig. 2b. Furthermore, we present various statistics about the annotations in Table 2.

3   Document Image Analysis

Document image analysis of digitized documents is generally a two-step process [19, 27] although one-step approaches have also been explored [13]. In two-step approaches, the first step involves segmenting the image to extract and classify its components (street signs or cars for street scene images, text lines for document images). In this paper, we focus our attention on the text line detection, elements that carry information relevant to our second task: the recognition and extraction of handwritten text.

Advances in image segmentation, not limited to document image analysis, mainly come from research based on challenges for natural scene image segmentation [10, 20]. As such, the Pascal VOC [14] or Microsoft COCO datasets [23] are mainly used as baseline datasets to enhance image segmentation processes.

---

[2] https://doc.callico.eu.

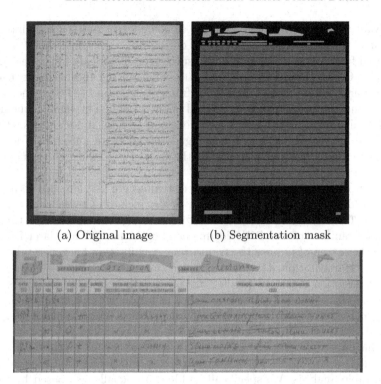

(a) Original image   (b) Segmentation mask

Fig. 2. Example of an image of a document with its annotations (Category n°1). Page header in blue, footer in orange, table header in pink and text lines in green. (Color figure online)

The detection of text lines has been widely explored in historical manuscript text books [9,26] and other historical documents of different natures, such as newspapers [25], meteorological tables [1] finding aids [33], as well as many other supports. With index tables, one can consider the issue as a two-class image segmentation task: we separate text lines from the background.

In this paper, we train and fine-tune state-of-the-art algorithms for the purpose of text-line detection. The used neural network models include: Fully Convolutional Networks (FCN), Region-based CNNs (R-CNN) and Transformers.

Fully Convolutional Networks (FCN) output pixel-level probability maps, from which the predicted elements can be extracted. dhSegment [28] or more recently Doc-UFCN [9] rely on this strategy to detect elements in document images. For both models, a post-processing task is needed to export masks or polygon coordinates of the detected components.

Other kinds of image segmentation algorithms come from studies that address real-time image segmentation of natural scenes. The most widely used state-of-the-art networks are two-step algorithms ('detect then segment' [16]). These are the Mask-RCNN [17] and PANet [24] models, with backbones based on ResNet and Feature Pyramid Networks (FPN) [22] and their derivatives. These models have been evaluated and compared on COCO challenges [16], and are fully integrated in popular toolkits such as Detectron2 or LayoutParser. Mask-RCNN has been prior used for document understanding such as on historical newspapers [25]. In contrast, YOLACT and YOLACT++ [10] are single-step approaches focusing on efficiency and increasing the number of frames per second (FPS), a metric that indicates the number of images processed in one second. This enables them to be used in real time applications. When processing historical documents, the FPS metric can aid in estimating the scaling potential of an automated document analysis method when confronted with the task of processing thousands, if not millions, of images.

Recent advances with the transformer architecture [35] have led to improvements within document image analysis fields, including table understanding. The TableTransformer [32] is a model for detecting tables and extracting table structure from images and PDF documents. SegFormer [36] and later DocSegTr [8] are other attempts to use the transformer architecture for general document and image segmentation. The latter approach focuses on document segmentation utilizing attention masks to predict instances with segmentation masks, while the former more generally predicts object instances with segmentation. Other transformer-type models like Pix2Seq [11] encode images and output a sequence of bounding box coordinates and the corresponding object classes.

In this paper, we evaluate and compare state-of-the-art image segmentation approaches on the index table dataset to build a baseline for historical handwritten table analysis. We specifically address the challenges posed by tabular data, which is not effectively handled by existing models and presents difficulties for both image segmentation and handwritten text recognition. Moreover, the quality of the latter depends on the efficiency of the document image analysis.

We evaluate the efficiency of the models using the metrics defined in Pascal VOC [14] and COCO [23]. The first is pixel-based and called IoU or Intersection over Union. It is a metric used in segmentation tasks to evaluate the detection of objects in images. Based on IoU thresholds, the mean AP (average precision) and its derivatives (AP_{50}, AP_{75}) are object based and evaluate the efficiency of object detection [23]. This type of ratio metric helps when comparing the predicted and ground truth segmentations. For example, an IoU of 1 indicates a perfect detection. We also compute the error value for the difference in the number of objects (DiCr – Difference in Count, error). This is the mean error based on the number of predicted objects when comparing predictions with corresponding ground truth masks. Zero is the best value, it means there is no difference in count between the prediction and the ground truth. Finally, we report the inference time in frames per second (FPS). The last two metrics become relevant as the number of detected lines increases, since missing or added predicted lines can lead to huge losses of information and more lines will increase inference time during later HTR processes. Inference time is also a key indicator, as digitization of historical collections can be carried out on massive amounts of data, leading to potentially lengthy and expensive processing.

4   Baselines for Text Line Extraction

In this section, we train different models on our tabular data. The aim of this research is to understand how the different models behave in the presence of historical documents, as most relevant models are designed for scene understanding or image analysis of modern documents. As such, text line extraction is often a prerequisite for document understanding and handwritten text recognition. Among the technologies mentioned in Sect. 3, we run baseline experiments using neural networks from three categories. First, U-shaped Fully Convolutional Networks [30] (U-FCN) that produce a single mask of pixel-level probabilities at the resolution of the input image. Second, Region-based CNNs (R-CNN), such as Mask-RCNN [17], detect Regions of Interest (RoI) in images to predict segmentations. Here, each detected instance comes with its own segmentation mask. Finally, recent advances with transformers for computer vision have proved their effectiveness on image segmentation and document understanding [8]. With this, we have chosen to focus our research on the model known as TableTransformer [32] which outputs bounding boxes for detected table components.

In the following section, we introduce the PARES dataset splits, pre-processing steps and baseline algorithms, and we comment on the results.

4.1   Data Splits and Pre-processing

Within our dataset, the category distribution is very unbalanced. The dataset is mainly composed of two different categories, C1 and C3, which represent about 90% (respectively 149 and 74 images) of the entire dataset. The models should learn general features to perform well on unseen data. Therefore, we have created a split with 80% of images in train, 10% in validation and 10% in test. We defined the split and the ratios of documents such that we will be able to train models on very unified data, and evaluate their abilities to generalize on unseen documents. The decision to assign an image to a split is still random, we only force proportion distribution. Since C1 and C3 are very similar and without many errors, we use them to train the models. The validation set contains C1 and C3 images, to check the learning on these categories, but also images from other categories. In the test set, we keep images with the unique peculiarities and damages. Table 3 gives details about the distribution of categories in each set.

Table 3. Category distribution in the split

	C1	C2	C3	C4	C5	C6	C7	Total
train	135	0	65	0	0	0	0	200
validation	8	0	5	4	5	0	3	25
test	6	2	4	5	4	1	3	25

In their works, Yang *et al.* [37] and Boillet *et al.* [9] preprocessed the input images by downsizing the images so that the longest size does not exceed respectively 384 and 768 pixels. The quality of the prediction is hence affected since the network has fewer features to map. We evaluate the impact of different input sizes on the quality of image segmentation. To do so, we downsize the images (Fig. 2a) and labels (Fig. 2b) to 512 and 768 pixels. The height of all the images in full resolution is around 4000 pixels, except for the documents belonging to the C4 and C5 categories, where the height is around 5000 pixels. This information is reported in Table 1 (page 6). The downsized image height is ≈13% of the original height (for 512 pixels) and ≈19% (for 768 pixels) for all categories except C4 and C5, where the ratios are ≈10% and ≈16%. While the latter resolution (768 pixels in height) was used to match the number of pixels used in Doc-UFCN, we chose the former after visual analysis of images smaller than 500 pixels showed large amounts of missing information in the images and labels due to resizing interpolation. Consequently, instead of using the 384 pixel value given by Yang *et al.*, we then used 512 pixels in height for the smaller resolution. We resize the labels and images using ImageMagick[3] with a nearest pixel interpolation and a point filter. To prevent elements from overlapping, when downsizing the segmentation masks, we used an square erosion kernel is of size 2. In the dataset [6], segmentation masks are eroded to prevent overlap, but the JSON files that describe the bounding boxes are not. The implementation of Doc-UFCN requires a square image as input. To address this, we introduced zero padding on the sides of the images to transform them into squares after resizing.

4.2   Implementations and Experiments

In this paper, we compare Doc-UFCN, a U-FCN network, with Mask-RCNN and TableTransformer, to test and understand how they behave for the task of table document image analysis. Doc-UFCN [9] and TableTransformer [32] have public implementations and are made for document analysis. We use them directly, as they provide command line tools to train and test the models on custom data. For Mask-RCNN, we implemented a model using PyTorch and released it on PyPi[4] as well as on Software Heritage [4].

Mask-RCNN and TableTransformer rely on a ResNet backbone and pretrained model weights are publicly available. We use these pretrained backbones and models as a starting point for training on our data. For Doc-UFCN, no such pretrained backbone models exist, so we trained the model from scratch.

For training, we propose two configurations. For the first, we fine-tune (Mask-RCNN, TableTransformer) or train (Doc-UFCN) directly to detect table lines from only the historical index table dataset with the split presented in Table 3. Results for this experiment are reported in Table 4. For the second configuration, we first pre-train the models on a large database of document images

---

[3] ImageMagick is a command-line image manipulation tool. https://imagemagick.org/.

[4] https://pypi.org/project/mask-rcnn-documents/.

Table 4. Baseline experiments on the split of the historical index table dataset. Doc-UFCN is trained from scratch. For other architectures, we start from the backbone weights.

Model	Parameters	Input size	Pixel metrics				Object metrics			DiCr	FPS
			IoU	P	R	F1	AP_{50}	AP_{75}	$mAP_{.5,.95}$		
Doc-UFCN	4.1 M	512	0.54	0.75	0.62	0.67	0.36	0.14	0.18	0.85	3.28
		768	0.55	0.73	0.64	0.67	0.39	0.21	0.21	1.15	1.86
Mask-RCNN	45.9 M	512	0.55	0.86	0.61	0.71	0.57	0.08	0.20	0.19	1.93
		768	0.59	**0.92**	0.62	0.74	**0.68**	0.11	0.24	**0.22**	1.59
TableTransformer	28.8 M	512	0.47	0.63	0.65	0.62	0.28	0.08	0.11	1.08	**8.01**
		768	**0.65**	0.81	**0.76**	**0.78**	0.56	**0.32**	**0.32**	0.31	3.43

Table 5. Baseline experiments on the split of the historical index table dataset. Models were pre-trained with the text lines dataset introduced and shared in [9].

Model	Parameters	Input size	Pixel metrics				Object metrics			DiCr	FPS
			IoU	P	R	F1	AP_{50}	AP_{75}	$mAP_{.5,.95}$		
Doc-UFCN	4.1 M	512	**0.66**	**0.91**	0.71	**0.79**	**0.65**	0.28	**0.34**	0.21	3.35
		768	0.64	**0.91**	0.69	0.77	0.60	**0.35**	**0.34**	0.44	1.90
Mask-RCNN	45.9 M	512	0.43	0.89	0.46	0.60	0.32	0.01	0.07	**0.18**	2.09
		768	0.44	0.90	0.46	0.61	0.32	0.00	0.07	0.20	1.77
TableTransformer	28.8 M	512	0.56	0.77	0.67	0.70	0.37	0.11	0.16	0.32	**7.87**
		768	0.64	0.75	**0.80**	0.77	0.56	0.30	0.31	0.30	3.52

annotated for the standard text line detection task (around 4,000 images in train, 1,300 in validation and 2,000 in test). They are the datasets used by Boillet et al. [9] and listed in the original paper in Table 2. Please refer to this paper to have more information on the datasets used to train the models and the model parameters. Then, we fine-tune these new model weights on the historical index table dataset. Given the limited number of 200 table images in the train set, we aim to determine whether fine-tuning with similar data types can enhance the final results. This approach allows the models to encounter a larger number of training examples of text lines, potentially leading to improved performance. The results of this configuration are shown in Table 5.

We train several models in different scenarios: with two images sizes (512 and 768 pixels in height) and three types of neural networks (U-FCN, R-CNN and Transformers). Training is done using two NVIDIA A40 GPUs and inference is done on a computer with an Intel(R) Core(TM) i7-10850H CPU @ 2.70 GHz and a NVIDIA Quadro T2000 Mobile GPU. It is the configuration of a workstation that could likely be used to perform a real document analysis without requiring extra GPUs. The number of epochs during training never exceeded 40 epochs when fine-tuning the models with a batch size of 4, and the training time never exceeded 2 h.

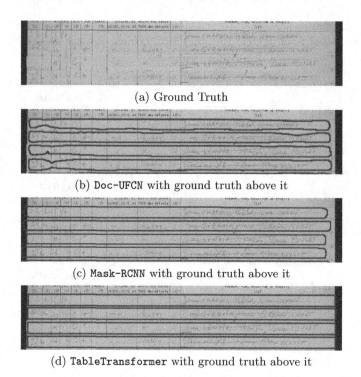

(a) Ground Truth

(b) `Doc-UFCN` with ground truth above it

(c) `Mask-RCNN` with ground truth above it

(d) `TableTransformer` with ground truth above it

Fig. 3. Superposition of manual annotations (in green) and preditions (in red), obtained by the models pre-trained on the large text lines dataset. For `Doc-UFCN` and `Mask-RCNN`, we show the contours of the lines extracted from the segmentation masks, and for `TableTransformer`, the predicted bounding box. (Color figure online)

4.3 Results

Depending on the model, the outputs are either segmentation masks or bounding boxes. `Doc-UFCN` outputs a single segmentation mask, as shown in Fig. 3b, and `Mask-RCNN` produces multiple masks, one for each detected instance. We merged them into a single mask during post-processing, shown in Fig. 3c, to compare the two predictions. The `TableTransformer` model outputs bounding boxes (Fig. 3d). We freely share the results of our experiments and the models for further analysis [5].

During inference, we feed the neural networks with images of the same height (512 or 768 pixels) as the one with which the model was trained. This is the resolution of the output. Since we are comparing segmentations at multiple scales, we upscale the predicted masks to the original image resolution before computing the evaluation metrics. Unlike previous work, we do not evaluate on small sub-resolutions.

We provide two types of results. First, we report in Table 4 the results of models trained from scratch on the index table images. In Table 5, we report the evaluation metrics obtained by the models pre-trained on a standard text line detection task, as described previously. We expect to see improvement in document segmentation as the model would have seen more examples of text lines. For each experiment, we provide both pixel and object metrics. To compute them, we use a free, publicly available software [9]. We keep only AP_{50} and AP_{75} as higher threshold values are not pertinent in our case. The primary information within a text line is typically the text itself, which often gets obscured by background pixels.

Observing Table 4, it becomes apparent that `TableTransformer` outperforms `Doc-UFCN` and `Mask-RCNN` in terms of pixel metrics for 768 pixel images and consistently surpasses `Doc-UFCN` in terms of object metrics. With regard to pixel metrics, `Mask-RCNN` and `Doc-UFCN` behave similarly, with comparable results. Enhancing the image resolution consistently leads to improved results; however, the effect is minimal with `Doc-UFCN`. The same pattern is observed in Table 5. The results on both resolutions are very comparable, indicating that `Doc-UFCN` is able to work well on smaller images. Also, pre-training `Doc-UFCN` using generic text lines proved to be highly beneficial, whereas the impact on other models appears to be minimal. When pre-trained with generic text lines, `Mask-RCNN` performs less well and the improvement on `TableTransformer` is not significant on 768 pixel images; however, it improves a lot on lower resolution images. Alternatively, when trained from scratch, `Mask-RCNN` appears to be more interesting as it performs better than `Doc-UFCN` and `TableTransformer` on small images. Furthermore, it is worth noting that the results obtained from `Mask-RCNN` are consistent across both resolutions. We postulate that this occurrence is attributed to the ResNet-50 backbone based on its deep feature masks which are 224×224 pixels. In contrast, the implementation of `Doc-UFCN` does not exhibit such a limitation, despite yielding comparable results. Nevertheless, it is evident with `TableTransformer` that higher image resolutions yield superior results. We hypothesize that these results are attributed to the attention mechanism in the transformer architecture that is more efficient than the Region of Interest (RoI) detection methods used in `Mask-RCNN` or pixel classification of `Doc-UFCN`. Furthermore, by generating a sequence of bounding box coordinates, the model guarantees the coherence of the coordinates in relation to the page layout. Since `TableTransformer` does not predict at a pixel level, small components (noise) within its predicted bounding box sequences are typically thresholded based on confidence values.

The number of layers and parameters of the models have an impact on the frame per second value. Additionally, reducing the resolution of images boosts the FPS of a given the model due to the reduced number of pixels to process in the input images. Contrary to the general expectation, we observe that `Doc-UFCN` outperforms `Mask-RCNN`, despite having significantly fewer parameters (10 times fewer) and fewer layers (three times fewer). Since `Doc-UFCN` is able to predict even better segmentation, it is a good candidate for the table line segmentation task for our dataset. `TableTransformer`, even with a high number of parameters compared to `Doc-UFCN`, performs relatively fast and the increase in speed follows the same ratio as `Doc-UFCN` whereas the increase in speed is very low with `Mask-RCNN`, probably due to the hypothesis we already mentioned before.

5   Conclusion

Alongside this paper, we share the PARES dataset, a historical dataset of 250 index tables images coming from the French National Archive [6]. Each image in PARES was meticulously annotated for document layout analysis with table headers, text lines, page headers, and footers using bounding polygons. The dataset annotations, presented as segmentation masks, are made available without any overlap between the elements, as eases the extraction of connected components. All identified components are labeled with different colors in segmentation masks to ease the conversion into the formats of your choice: ALTO, PageContent or COCO for instance. The documents are homogeneous (90% are based on a single physical paper template), but we identified variations in each, differences that might fail automatic methods to automatically detect and segment text lines. To that extent, we propose and share a dataset split that focuses on unique document characteristics.

We experimented with three types of neural networks: a U-shaped FCN (`Doc-UFCN`), a region-based CNN (`Mask-RCNN`) and a Transformer (`TableTransformer`) to test their ability to extract table text lines from our historical documents. Their implementations were already public, except for `Mask-RCNN`, which was easily implemented with PyTorch[5]. We release our own version of Software Heritage [4]. The two others are very promising and recent advances with Transformers for document analysis [11,13] lead us to the conclusion that, given sufficient data, the results of these segmentation networks will increase in the domain of historical document analysis. We also foresee the design of a single Transformer-based neural network that could detect and segment documents (by predicting bounding box coordinates and their classes), as well as the handwritten text, all in one.

Acknowledgements. The authors would like to thank the people of Teklia for providing the infrastructure to annotate document (https://callico.teklia.com). This work was supported by the French government in the framework of the France Relance program and by the TEKLIA company. Full gratitude is expressed to Isabelle Séguy, researcher at INED (Institut national d'études démographiques) and the institution who allowed us to use and share the original images of the PARES dataset.

References

1. Andrés, J., Prieto, J.R., Granell, E., Romero, V., Sánchez, J.A., Vidal, E.: Information extraction from handwritten tables in historical documents. In: Uchida, S., Barney, E., Eglin, V. (eds.) DAS 2022. LNCS, vol. 13237, pp. 184–198. Springer, Cham (2022). https://doi.org/10.1007/978-3-031-06555-2_13

---

[5] https://pytorch.org/vision/main/models/mask_rcnn.html.

2. Bernard, G.: `doc-ufcn-test` (2023). https://archive.softwareheritage.org/swh:1:dir:7ca17e4a36ff25cf4d68513a2af99074a3af4f3f

3. Bernard, G.: `doc-ufcn-utilities` (2023). https://archive.softwareheritage.org/swh:1:dir:ca5daf53c31def70e46c9aa8f887abe60cdd1d27

4. Bernard, G.: `mask-rcnn-documents` (2023). https://archive.softwareheritage.org/swh:1:dir:981ec0052f93e37505eba3d47e085a255483441f

5. Bernard, G., Wall, C.: Experiments of 'Line Detection in Historical Index Tables: Evaluations on a New French PArish REcord Survey Dataset (PARES) (2023). https://doi.org/10.5281/zenodo.8334664

6. Bernard, G., Wall, C., Boillet, M., Coustaty, M., Kermorvant, C., Doucet, A.: Pares: Parish registry survey - historical census table dataset (19th, 20th centuries) - france (2023). https://doi.org/10.5281/zenodo.8337504

7. Biraben, J.N., Brouard, N., Blanchet, D.: Pour reconstituer le mouvement de la population aux xvie et xviie siècles. Annales de Démographie Historique **1980**(1), 39–52 (1980). https://doi.org/10.3406/adh.1980.1452,https://www.persee.fr/doc/adh_0066-2062_1980_num_1980_1_1452, included in a thematic issue : La démographie avant les démographes (1500-1670)

8. Biswas, S., Banerjee, A., Lladós, J., Pal, U.: Docsegtr: an instance-level end-to-end document image segmentation transformer. CoRR abs/2201.11438 (2022). https://arxiv.org/abs/2201.11438

9. Boillet, M., Kermorvant, C., Paquet, T.: Robust text line detection in historical documents: learning and evaluation methods. Int. J. Doc. Anal. Recogn. (IJDAR) **25**, 95–114 (2022). https://doi.org/10.1007/s10032-022-00395-7

10. Bolya, D., Zhou, C., Xiao, F., Lee, Y.J.: YOLACT++: better real-time instance segmentation. IEEE Trans. Pattern Anal. Mach. Intell. **44**, 1108–1121 (2022). https://doi.org/10.1109/TPAMI.2020.3014297

11. Chen, T., Saxena, S., Li, L., Fleet, D.J., Hinton, G.E.: Pix2seq: a language modeling framework for object detection. CoRR abs/2109.10852 (2021). https://arxiv.org/abs/2109.10852

12. Constum, T., et al.: Popp datasets: datasets for handwriting recognition from French population census. https://doi.org/10.5281/zenodo.6581158

13. Coquenet, D., Chatelain, C., Paquet, T.: DAN: a segmentation-free document attention network for handwritten document recognition. IEEE Trans. Pattern Anal. Mach. Intell. 1–17 (2023). https://doi.org/10.1109/TPAMI.2023.3235826

14. Everingham, M., Van Gool, L., Williams, C.K.I., Winn, J., Zisserman, A.: The Pascal Visual Object Classes (VOC) challenge. Int. J. Comput. Vis. **88**, 303–338 (2010). https://doi.org/10.1007/s11263-009-0275-4

15. Fleury, M., Henry, L.: Pour connaître la population de la france depuis louis xiv. - plan de travaux par sondage. Population 13(4), 663–686 (1958). https://doi.org/10.2307/1525088, https://www.persee.fr/doc/pop_0032-4663_1958_num_13_4_5737

16. Gu, W., Bai, S., Kong, L.: A review on 2D instance segmentation based on deep neural networks. Image Vis. Comput. **120**, 104401 (2022). https://doi.org/10.1016/j.imavis.2022.104401

17. He, K., Gkioxari, G., Dollár, P., Girshick, R.: Mask R-CNN. In: Proceedings of the IEEE International Conference on Computer Vision (ICCV) (2017)

18. Hervé, D., Eva, L., Florian, K.: READ ABP Table datasets. https://doi.org/10.5281/zenodo.1226879

19. Kiessling, B.: CurT: end-to-end text line detection in historical documents with transformers. In: Porwal, U., Fornés, A., Shafait, F. (eds.) ICFHR 2022. LNCS, vol. 13639, pp. 34–48. Springer, Cham (2022). https://doi.org/10.1007/978-3-031-21648-0_3

20. Kirillov, A., He, K., Girshick, R., Rother, C., Dollár, P.: Panoptic Segmentation. In: Proceedings of the IEEE International Conference on Computer Vision (ICCV) (2019)
21. LECTAUREP, Rostaing, A., Durand, M., Chagué, A.: Notaires de Paris - Répertoires, ground truth for various Parisian registries of notary deeds (French 19th and 20th centuries). https://doi.org/10.5072/zenodo.977691
22. Lin, T.Y., Dollar, P., Girshick, R., He, K., Hariharan, B., Belongie, S.: Feature pyramid networks for object detection. In: 2017 IEEE Conference on Computer Vision and Pattern Recognition (CVPR), pp. 936–944. IEEE (2017). https://doi.org/10.1109/CVPR.2017.106
23. Lin, T.-Y., et al.: Microsoft COCO: common objects in context. In: Fleet, D., Pajdla, T., Schiele, B., Tuytelaars, T. (eds.) ECCV 2014. LNCS, vol. 8693, pp. 740–755. Springer, Cham (2014). https://doi.org/10.1007/978-3-319-10602-1_48
24. Liu, S., Qi, L., Qin, H., Shi, J., Jia, J.: Path aggregation network for instance segmentation. In: 2018 IEEE/CVF Conference on Computer Vision and Pattern Recognition, pp. 8759–8768 (2018). https://doi.org/10.1109/CVPR.2018.00913
25. Michael, J., Weidemann, M., Laasch, B., Labahn, R.: ICPR 2020 competition on text block segmentation on a NewsEye dataset. In: Del Bimbo, A., et al. (eds.) ICPR 2021. LNCS, vol. 12668, pp. 405–418. Springer, Cham (2021). https://doi.org/10.1007/978-3-030-68793-9_30
26. Neche, C., Belaid, A., Kacem-Echi, A.: Arabic handwritten documents segmentation into text-lines and words using deep learning. In: 2019 International Conference on Document Analysis and Recognition Workshops (ICDARW), pp. 19–24. IEEE (2019). https://doi.org/10.1109/ICDARW.2019.50110
27. Nion, T., et al.: Handwritten information extraction from historical census documents. In: 2013 12th International Conference on Document Analysis and Recognition, pp. 822–826. IEEE (2013). https://doi.org/10.1109/ICDAR.2013.168
28. Oliveira, S.A., Seguin, B., Kaplan, F.: dhSegment: a generic deep-learning approach for document segmentation. In: 2018 16th International Conference on Frontiers in Handwriting Recognition (ICFHR), pp. 7–12 (2018). https://doi.org/10.1109/ICFHR-2018.2018.00011
29. PRHLT: HisClima Dataset. https://doi.org/10.5281/zenodo.7442971
30. Ronneberger, O., Fischer, P., Brox, T.: U-Net: convolutional networks for biomedical image segmentation. In: Navab, N., Hornegger, J., Wells, W.M., Frangi, A.F. (eds.) MICCAI 2015. LNCS, vol. 9351, pp. 234–241. Springer, Cham (2015). https://doi.org/10.1007/978-3-319-24574-4_28
31. Séguy, I.: La population de la France de 1670 à 1829: l'enquête Louis Henry et ses données. Ined (2001)
32. Smock, B., Pesala, R., Abraham, R.: PubTables-1M: towards comprehensive table extraction from unstructured documents. In: 2022 IEEE/CVF Conference on Computer Vision and Pattern Recognition (CVPR), pp. 4634–4642 (2021)
33. Tarride, S., Boillet, M., Moufflet, J.F., Kermorvant, C.: Simara: a database for key-value information extraction from full pages. arXiv preprint arXiv:2304.13606 (2023)
34. Van Dormolen, H.: Metamorfoze Preservation Imaging Guidelines. National programme for the preservation of paper heritage 5(1), 162–165 (2012). https://doi.org/10.2352/issn.2168-3204.2008.5.1.art00032
35. Vaswani, A., et al.: Attention is all you need. In: Guyon, I., et al. (eds.) Advances in Neural Information Processing Systems, vol. 30. Curran Associates, Inc. (2017). https://proceedings.neurips.cc/paper_files/paper/2017/file/3f5ee243547dee91fbd053c1c4a845aa-Paper.pdf

36. Xie, E., Wang, W., Yu, Z., Anandkumar, A., Alvarez, J.M., Luo, P.: SegFormer: simple and efficient design for semantic segmentation with transformers. In: Neural Information Processing Systems (NeurIPS) (2021)
37. Yang, X., Yumer, E., Asente, P., Kraley, M., Kifer, D., Giles, C.L.: Learning to extract semantic structure from documents using multimodal fully convolutional neural network. In: 2017 IEEE Conference on Computer Vision and Pattern Recognition (CVPR), pp. 4342–4351 (2017). https://doi.org/10.1109/CVPR.2017.462

Benchmarking NAS for Article Separation in Historical Newspapers

Nancy Girdhar$^{(\boxtimes)}$ [iD], Mickaël Coustaty [iD], and Antoine Doucet [iD]

L3i, University of La Rochelle, La Rochelle 17000, France
{nancy.girdhar,mickael.coustaty,antoine.doucet}@univ-lr.fr

Abstract. The digitization of historical newspapers is a crucial task for preserving cultural heritage and making it accessible for various natural language processing and information retrieval tasks. One of the key challenges in digitizing old newspapers is article separation, which consists of identifying and extracting individual articles from scanned newspaper images and retrieving the semantic structure. It is a critical step in making historical newspapers machine-readable and searchable, enabling tasks such as information extraction, document summarization, and text mining. In this work, we assess *NewsEye Article Separation* (NAS), a multilingual dataset for article separation in historical newspapers. It consists of scanned newspaper pages from the 19th and 20th centuries and annotation files in German, Finnish, and French. Moreover, the dataset is challenging due to the varying layouts and font styles, which makes it difficult for models to generalize to unseen data. Also, we introduce new metrics of *article error rate*, *article coverage score*, *proper predicted article*, and *segmentation* to evaluate the performance of the models trained on the NAS to highlight the relevance and challenges of this dataset. We believe that NAS, which is publicly available, will be a valuable resource for researchers working on historical newspaper digitization.

Keywords: multilingual · datasets · article separation · historical documents · diachronic newspapers

1 Introduction

Historical newspapers are a rich source of information for understanding the past and preserving cultural heritage, making them valuable resources for researchers in various fields, such as history, sociology, and linguistics. They provide a wealth of information on various aspects of society, such as politics, economy, culture, and daily life. Digitizing historical newspapers is a crucial task for making this information accessible for research and education. Nevertheless, the process of making historical newspapers machine-readable and searchable is critical due to the large amount of data, the varying quality and resolution of the images, and the complexity of the page layouts. One of the key steps in this process is *article separation* which involves identifying and extracting individual articles from

D. H. Goh et al. (Eds.): ICADL 2023, LNCS 14457, pp. 76–88, 2023.
https://doi.org/10.1007/978-981-99-8085-7_7

scanned images of newspaper pages [2,4,18]. Being able to automatically separate articles within a newspaper page is crucial for a wide range of applications, including text retrieval, digital preservation, and document understanding.

Although the task of article separation is important, very few studies have attempted to address the problem of segmenting articles in historical newspapers [15]. One of these studies involves identifying *lines, text, images*, and *headings* in the newspaper layout and then applying a set of rules for article separation in old newspapers [11]. Another rule-based approach for article separation considers visual features such as *layout, font, spacing*, and other visual elements. However, this method has limitations in its ability to handle variations in the layout and format of historical newspapers [18]. More recently, deep learning-based methods have been proposed for article separation in newspapers. One such study utilizes a *fully convolutional network* (FCN) architecture to extract features from an input image and then distinguishes articles from other elements on a newspaper page [12]. However, most of these studies that have tackled the task of article segmentation in historical newspapers have relied on contemporary datasets to handle the historical data [5,12,17,20]. Nonetheless, building tools on contemporary resources for separating articles from historical text is not very suitable as historical data generated by OCR engines on scanned images is more prone to noise compared to contemporary data, not to mention the varying historic layouts and ancient font styles that are not in use anymore [21]. A summary of existing studies on article separation in historical newspapers is presented in Table 1.

Table 1. Article separation in historical newspapers (*Lang*: Language; *VAS*: Visual features based Article Separation; *HN*: Historical Newspapers; *CN*: Contemporary Newspapers; *CRF*: Conditional Random Field; *MM*: Markov Model; *A*: Accuracy; *P*: Precision; *R*: Recall; *F1*: F_score; *mCS*: mean Completeness Score; *mDER*: mean Diarization Error Rate).

[Ref]	Method	Approach	Dataset					Results
			Name	Type	Source	Pages	Lang	(%)
[11]	VAS	Rule-based	TO VIMA	HN	Private	100	Greek	P: 75.20 R: 77.15
Limitation(s):								
Semantic cues could be relevant but are currently not utilized for article separation tasks.								
[18]	VAS	CRF+Rule- based	Journal De Rouen	HN	Private	42	French	A: 85.84
Limitation(s):								
Performance measured on limited dataset size.								
[12]	VAS	FCN	ARGUS DATA INSIGHTS Schweiz AG	CN	Private	426	–	mCS: 54.44 mDER: 13.78
Limitation(s):								
Cannot differentiate between article-text and an ad-image.								
Can recognize rectangular shapes only.								
Implemented on a contemporary dataset, not on historical data.								
[3]	VAS	Fixed point	–	CN	Private	45	English	A: 96
Limitation(s):								
Performance measured on limited dataset size.								
Implemented on a contemporary dataset, not on historical data.								
[16]	VAS	2D MM	Fairfax Media	CN	Private	3332	English	F1: 92.9
Limitation(s):								
Lack of consideration for visual cues, such as horizontal and vertical rules.								
Approximated 2D Markov model may overlook intricate dependencies.								
Implemented on a contemporary dataset, not on historical data.								

Currently, there is a lack of benchmark datasets and evaluation metrics as existing datasets are either limited in terms of the languages, time period, and newspapers they cover, or they are not publicly accessible [8,15,18]. This limits the ability of researchers to develop and evaluate different article separation models to advance the state-of-the-art in this field. For all aforementioned reasons, it is significant to build resources that are specifically designed for historical newspapers that can serve as a learning base to train new models and to compare the performance of existing models.

To address this gap, we assess a multilingual dataset for article separation in historical newspapers that we refer to as "NAS" (*NewsEye Article Separation*) [13]. We also introduce new evaluation metrics to measure the performance of models trained on this dataset. The NAS dataset includes a diverse set of historical newspapers in multiple languages published in the 19th and early 20th centuries. The large-scale annotations are carried out using OCR on scanned images on various newspaper pages for each language. The dataset is designed to be challenging as it includes a variety of layouts (showcased in Fig. 1) and font styles in historical newspapers, making it hard for models to apply their learning to new data. Besides the newly introduced evaluation metrics, our evaluation of the dataset also includes the use of standard metrics for article separation tasks, making the NAS dataset unique in its scope and coverage. The NAS is publicly available for download and use, which will facilitate further research in the field of natural language processing (NLP) and information retrieval (IR) on historical newspapers.

Fig. 1. Sample images of various historical newspaper layouts included in the NAS dataset. French *Le Gaulois* newspaper (Left), Finnish *Suometar* newspaper (Middle), and German *Freie Presse* newspaper (Right).

The rest of the paper is organized as follows: Sect. 2 describes the details of the annotation process and the statistics for the presented NAS dataset. Section 3 introduces proposed evaluation measures to evaluate models trained on the presented dataset. Section 4 describes the experimental setup and evaluation results for the article separation task. Finally, Sect. 5 concludes the presented work.

2   The NAS Dataset

The NAS dataset is a vast diverse multilingual collection of digitized items extracted from the archives of European national libraries as a component of the NewsEye Project[1]. NAS builds on corpora from three European National Libraries: The *Austrian National Library* (ONB), the *National Library of Finland* (NLF), and the *National Library of France* (BNF). The dataset includes scanned newspaper images in the PAGE format and the description of each corpus detailing the archive source, the composition of newspapers, and their timeline is provided in Table 2.

Table 2. NAS data collection sources and acquisition timeline.

Corpus	Archive	Newspaper (Timeline)
ONB[a]	The Austrian National Library	Innsbrucker Nachrichten (Mittags-Zeitung) (1864–1939), Neue freie Presse (1864–1939), Arbeiter-Zeitung (1895–1939), Illustrierte Kronen Zeitung (1911–1939)
NLF[b]	The National Library of Finland	**Finnish dataset:** Suometar (1847–1866), Sanomia Turusta (1850–1900), Uusi Suometar (1869–1918), Aura (1880–1896), Helsingin Sanomat (1904–1918), Uusi Aura (1897–1918), Päivälehti (1889–1904) **Swedish dataset:** Hufvudstadsbladet (1864–1918), Västra Finland (1895–1918), åbo Underrättelser (1824–1918)
BNF[c]	The National Library of France	Le Matin (1884–1944), La Presse (1850–1890), Le Gaulois (1868–1900), La Fronde (1897–1929), L'Oeuvre (1915–1944), Marie-Claire (1937–1944)

[a] https://www.onb.ac.at
[b] https://www.kansalliskirjasto.fi
[c] https://www.bnf.fr

2.1   Annotation Guidelines

The annotation guidelines for the NAS dataset were developed with the intention of meeting the needs of its users and aligning with the NewsEye project [9,13,14]. For the ground truth, the PAGE format [19] was adopted and the annotation

---

[1] https://www.newseye.eu/.

process was done using the Transkribus[2] platform, which is open-source software for the transcription and annotation of historical documents [6]. The annotations were done in two stages: *first*, the layout elements such as text lines and regions were annotated; and *second*, the article boundaries were annotated based on the layout elements.

Each *region* on the scanned image is marked with a *unique identifier* (ID) on the PAGE file. A region is defined by its *attributes, coordinates outline* (polygon), and *type*. The baselines are one of the key factors for the article separation task and for that, a ground truth file includes three substantial pieces of information about the *baseline's coordinates*, their *reading order*, and the *baseline's article Ids* which they are part of. However, it is important to note that while a *reading order* is provided, it was not corrected during the truthing phase. Therefore, it cannot be utilized for training or evaluating a model. Instead, it primarily serves as a technical necessity of the PAGE format rather than a reliable indicator of the actual reading order.

The key points of the annotation guidelines are detailed as follows:

– A *news item* encompasses not only *articles*, but also includes *advertisements*, *classified ads*, and other graphical elements. In the PAGE file, *articles* are formed by their corresponding *TextLines*. Thus, any graphical elements or advertisements cannot be part of an article since these elements do not have the *'custom'* attribute with an article id.

– The article information is contained within the *TextLine* element, which is always nested inside a *TextRegion* in the PAGE file. This information is stored in the *'custom'* attribute, which specifies the article to which the text line belongs. For example, if multiple text lines have the same id in the *'custom'* attribute, it indicates that they belong to the same unique article.

Figure 2 presents the various annotated regions. A *region* is classified into *Text, Image, Table, Advert, Separator*. The *'points'* represent the pixel coordinates of that region in a newspaper page. The details of these regions are as follows:

– *TextRegion*: Text regions are marked at the text block level, which is non-overlapping.

– *ImageRegion*: A text region is drawn for an image/picture.

– *TableRegion*: For a table, two regions are drawn: *table* and *text* of the same size. The reason for additional text regions is due to the fact, that *TextLines* in the PAGE format can only be placed within *TextRegions*. The additional text regions are included to capture the textual content within the table.

– *AdvertRegion*: This includes advertisements and classified ads.

– *SeparatorRegion*: Both horizontal and vertical separators that were obvious are marked as separator regions.

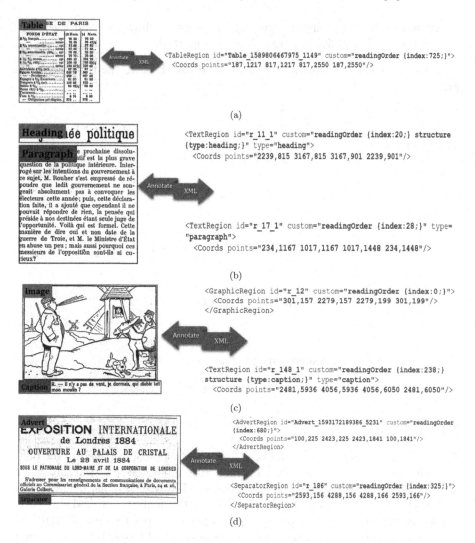

Fig. 2. Illustration of various annotated regions in an article: (a) Table, (b) Heading and Paragraph, (c) Image and Caption, and (d) Advertisement and Separator.

In addition to this, a *TextRegion* further consists of four structure tags *paragraph, caption, heading, enumeration* as illustrated in Fig. 2:

– *Paragraph*: The ordinary blocks of text are labeled with the *'paragraph'* tag.

– *Caption*: Captions are marked below the graphics and pictures.

– *Heading*: Headings and sub-headings both are marked with the *'heading'* tag.

---

[2] https://transkribus.eu/Transkribus.

– *Enumeration*: The structure type *'enumeration'* is drawn around the entire text region after individual text blocks are marked.

An excerpt from a subsequently annotated PAGE XML file is presented in Fig. 3.

```xml
<?xml version='1.0' encoding='UTF-8' standalone='yes'?>
  <Page imageFilename="18680715_1-0001.jpg" imageWidth="5362" imageHeight="7363">
    <ReadingOrder>
      <OrderedGroup id="ro_1607341595266" caption="Regions reading order">
        <RegionRefIndexed index="0" regionRef="r_1_1"/>
      </OrderedGroup>
    </ReadingOrder>
     <SeparatorRegion id="r_41" custom="readingOrder {index:190;}">
     <Coords points="3097,70 3283,70 3283,77 3097,77"/>
     </SeparatorRegion>
    <TextRegion id="r_1_1" custom="readingOrder {index:0;}" type="paragraph">
      <Coords points="551,179 974,179 974,210 551,210"/>
        <TextLine id="r_1_111" custom="readingOrder {index:0;} structure {id:a2; type:article;}">
         <Coords points="568,252 593,252 618,252 643,252 669,252 694,252 719,252 744,252 770"/>
         <Baseline points="568,202 593,202 618,202 643,202 669,202 694,202 719,202 744,202 770"/>
          <TextEquiv>
            <Unicode>Le service de distribution du GAULOIS,</Unicode>
          </TextEquiv>
        </TextLine>
        <TextEquiv>
          <Unicode>Le service de distribution du GAULOIS,</Unicode>
        </TextEquiv>
    </TextRegion>
  </Page>
```

Fig. 3. Sample excerpt of an annotation PAGE.

2.2   Statistics

The NAS dataset features a total of 613 scanned newspaper page images published from the 19th and early 20th century with annotated text. Initially, there were 16,498 text blocks in ONB (German), 28,447 in NLF (Finnish), and 73,376 text blocks in BNF (French) [13]. However, given the quality of ground truth text block annotations, preprocessing is required prior to working with the dataset. The preprocessing step primarily involved removing text blocks from the ground truth annotations that lacked baselines or article tags. The significant number of removed text blocks reflects the overall quality of the provided ground truth annotations.

The details of each dataset before and after processing of text blocks are mentioned in Table 3. To be precise, the dataset contains 230 pages of ONB, 200 pages of NLF, and 183 pages of BNF newspapers. It is worth mentioning that the ONB dataset exhibits the highest quality, as indicated by the relatively low number of removed text blocks.

The current section has detailed the guidelines and statistical details of the NAS dataset. The subsequent section focuses on the performance evaluation measures for assessing the effectiveness of approaches trained on the NAS dataset for the article separation task.

Table 3. Statistical overview of multilingual NAS dataset

Dataset	Language	Pages	Text Blocks	W_B	W_AT	Text Blocks (final)
ONB[d]	German	230	16,498	0	45	16,454
NLF[e]	Finnish	200	28,447	739	25	27,683
BNF[f]	French	183	73,376	10,153	661	62,562

W_B=Without Baselines, W_AT=Without Article Tags
[d] ONB: https://zenodo.org/record/5654907
[e] NLF: https://zenodo.org/record/5654858
[f] BNF: https://zenodo.org/record/5654841

3   Performance Evaluation Measures

In this section, we introduce new performance evaluation measures specifically tailored for assessing that the results correspond to the end-user expectations on the NAS dataset: *article error rate, article coverage score, proper predicted article*, and *segmentation*[3]. In addition to these novel metrics, the NAS dataset can also be evaluated using standard evaluation measures such as F_1 _ $score$, *accuracy*, and *intersection over union* (IoU). However, despite being widely used as a benchmark, particularly the IoU, these metrics have limitations. They are sensitive to threshold values, do not account for complex shapes and localization accuracy, and can produce high scores even if the predicted segment is not accurately aligned with the ground truth. Thus, for all these reasons, solely IoU is not enough to comprehensively evaluate overall model performance. Therefore, it is essential to have reliable and comprehensive evaluation metrics to accurately assess the performance of models.

3.1   Article Error Rate

The first of these new metrics is the ***article error rate*** (AER) to evaluate *"How much error incurred in identifying the relevant text regions of an article ?"*. AER signifies the mismatch in the predicted text regions of an article x and the actual (ground truth) text regions of the article x. This metric takes into account both Type-I and Type-II errors: (i) text region r predicted to belong to the article x but according to ground truth it does not (i.e. *Type-I* error) and (ii) text region r which belongs to article x but not predicted by the model (i.e. *Type-II* error).

Given an article x, PTR_x is the set of predicted text regions in article x and GTR_x is the set of actual text regions (ground truth) of article x. Then, the error rate in the prediction of article x is calculated as Eq. (1).

$$AER_x = \frac{|PTR_x \oplus GTR_x|}{|PTR_x \cup GTR_x|} \qquad (1)$$

---

[3] https://github.com/NancyGirdhar/AS_EvaluationMetrics.

This equation Eq. (1) can be rewritten as Eq. (2).

$$AER_x = \frac{|(PTR_x - GTR_x) \cup (GTR_x - PTR_x)|}{|PTR_x \cup GTR_x|} \quad (2)$$

Here, $PTR_x - GTR_x$ corresponds to the set difference between two sets, PTR_x and GTR_x.

Given n articles, where n is the cardinality of union between sets of ground truth articles and predicted articles respectively, the **mean article error rate** (mAER) is computed as Eq. (3).

$$mAER = \sum_{x=1}^{n} \frac{AER_x}{n} \quad (3)$$

Let P and GT symbolize the model's predicted articles set and ground truth articles set respectively, and R denotes the set of all text regions. a_x^P and a_x^{GT} corresponds to predicted and actual text regions of xth article respectively. For instance, consider $P = \{a_1, a_2, a_3\}$, $GT = \{a_1, a_2\}$ (over-segmentation since the number of predicted articles is more than the number of ground truth articles) and $R = \{r_1, r_2, r_3, r_4, r_5\}$.

Now, for each article a_x, assume the predicted and ground truth text regions as $a_1^P = \{r_1, r_2, r_5\}$, $a_1^{GT} = \{r_1, r_4, r_5\}$, $a_2^P = \emptyset$, $a_2^{GT} = \{r_3\}$, $a_3^P = \{r_7\}$, $a_3^{GT} = \emptyset$.

Note: Here, $a_2^P = \emptyset$ represents 2nd article does not exist in predicted articles set and similarly, 3rd article does not exist in ground truth articles set.

Using Eq. (1) and (3), the model's error rate in the prediction of text regions per article is $AER_{a_1} = 2/3 = 0.667$, $AER_{a_2} = 1/1 = 1$ and $AER_{a_3} = 1/1 = 1$ and the average error rate across all articles will be $mAER = 2.67/3 = 0.89$.

3.2   Article Coverage Score

The second new evaluation metric is **article coverage score** (ACS) to quantify *"How many regions of an article are successfully extracted?"* or alternatively, *"To what extent is an article covered in terms of identifying its regions?"*. ACS is derived from the *article error rate* metrics and indicates the correctness of the model's prediction and extraction of text regions within an article. This is calculated using Eq. (4):

$$ACS_x = 1 - AER_x \quad (4)$$

Given n articles, **mean article coverage score** (mACS) is computed as mentioned in Eq. (5):

$$mACS = 1 - \sum_{x=1}^{n} \frac{AER_x}{n} \quad (5)$$

3.3   Proper Predicted Article

The third introduced evaluation metric is **proper predicted article** (PPA) to calculate *"How many articles are predicted perfectly?"*. PPA is the ratio of the count of accurately predicted articles to the total number of ground truth articles. An article is said to be an **exact predicted article** if and only if (*iff*) it satisfies the following constraint:

$$\{\forall x, \quad r|\ r \in PTR_x \quad \text{and} \quad \exists\ y \in GTR_x \quad \text{such that} \quad |PTR_x| = |GTR_x|\}$$

where, x denotes articles, r denotes text regions, PTR_x and GTR_x represent the set of predicted and ground truth text regions of article x respectively.

For a single page p of the newspaper, the **proper predicted article** (*PPA*) is computed as Eq. (6).

$$PPA_p = \frac{|Exact\ Predicted\ Articles|}{|Ground\ Truth\ Articles|} \tag{6}$$

For a multi-page newspaper with P pages, the **mean proper predicted article** (*mPPA*) is calculated as Eq. (7).

$$mPPA = \frac{\sum_{p=1}^{P} PPA_p}{P} \tag{7}$$

Assume $|GT_x| = 3$ (total ground truth articles), the predicted and ground truth text regions are as $a_1^P = \{r_1, r_2\}$, $a_1^{GT} = \{r_1, r_2\}$; $a_2^P = \{r_4, r_5, r_6\}$, $a_2^{GT} = \{r_4, r_5\}$; $a_3^P = \{r_7, r_8\}$, $a_3^{GT} = \{r_6, r_7, r_8, r_9\}$, $a_4^P = \{r_9\}$, $a_4^{GT} = \emptyset$. According to the definition of the *exact predicted article*, only a_1 article satisfies the constraint. Thus, $PPA = 1/3 = 0.333$.

3.4   Segmentation

The last evaluation metric presented is **segmentation** that corresponds to *"How well the approach can isolate the different articles?"*. Segmentation (Seg) of an article is the proportion of predicted text regions belonging to an article x compared to the actual number of text regions belonging to the article x. A value greater than 1 signifies over-segmentation and a value less than 1 signifies under-segmentation (aggregation of text regions that do not belong to the same article). Consequently, a higher segmentation score indicates a better ability to separate the articles, while a lower score suggests a less accurate segmentation. The segmentation for x^{th} article can be computed as Eq. (8).

$$Seg_x = \frac{|PTR_x|}{|GTR_x|} \tag{8}$$

The overall **mean segmentation** score (mSeg) of n articles can be calculated using Eq. (9).

$$mSeg = \sum_{x=1}^{n} \frac{Seg_x}{n} \tag{9}$$

4   Experiments and Results

This section presents the experimental results of the article separation task conducted on the NAS dataset, utilizing the proposed evaluation metrics for the NewsEye baseline model[4]. The experimental setup involved training Graph Neural Network (GNN) models using BERT (Bidirectional Encoder Representations from Transformers) features. The models were trained on permutations of all three datasets, following a similar approach as described in [7]. The training, validation, and testing processes utilized a random selection of relevant test sets. The output obtained from the trained GNN models was then passed through various clustering algorithms with the objective of reconstructing the original news articles, thereby accomplishing the article separation task. Three distinct clustering techniques, namely *Greedy*, *DBSCAN* (Density-Based Spatial Clustering of Applications with Noise), and *Hierarchical*, were employed in the experiments. A threshold of 0.8 was set for each clustering method, adhering to the recommendations in [1, 10].

Table 4 presents the baseline approach results for the article separation task [13] on the proposed evaluation metrics. Among the different clustering algorithms, the *DBSCAN* clustering method obtains the highest mACS score (lowest mAER score) for the German (ONB) dataset. On the other hand, the *Hierarchical* clustering algorithm performs better for the Finnish (NLF) and French (BNF) datasets. However, it is worth noting that none of these clustering algorithms were able to fully reconstruct the news articles, as indicated by the low-performance results obtained for the mPPA metric.

Table 4. Baseline [13] results for article separation task on NAS dataset.

Dataset	Algorithm	Evaluation		
		mACS	mAER	mPPA
ONB	DBSCAN	**0.5844**	**0.4156**	**0.1914**
	Greedy	0.5360	0.4640	0.1736
	Hierarchical	0.5545	0.4455	0.1659
NLF	DBSCAN	0.3751	0.6249	**0.0662**
	Greedy	0.3275	0.6725	0.0548
	Hierarchical	**0.3823**	**0.6177**	0.0615
BNF	DBSCAN	0.4470	0.5530	0.1057
	Greedy	0.3568	0.6432	0.0940
	Hierarchical	**0.5382**	**0.4618**	**0.1393**

---

[4] https://github.com/CITlabRostock/citlab-article-separation-new.

5 Conclusions

The task of separating articles in newspapers, aimed at semantically classifying textual and non-textual components for information retrieval, is a significant yet challenging endeavor. One of the crucial aspects of article separation is the scarcity of publicly available datasets and performance evaluation strategies. This work presents a new multilingual annotated dataset, NAS, along with novel evaluation measures, providing valuable resources for digitizing historical newspapers. The dataset is extracted from multiple national European library collections and includes a diverse range of old press publications in *German, Finnish,* and *French* published from the 19th and early 20th century. The detailed annotation guidelines are made publicly accessible for research purposes. The introduced evaluation metrics, in addition to standard metrics, allow for a better understanding and comparison of model performance trained on this dataset.

The NAS dataset, unique in its scope and coverage, is a valuable benchmark resource for researchers in the field of information retrieval and digitizing historical collections. It is publicly accessible to researchers (ONB, NLF, BNF) and we hope its availability will foster further research in this area.

Acknowledgement. This work has been supported by the ANNA (2019-1R40226), TERMITRAD (AAPR2020-2019-8510010), Pypa (AAPR2021-2021-12263410), and Actuadata (AAPR2022-2021-17014610) projects funded by the Nouvelle-Aquitaine Region, France. We would also like to thank our colleagues Max Weidemann, Johannes Michael, and Roger Labahn for their review, valuable suggestions, and insightful comments, which greatly contributed to the improvement of this manuscript.

References

1. Andrade, G., Ramos, G., Madeira, D., Sachetto, R., Ferreira, R., Rocha, L.: G-DBscan: a GPU accelerated algorithm for density-based clustering. Procedia Comput. Sci. **18**, 369–378 (2013)
2. Augusto Borges Oliveira, D., Palhares Viana, M.: Fast CNN-based document layout analysis. In: Proceedings of the IEEE International Conference on Computer Vision Workshops, pp. 1173–1180 (2017)
3. Bansal, A., Chaudhury, S., Roy, S.D., Srivastava, J.: Newspaper article extraction using hierarchical fixed point model. In: 2014 11th IAPR International Workshop on Document Analysis Systems, pp. 257–261. IEEE (2014)
4. Buntinx, V., Kaplan, F., Xanthos, A.: Layout analysis on newspaper archives. In: Digital Humanities 2017, pp. 409–412 (2017)
5. Cohen, R., Asi, A., Kedem, K., El-Sana, J., Dinstein, I.: Robust text and drawing segmentation algorithm for historical documents. In: Proceedings of the 2nd International Workshop on Historical Document Imaging and Processing, pp. 110–117 (2013)
6. Colutto, S., Kahle, P., Guenter, H., Mühlberger, G.: Transkribus. A platform for automated text recognition and searching of historical documents. In: 2019 15th International Conference on eScience (eScience), pp. 463–466. IEEE (2019)

7. Devlin, J., Chang, M.W., Lee, K., Toutanova, K.: Bert: pre-training of deep bidirectional transformers for language understanding. arXiv preprint arXiv:1810.04805 (2018)
8. Doermann, D., Zotkina, E., Li, H.: Gedi-a groundtruthing environment for document images. In: Ninth IAPR International Workshop on Document Analysis Systems (DAS 2010). Citeseer (2010)
9. Doucet, A., et al.: Newseye: a digital investigator for historical newspapers. In: 15th Annual International Conference of the Alliance of Digital Humanities Organizations, DH 2020 (2020)
10. Ester, M., Kriegel, H.P., Sander, J., Xu, X., et al.: A density-based algorithm for discovering clusters in large spatial databases with noise. In: KDD, vol. 96, pp. 226–231 (1996)
11. Gatos, B., Mantzaris, S., Chandrinos, K., Tsigris, A., Perantonis, S.J.: Integrated algorithms for newspaper page decomposition and article tracking. In: Proceedings of the Fifth International Conference on Document Analysis and Recognition. ICDAR'99 (Cat. No. PR00318), pp. 559–562. IEEE (1999)
12. Meier, B., Stadelmann, T., Stampfli, J., Arnold, M., Cieliebak, M.: Fully convolutional neural networks for newspaper article segmentation. In: 2017 14th IAPR International Conference on Document Analysis and Recognition (ICDAR), vol. 1, pp. 414–419. IEEE (2017)
13. Michael, J., Weidemann, Max, L.R., Doucet, A.: Newseye: a digital investigator for historical newspapers (2022). https://www.newseye.eu/fileadmin/deliverables/NewsEye-T23-D27-ArticleSeparation-c-final-Submitted-v6.0.pdf. Accessed on 26 May 2023
14. Michael, J., Weidemann, M., Laasch, B., Labahn, R.: ICPR 2020 competition on text block segmentation on a NewsEye dataset. In: Del Bimbo, A., Cucchiara, R., Sclaroff, S., Farinella, G.M., Mei, T., Bertini, M., Escalante, H.J., Vezzani, R. (eds.) ICPR 2021. LNCS, vol. 12668, pp. 405–418. Springer, Cham (2021). https://doi.org/10.1007/978-3-030-68793-9_30
15. Naoum, A.: Article Segmentation in Digitised Newspapers. Ph.D. thesis (2020)
16. Naoum, A., Nothman, J., Curran, J.: Article segmentation in digitised newspapers with a 2d Markov model. In: 2019 International Conference on Document Analysis and Recognition (ICDAR), pp. 1007–1014. IEEE (2019)
17. Oliveira, S.A., Seguin, B., Kaplan, F.: dhsegment: a generic deep-learning approach for document segmentation. In: 2018 16th International Conference on Frontiers in Handwriting Recognition (ICFHR), pp. 7–12. IEEE (2018)
18. Palfray, T., Hebert, D., Nicolas, S., Tranouez, P., Paquet, T.: Logical segmentation for article extraction in digitized old newspapers. In: Proceedings of the 2012 ACM Symposium on Document Engineering, pp. 129–132 (2012)
19. Pletschacher, S., Antonacopoulos, A.: The page (page analysis and ground-truth elements) format framework. In: 2010 20th International Conference on Pattern Recognition, pp. 257–260. IEEE (2010)
20. Zheng, S.,et al.: Rethinking semantic segmentation from a sequence-to-sequence perspective with transformers. In: Proceedings of the IEEE/CVF Conference on Computer Vision and Pattern Recognition, pp. 6881–6890 (2021)
21. Zhu, W., Sokhandan, N., Yang, G., Martin, S., Sathyanarayana, S.: Docbed: a multi-stage ocr solution for documents with complex layouts. In: Proceedings of the AAAI Conference on Artificial Intelligence, vol. 36, pp. 12643–12649 (2022)

STRAS: A Semantic Textual-Cues Leveraged Rule-Based Approach for Article Separation in Historical Newspapers

Nancy Girdhar$^{(\boxtimes)}$, Mickaël Coustaty , and Antoine Doucet

L3i, University of La Rochelle, 17000 La Rochelle, France
{nancy.girdhar,mickael.coustaty,antoine.doucet}@univ-lr.fr

Abstract. The digitization of historical documents is a critical task for preserving cultural heritage and making vast amounts of information accessible to the wider public. One of the challenges in this process is separating individual articles from old newspaper images, which is significant for text analysis and information retrieval. In this work, we present a novel approach, *Semantic Textual-cues leveraged Rule-based approach for Article Separation* (STRAS) in historical newspapers. The presented approach, STRAS, involves utilizing textual information by extracting text region embeddings using scanned input images and their corresponding *PAGE* format files. The text regions with similar contextual embeddings are then categorized and articles are separated based on a defined rule set. The presented approach is tested on *French* and *Finnish* newspapers of the 19th and early 20th centuries. Besides this, novel metrics are introduced specifically for the article separation task: *article error rate* (AER), *article coverage score* (ACS), and *proper predicted article* (PPA). Our study evaluates the performance of various models, including *skip-gram* (sgSTRAS), *continuous-bag-of-words* (cbowSTRAS), *FastText* (ftSTRAS), and *pre-trained SpaCy* model (preSTRAS), and the results show that the sgSTRAS model achieves the highest *mean ACS* scores of 0.8343 and 0.8611 on the *French* and *Finnish* datasets, respectively, outperforming all other models. Our findings demonstrate that the semantic textual features contain valuable information, and the selection of an appropriate embedding method significantly influences the overall performance of the proposed approach to segment articles. To the best of our knowledge, this is the first study that applies a semantic textual similarity rule-based approach for article separation in historical newspapers, filling a gap in the existing literature and opening up new avenues for further research in this area.

Keywords: semantic analysis · logical segmentation · article separation · historical newspaper · article extraction · text embedding

D. H. Goh et al. (Eds.): ICADL 2023, LNCS 14457, pp. 89–105, 2023.
https://doi.org/10.1007/978-981-99-8085-7_8

1   Introduction

Historical newspapers provide valuable insights into the past and are essential for text mining, information retrieval, text analysis, and historical research. Document digitization makes it possible to access and study these valuable resources to understand the social, cultural, and political context of a particular period. However, these newspaper documents are often difficult to read and analyze due to their diverse content, various quality degradation factors, and the lack of standardized formats. One of the key challenges in digitizing old newspapers is the task of *article separation*, which involves logically segmenting a newspaper page into individual articles. The approaches to article separation (AS) can broadly be categorized into two main categories based on *visual-cues* and *textual-cues*. The V*isual-cues*-based A*rticle* S*eparation*(VAS) approaches depend on the visual features (such as *pixel-value*) of newspaper structure, on the other hand, T*extual-cues*-based Article S*eparation* (TAS) approaches assimilate textual features (such as *text-similarity*) to extract the similar segments that are possibly related to a particular article.

Most of the existing approaches to aggregate the individual segments of an article in historical newspapers fall under the umbrella of VAS approaches [1,14,29], however, these *layout-dependent* methods often fail when dealing with newspapers from different periods, regions, or non-standard layouts. Moreover, many of these studies primarily experimented with contemporary data and may not be suitable for historical newspapers as unlike modern newspapers, old historical newspapers come with many additional challenges, some of which are detailed as follows:

   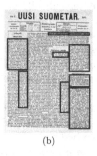

(a)   (b)

Fig. 1. Text line detection results of Doc-UFCN on (a) BNF and (b) NLF dataset pages. The purple-colored rectangular boxes spotlight the uncaptured text.

- *Layout Challenges*: The handling of historic newspapers for information extraction is more challenging compared to contemporary newspapers due to their differences in *source quality, diverse formatting*, and *varied layouts* [21]. In contrast to contemporary newspapers, the quality of historical newspapers is much more depreciated due to facsimiles (*skew, slant, rotated-text*, etc.) and environmental and time deterioration factors (such as *blur, ink bleed, jitter, noise*, etc.) [12,18,32] which can affect the visual cues of the newspaper layout and, consequently, the overall performance of VAS methods. Figure 1, showcases the text line detection results of the Doc-UFCN model [4] applied to historical newspapers that clearly exhibit significant data loss, indicating the model's inability to capture the text in these old documents.

– **Language Diversity and Evolution**: Additionally, along with the much higher variability and diversity in the historical newspapers than contemporary newspapers, as they span for a long enough time period, it is much more difficult to handle and process these old documents for information retrieval and natural language processing (NLP) tasks [28]. Furthermore, these historic newspapers are prone to be affected by language change and evolution, particularly in the case of Western European languages which only adopted modern spelling standards in the 18th or 19th centuries [13,20]. It is difficult for VAS models to capture the specific nuances of language usage in historical documents, such as archaic or colloquial language. Thus, taking account of textual-based semantic cues becomes even more important to improve the outcomes of AS methods for the mass digitization of historical newspapers [11].

To address the existing approaches' shortcomings and comprehend the literature gap, we present a novel approach that identifies potentially related segments (*text regions*) based on their textual semantic similarity and aggregates them together utilizing rules derived from the fundamental syntactic structure of a language to segment articles from newspapers of a historic era. Our *layout-independent* approach is motivated by the need for a flexible and adaptable method that can handle the varying layouts and formats of historical newspapers and is also applicable to processing contemporary newspapers.

The contribution of this paper is three-fold:

i. We present a novel method, *Semantic Textual-cues leveraged Rule-based Article Separation* (STRAS), that addresses the challenges posed by the varying layouts and formats of these documents to address the tasks of article extraction and separation in historical newspapers.
ii. We compare the results of our proposed approach with the baseline article separation model presented in [22] on historical datasets of French and Finnish newspapers.
iii. Besides the gold standard evaluation, we have introduced new metrics to further assess and validate the efficacy of the proposed approach for the article separation task.

The rest of the paper is organized as follows. Section 2 presents preliminary background and is followed by a brief overview of similar works in this field in Sect. 3. Section 4 elaborates on the proposed semantic rule-based approach in detail. To evaluate it, Sect. 5 describes the dataset and evaluation metrics, while Sect. 6 describes the experimental setup and evaluation results with a discussion on the implications of our work. Finally, Sect. 7 concludes the work presented with some future outlooks.

2   Preliminaries

This section presents background concepts related to the article separation task to provide context for the presented research and to establish a foundation for the subsequent sections of the paper.

2.1   Word Embedding Methods

Word embeddings play a crucial role in representing and understanding the semantic relationships and contextual information of words. These are numerical representations of words in a high-dimensional vector space, where each dimension captures a specific feature or semantic property of the word. In this work, we have utilized three popular models for generating word embeddings: *Skip-Gram* (SG) [23], *Continuous Bag-of-Words* (CBoW) [23], and *FastText* (FT) [6].

While there also exist *sentence embedding* learning methods [7,31] that have gained attention in recent years for capturing the semantic meaning of entire sentences, we have chosen to focus solely on word embedding methods for generating the embeddings of text regions in our proposed methodology. The primary reason for this decision is the inherent nature of AS in historical newspapers. Given that the task involves grouping and combining text regions to form articles, the contextual information provided by word embeddings is more suitable for capturing the nuanced relationships between words within a specific region. Additionally, considering the computational complexity associated with training sentence embedding models on large historical newspaper datasets, we believe that word embeddings provide a reasonable representation of the text regions for our AS task.

2.2   Pre-trained Language Models

Another popular approach to learning word embeddings is by using pre-trained language models. Language models (LMs) are a crucial component of NLP tasks that utilize deep-learning techniques to learn contextual representations of words and phrases. Pre-trained LMs have revolutionized the field of NLP by providing a robust starting point for various tasks. Typically trained on massive text data using unsupervised learning methods, these models can learn to capture the semantic meaning of words and phrases, as well as their context within sentences and documents.

2.3   Newspaper Layout Analysis

– *Article Separation Task:* The task of logical partitioning of a newspaper into distinct articles by segmenting and extracting relevant regions and further aggregating regions that belong together forming an article.
  • *VAS* (*V*isual-cues-based *A*rticle *S*eparation) entails extracting and segmenting the articles based on the information about the layout structure

including the details of the *pixel value, font type, font size*, etc. These *layout-dependent* approaches mainly rely on visual elements to perform article segmentation and extraction tasks from newspapers.

- **TAS** (***T****extual*-cues-based **A**rticle **S**eparation) approaches include methods that exploit logical information from the text itself to segment the newspaper into articles. These *layout-independent* approaches compute the semantic similarity between text regions of the newspapers (i.e. *text embedding similarity*) to extract newspaper articles.

- **Article Definition:** An *article* is typically composed of segments (text regions) or a combination of segments and images, where each segment is comprised of a group of text lines that can span multiple columns or even extend to another page. In this work, we defined an *article* as a unit that includes at least one text entity i.e. *text region*. Specifically, our model is focused on the scenario where articles span multiple columns within a single newspaper page.

3   Related Work

Article separation (AS) in historical documents has been a subject of interest in the field of document analysis and digitization. Despite this, there have only been a limited number of studies addressing this task with most existing methods focusing on contemporary documents and not historical ones. Nonetheless, few approaches have addressed the task of article separation in historical newspapers. After the breakthrough success of the ImageNet 2D image classification task [17,30], deep learning (DL) techniques, particularly *CNNs*, have revolutionized various areas of image processing [19,27]. More recently, methods based on DL have been proposed for text line detection [5], and article separation in historical documents. A summary of existing studies on article separation in historical newspapers is presented in Table 1.

One of the studies on layout analysis adopted a U-shaped model, Doc-UFCN, that employs a *fully convolutional network* (FCN) architecture to identify objects in historical documents [4]. The work considered the task of text line detection as a classification problem at the pixel level and the model generates pixel-level labeling of the input images. Similarly, an FCN architecture is utilized to extract features from an input image and then distinguish articles from other elements on a newspaper page [21]. Despite achieving state-of-the-art results, their method is memory-intensive during training and requires a high-performance GPU. Further, while this method is flexible and adaptable, it requires a large amount of labeled data for training, making it, thus, less suitable for historical newspapers where labeled data is limited. Also, the approach was tested on a contemporary dataset that recognizes rectangular shapes only. Furthermore, it is unclear how well it would perform when faced with noisy, complex, and irregular layouts of historical newspaper datasets, which can be degraded and have varied layouts and formats.

Table 1. Article separation in historical newspapers (*Lang*: Language; *HN*: Historical Newspapers; *CN*: Contemporary Newspapers; *CRF*: Conditional Random Field; *MM*: Markov Model; *A*: Accuracy; *P*: Precision; *R*: Recall; *F1*: F_score; *mCS*: mean Completeness Score; *mDER*: mean Diarization Error Rate).

[Ref]	Method	Approach	Dataset					Results
			Name	Type	Source	Pages	Lang	(%)
[11]	VAS	Rule-based	TO VIMA	HN	Private	100	Greek	P: 75.20 R: 77.15
Limitation(s):								
Semantic cues could be relevant but are currently not utilized for article separation tasks.								
[29]	VAS	CRF + Rule- based	Journal De Rouen	HN	Private	42	French	A: 85.84
Limitation(s):								
Performance measured on limited dataset size.								
[21]	VAS	FCN	ARGUS DATA INSIGHTS Schweiz AG	CN	Private	426	–	mCS: 54.44 mDER: 13.78
Limitation(s):								
Cannot differentiate between article-text and an ad-image.								
Can recognize rectangular shapes only.								
Implemented on a contemporary dataset, not on historical data.								
[3]	VAS	Fixed point	–	CN	Private	45	English	A: 96
Limitation(s):								
Performance measured on limited dataset size.								
Implemented on a contemporary dataset, not on historical data.								
[26]	VAS	2D MM	Fairfax Media	CN	Private	3332	English	F1: 92.9
Limitation(s):								
Lack of consideration for visual cues, such as horizontal and vertical rules.								
Approximated 2D Markov model may overlook intricate dependencies.								
Implemented on a contemporary dataset, not on historical data.								

Another approach to extracting articles is based on identifying *lines*, *text*, *images*, and *headings* in the newspaper layout, and then applying a set of rules for AS in old newspapers. However, their rule set is not dynamic and adaptable for various newspaper layouts [11]. A similar rule-based approach for article separation considered visual information such as *layout*, *font*, *spacing*, and other visual elements [29]. The method used a set of hand-crafted rules to extract articles from a newspaper page based on these visual features. Although this method was effective, it was limited in its ability to handle variations in the layout of historical newspapers.

4   Proposed Methodology

This section provides a detailed description of the proposed STRAS (*Semantic Textual-cues leveraged Rule-based Article Separation*) methodology for semantically extracting the articles from historical newspaper pages. Our approach to article separation is based on a set of rules and works on textual features, specifically the textual context, using basic syntactical grammar rules and language structure. The algorithm takes as input *PAGE* format files in *ALTO* format and the original scanned newspaper images in formats such as *.jpg*, *.png*, or *.tif*. Thus, our approach is more generic and layout-independent and is applicable to both historical and contemporary datasets.

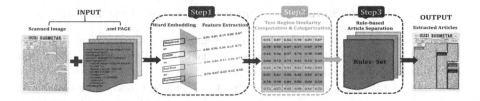

Fig. 2. Framework of the proposed STRAS methodology.

To summarize, the overall STRAS approach consists of the following three steps, as illustrated in Fig. 2, and described in further detail in this section:

- Extracting embeddings of text regions using trained or pre-trained language models.
- Computing inter-text-region similarity and categorizing each text region into dependent or independent, and further, sub-categorizing dependent regions into source or non-source regions.
- Recursively aggregating text regions of an article based on defined rules.

4.1 Text-Region Embedding Generation

The first step of the proposed STRAS method involves leveraging trained or pre-trained language models to learn word embeddings of the text regions and compute similarity scores between them. For this, we tailored the approach of *text embedding map* to generate word embeddings (in our case text region embeddings) [33]. We have considered a text region as the minimum unit that conveys certain semantic meaning, and represent it using a low-dimensional vector. Our text region embedding is built by averaging embeddings for individual sentences (text lines). This is a simple yet effective method that has been shown to be useful in many applications, including sentiment analysis [15] and text classification [16]. Using such embeddings, we created a *text embedding map* for each annotated text region consisting of multiple text lines in a scanned newspaper image. Specifically, our text region embedding is learned using *primary* word embedding methods (*SG*, *CBoW*, and *FT*), and we have trained them on our dataset for text embedding generation and similarity score computation.

Another way we opted to generate embeddings is by using *pre-trained* LMs. We chose *SpaCy's* pre-trained LMs on news articles in *French* and *Finnish* to learn text region embeddings. The relevance to select these models lies in the fact that we are working with historical newspaper datasets in these languages. As these models have been trained on contemporary newspaper datasets, they offer a baseline representation of semantic meaning for words and phrases in these languages. Using these models, we can extract embeddings that capture the semantic meaning of the text in our historical newspaper datasets, which is critical for accurate article separation.

4.2 Text-Regions Similarity Computation and Categorization

After embedding generation, for each text region embedding, cosine similarity is utilized to calculate the text region similarity index. A threshold is set based on empirical analysis and thereafter, text region categorization is done based on the fundamental language syntactical structure. This approach is more reliable than visual cues since it relies on the actual content of the articles and can adapt to different newspaper styles and layouts. Furthermore, semantic rules can be customized to fit the specific needs of different projects, allowing for greater flexibility in processing historical newspapers. For this, we have defined categories: *dependent* and *independent text regions* and subcategories *source* and *non-source text regions* into which text regions are segregated. The definitions of these categories and the rules applied are detailed in Table 2.

Table 2. Defined rules for text regions categorization.

Independent Text Regions
A text region is considered an *independent text region* if it satisfies any of the following conditions: –The text region with a length of fewer than 3 words. – The text region does not have semantic similarity with any other text regions.

Dependent Text Regions
A text region is considered to be a *dependent text region* if it has a semantic similarity with another text region (where the similarity is equal to or greater than the predetermined threshold value) and meets any of the following criteria: – The text region starts with a lower letter casing and/or does not end with a period mark (.). – The text region starts with an upper letter casing and does not end with a period mark (.).

Source Text Regions
A dependent text region is considered a *source text region* if it starts from an upper letter casing.

non-Source Text Regions
A dependent text region is considered a *non-source text region* if it does not start with an upper letter casing

4.3 Rule-Based Article Extraction

The final step involves connecting individual text regions that belong to the same article. The step-by-step procedure connecting text regions of an article is detailed in Algorithm 1, and the notations used are presented in Table 3.

Table 3. Notations used in Algorithm 1 (Merged Regions List Generation).

Notation	Description
I	Image of a newspaper page.
D	Annotated XML file of Image I.
B	The set of text regions in XML file D. For each $region \in \{r_0, r_1, ..., r_{(|R|-1)}\}$ and $i_{pos} \in \{0, 1, ..., (|R| - 1)\}$, where, $|R|$ is the total number of regions in D. Each i_{pos} corresponds to the index of each $region$.
$BBox$	The set of bounding boxes. For each region defined by $bbox = (x, y, w, h)$ where x and y are horizontal and vertical positions respectively, w and h are the width and height of a region.
IR	The set of $independent\ text\ regions$.
DR	The set of $dependent\ text\ regions$.
SR	The set of $source\ text\ regions$.
NSR	The set of $non\text{-}source\ text\ regions$.
CS	The contextual similarity score matrix of size $|R| \times |R|$.
CS_i	The contextual similarity score list of ith text region.
$\triangledown$	The threshold value for region contextual similarity score.
$traverseDepFlag$	The list of size $|R|$ consists binary value $(0/1)$, where 1 represents a traversed dependent region.
$traverseSrcFlag$	The list of size $|R|$ consists binary value $(0/1)$, where 1 represents a traversed source region.
CP	The list of semantically connected pairs of regions $[(r_i, r_j), ...,]$.
T	The list of connected merged regions. For each pair of $CP \in [(r_i, r_j), (r_j, r_k), ...,]$, generate $T = [(r_i, r_j, r_k), ...,]$

5   Datasets and Performance Evaluations Metrics

This section provides the details of the data used for conducting experiments and evaluation metrics opted for comparative performance analysis of the proposed approach.

5.1   Data

For experimental purposes, we selected two classical historical newspapers datasets in *French* and *Finnish* languages that cover a span of about 200 years, obtained from digital libraries during the international research project NewsEye [9]. These datasets were collected through the national libraries of France (BNF), Finland (NLF), and German (ONB)[1] [22]. They comprise four corpora (*French, Swedish, German*, and, *Finnish*), with the *French* one composed of digitized archives of nine newspapers (i.e., *L'Oeuvre, La Fronde, La Presse, Le Matin, Marie-Claire, Ce soir, Marianne, Paris Soir* and *Regards*) from 1854 to 1946

---

[1] BNF: https://bnf.fr; NLF: https://kansalliskirjasto.fi; ONB: https://onb.ac.at.

and the *Finnish* corpora consisting digitized archives of seven newspapers (i.e., *Suometar, Sanomia Turusta, Uusi Suometar, Aura, Helsingin Sanomat, Uusi Aura, Päivälehti*) from 1824-1918. Table 4 details statistics about the dataset.

Algorithm 1 Merged Regions List Generation

Input: Image file (I) and its annotated XML file (D).
Output: Merged regions ($BBox$) list.

Step 1: Read the XML file and extract text regions.
Step 2: Compute similarity among text regions using a trained or pre-trained language model and generate a contextual similar region list (CS) for each region.
Step 3: Split the text regions into Independent(IR) and Dependent Regions (DR) respectively.
Step 4: Split Dependent Regions (DR) into Source (SR) and Non-Source Regions (NSR).
Step 5: **for** each region r in DR **do**
  if r in SR **then**
    Create an empty list connectSrc[r].
    Set the traverseSrcFlag[r] = r
    Compute CS(r)
    if (($r + 1$) in $CS(r)$) and (($r + 1$) in DR) **then**
      Append $r + 1$ in connectSrc[r]
      Set traverseDepFlag[$r + 1$] = r
    end if
  end if
end for
Step 6: Identify the consecutive connected pairs list (CP) based on contextual similarity.
Step 7: Connect Transitive Regions (T)
  for each region pair (r_i, r_j) in CP **do**
    if exist region pair (r_j, r_k) in CP **then**
      Merge regions[(r_i, r_j, r_k)]
    end if
  end for
Step 8: Create a $BBox$ list & append the IR list and T list

5.2 Evaluation Metrics

For results analysis, in addition to the standard *intersection over union* (IoU) metric, we have introduced novel evaluation metrics[2] for the AS task, to assess the performance based on various aspects including *error, article coverage*, and *prediction accuracy* of an article, considering the fact that IoU metric is prone to being sensitive to threshold values, does not account for complex shapes and

Table 4. Statistical description of the dataset (*Lang*: Language; *TR*: Text Regions; *W_B*: Without Baselines; *W_AT*: Without Article Tags; *F_TR*: Final Text Regions; *AC*: Article Count).

Dataset	Lang	Pages	TR	W_B	W_AT	F_TR	AC
BNF	French	183	73,376	10,153	661	62,562	3,061
NLF	Finnish	200	28,447	739	25	27,683	3,282

---

[2] https://github.com/NancyGirdhar/AS_EvaluationMetrics.

localization accuracy, and may yield high scores even if the predicted segment is not correctly aligned with the ground truth. Thus, relying solely on IoU to evaluate overall model performance is inadequate.

- **Article Error Rate** (AER): The first new metric AER is introduced to evaluate *"How much error incurred in identifying the relevant text regions of an article ?"*, which indicates the discrepancy between the predicted text regions and the actual text regions of an article x. This metric takes account of both Type-I and Type-II errors (i) when a TR is predicted to belong to the article x, but according to the ground truth, it does not. (ii) when a TR belongs to the article x, but it is not predicted by the model. Given an *article* x, PTR_x is the set of *predicted text regions* in article x and GTR_x is the set of *actual text regions* (ground truth) of article x. Then, the error rate in the prediction of article x is calculated as Eq.(1).

$$AER_x = \frac{|PTR_x \oplus GTR_x|}{|PTR_x \cup GTR_x|} \tag{1}$$

Assume n articles, where n is the cardinality of union between sets of ground truth and predicted articles respectively, the **mean article error rate** ($mAER$) is computed as Eq.(2)

$$mAER = \sum_{x=1}^{n} \frac{AER_x}{n} \tag{2}$$

- **Article Coverage Score** (ACS): Another metric ACS is introduced to calculate *"How many regions of an article are extracted ?"* or in other words, *"How much proportion of an article is covered in terms of identifying its regions ?"*. This metric is derived from the *article error rate* and signifies the accuracy of the model's prediction and extraction of text regions within an article. Given n articles, **mean article coverage rate** ($mACR$) is calculated as Eq.(3).

$$mACS = 1 - \sum_{x=1}^{n} \frac{AER_x}{n} \tag{3}$$

- **Proper Predicted Article** (PPA): The last introduced metric PPA is to retort *"How many articles are predicted perfectly ?"*, which calculates the ratio of correctly predicted articles to the total number of articles in the ground truth set. An *article* is said to be an **exact predicted article** if and only if (*iff*) it satisfies constraint as given in Eq.(4).

$$\forall x, \ TR|TR \in PTR_x \text{ and } \exists y \in GTR_x \text{ such that } |PTR_x| = |GTR_x| \tag{4}$$

Given a multi-page newspaper with P pages, **mean proper predicted article** ($mPPA$) is computed as Eq.(5).

$$mPPA = \frac{\sum_{p=1}^{P} \frac{|Exact\ Predicted\ Articles_p|}{|Ground\ Truth\ Articles_p|}}{P} \tag{5}$$

6 Experiments and Results

This section details the experimental settings, comparative analysis, and discusses the results obtained by the proposed approach across various performance evaluation measures. Additionally, we examine the impact of the embedding generation step on the proposed article separation approach.

6.1 Experimental Settings and Comparative Analysis

For text embedding extraction, we used the pre-trained models from the $SpaCy^{3,4}$ library. In addition to obtaining embeddings from these pre-trained models (preSTRAS), we also trained our own models to generate embeddings on the dataset. The training was performed for 100 epochs, with a vector-dimension size of 300, using the *skip-gram* (sgSTRAS), *continuous bag-of-words* (cbow-STRAS), and *FastText* (ftSTRAS) approaches. For experimental purposes, for each model (pre-trained or trained), an empirical threshold of 0.9 is set (which is a common practice) to compute cosine similarity among the generated text region embeddings.

For comparative analysis, we have compared our approach with the News-Eye's [22] baseline for article separation (AS) task[5]. Their AS baseline approach involved training Graph Neural Network (GNN) models utilizing BERT (Bidirectional Encoder Representations from Transformers) features, similar to [8]. Subsequently, the output obtained from the trained GNN models was passed through different clustering algorithms: *Greedy* (greedyAS), *Density-Based Spatial Clustering of Applications with Noise* (dbscanAS), and *Hierarchical* (hierarchicalAS) to reconstruct the original news articles with a clustering hyperparameter threshold set to 0.8 [2,10].

6.2 Results Discussion

Table 5 presents a comprehensive comparison of the results achieved by the proposed STRAS approach and the AS baseline approach for the article separation task. The results clearly demonstrate the superiority of the proposed STRAS approach over the baseline approach in terms of both metrics, with particular emphasis on the mPPA score. The achieved mPPA score for the baseline approach is relatively low, suggesting that none of the clustering algorithms employed in the baseline approach were capable of fully reconstructing the original news articles.

Furthermore, comparing the performance of the proposed STRAS approach across the datasets, we observe that the *sgSTRAS* model consistently outperforms other models on both the BNF and NLF datasets. The *cbowSTRAS* model, despite being outperformed by *sgSTRAS*, still achieves competitive results by

---

[3] https://spacy.io/models/fr#fr_core_news_lg.
[4] https://spacy.io/models/fi#fi_core_news_lg.
[5] https://github.com/CITlabRostock/citlab-article-separation-new.

Table 5. Results on historical newspaper datasets for article separation task (*pre*: pre-trained; *sg*: skip-gram; *cbow*: continous bag-of-words; *ft*: fasttext). In the column *Model*, * superscript indicates AS baseline.

Dataset	Model	mACS	mPPA	mIoU
BNF [24]	preSTRAS	0.8006	0.6347	0.7878
	ftSTRAS	0.7984	0.6122	0.7867
	cbowSTRAS	0.8067	0.6310	0.7997
	sgSTRAS	**0.8343**	**0.7003**	**0.8238**
	dbscanAS*	0.4470	0.1057	–
	greedyAS*	0.3568	0.0940	–
	hierarchicalAS*	0.5382	0.1393	–
NLF [25]	preSTRAS	0.7905	0.6065	0.8247
	ftSTRAS	0.8271	0.7001	0.8664
	cbowSTRAS	0.8552	**0.7924**	0.8687
	sgSTRAS	**0.8611**	0.7857	**0.8774**
	dbscanAS*	0.37511	0.0662	–
	greedyAS*	0.3275	0.0548	–
	hierarchicalAS*	0.3823	0.0615	–

leveraging local word dependencies and contextual information. Based on the results mentioned in Table 5, we present our findings on two prime factors that are detailed as follows:

– **Effectiveness of Pre-trained Word Embeddings** The *preSTRAS* model, which utilizes pre-trained embeddings achieves relatively lower scores compared to *sgSTRAS* and *cbowSTRAS*. This could be attributed to the limitations of pre-trained embeddings in capturing the specific linguistic characteristics and semantic nuances present in historical newspaper texts. These models may struggle to capture the fine-grained contextual information necessary for precise article separation.
– **Effect of Trained Word Embeddings** Among the different trained models evaluated, the skip-gram embeddings (*sgSTRAS*) consistently outperform other models on both datasets. This can be argued as SG models excel at capturing contextual information and fine-grained semantic relationships between words. Since historical newspaper datasets contain complex language patterns and contextual dependencies, SG embeddings are better equipped to handle such challenges. The CBoW embeddings (*cbowSTRAS*) also demonstrated competitive performance, particularly in terms of mACS and mIoU on both datasets. Since, CBoW models aim to predict the current word based on the context, making them suitable for capturing local word dependencies and hence, CBoW embeddings have proven to be effective in discerning arti-

cle boundaries in historical newspaper datasets. The FastText embeddings (*ftSTRAS*) exhibit moderate performance in the AS task. It may be due to the fact that FT models incorporate subword information, which is advantageous when dealing with morphologically rich languages or out-of-vocabulary words, however, in the case of historical newspaper datasets, where contextual information and semantic nuances play a significant role, the FT embeddings might not be able to capture the relevant information as effectively as SG or CBoW models.

Figure 3 presents the illustration of article separation results obtained based on trained and pre-trained text embedding generation models. It is clear from the results that the selection of the appropriate embedding method plays a significant role in the overall model's performance for the article separation task. Skip-gram and CBoW embeddings emerge as strong candidates, considering their ability to capture contextual information and handle morphologically rich languages, respectively. Hence, it can be concluded that the model trained on domain-specific data enhances the performance of the approach for article separation compared to the pre-trained models. The findings contribute to the development of effective models for text region article separation tasks in the field of historical newspaper analysis.

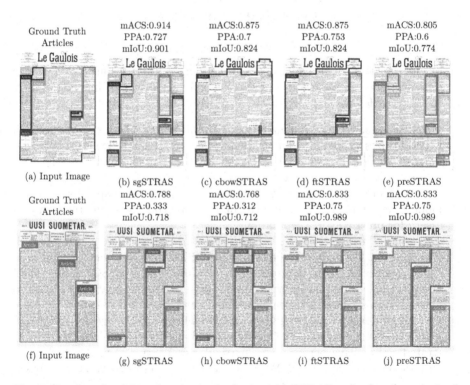

Fig. 3. Results of article separation task obtained by STRAS trained and pre-trained embedding rule-based approach on (a)-(e) BNF and (f)-(j) NLF datasets.

7 Conclusions and Future Outlook

In this work, we introduced STRAS, as one of the first studies that applies a semantic textual similarity rule-based approach for article separation in historical newspapers. Our approach leverages trained and pre-trained models to learn embeddings and utilizes textual cues and language syntax grammar rules for article separation. A key strength of our proposed approach is its layout independence, enabling its application to diverse newspaper layouts, which is a critical challenge in article separation tasks. We conducted experiments on *French* and *Finnish* historical newspaper datasets obtained from the NewsEye project, comprising 183 and 200 pages, respectively. Our approach demonstrated substantial initial results in terms of standard *mIoU* and the novel metrics of *mACS* and *mPPA*, showcasing its effectiveness in accurately segmenting articles with complex layouts, including those with multi-column structures. Additionally, our proposed approach demonstrated a significant improvement over the baseline article separation approach on both metrics, particularly in terms of *mPPA* score, where STRAS achieved performance that was five times better compared to the AS baseline. Furthermore, our findings indicate that training models on domain-specific data improve the approach's performance compared to utilizing pre-trained models, while pre-trained models still offer computational efficiency and benefit from extensive training data. It is worth mentioning that this study focused on single-page article segmentation, and future research will explore multi-page article separation and the integration of textual and visual features to enhance segmentation performance.

Acknowledgements. This work has been supported by the ANNA (2019-1R40226), TERMITRAD (AAPR2020-2019-8510010), Pypa (AAPR2021-2021-12263410), and Actuadata (AAPR2022-2021-17014610) projects funded by the Nouvelle-Aquitaine Region, France.

References

1. An, C., Yin, D., Baird, H.S.: Document segmentation using pixel-accurate ground truth. In: 2010 20th International Conference on Pattern Recognition, pp. 245–248. IEEE (2010)
2. Andrade, G., Ramos, G., Madeira, D., Sachetto, R., Ferreira, R., Rocha, L.: G-DBSCAN: a GPU accelerated algorithm for density-based clustering. Procedia Comput. Sci. **18**, 369–378 (2013)
3. Bansal, A., Chaudhury, S., Roy, S.D., Srivastava, J.: Newspaper article extraction using hierarchical fixed point model. In: 2014 11th IAPR International Workshop on Document Analysis Systems, pp. 257–261. IEEE (2014)
4. Boillet, M., Kermorvant, C., Paquet, T.: Multiple document datasets pre-training improves text line detection with deep neural networks. In: 2020 25th International Conference on Pattern Recognition (ICPR), pp. 2134–2141. IEEE (2021)
5. Boillet, M., Kermorvant, C., Paquet, T.: Robust text line detection in historical documents: learning and evaluation methods. IJDAR **25**, 95–114 (2022)

6. Bojanowski, P., Grave, E., Joulin, A., Mikolov, T.: Enriching word vectors with subword information. Trans. Assoc. Comput. Linguist. **5**, 135–146 (2017)

7. Conneau, A., Kiela, D., Schwenk, H., Barrault, L., Bordes, A.: Supervised learning of universal sentence representations from natural language inference data. arXiv preprint arXiv:1705.02364 (2017)

8. Devlin, J., Chang, M.W., Lee, K., Toutanova, K.: Bert: pre-training of deep bidirectional transformers for language understanding. arXiv preprint arXiv:1810.04805 (2018)

9. Doucet, A., et al.: NewsEye: a digital investigator for historical newspapers. In: 15th Annual International Conference of the Alliance of Digital Humanities Organizations, DH 2020 (2020)

10. Ester, M., Kriegel, H.P., Sander, J., Xu, X., et al.: A density-based algorithm for discovering clusters in large spatial databases with noise. In: KDD 1996: Proceedings of the Second International Conference on Knowledge Discovery and Data Mining, vol. 96, pp. 226–231 (1996)

11. Gatos, B., Mantzaris, S., Chandrinos, K., Tsigris, A., Perantonis, S.J.: Integrated algorithms for newspaper page decomposition and article tracking. In: Proceedings of the Fifth International Conference on Document Analysis and Recognition. ICDAR'99 (Cat. No. PR00318), pp. 559–562. IEEE (1999)

12. Gatos, B., Pratikakis, I., Perantonis, S.J.: Efficient binarization of historical and degraded document images. In: 2008 The Eighth IAPR International Workshop on Document Analysis Systems, pp. 447–454. IEEE (2008)

13. González-Gallardo, C.E., Boros, E., Giamphy, E., Hamdi, A., Moreno, J.G., Doucet, A.: Injecting temporal-aware knowledge in historical named entity recognition. In: Kamps, J., et al. Advances in Information Retrieval. ECIR 2023. Lecture Notes in Computer Science, vol. 13980, pp. 377–393. Springer, Cham (2023). https://doi.org/10.1007/978-3-031-28244-7_24

14. Hebert, D., Paquet, T., Nicolas, S.: Continuous CRF with multi-scale quantization feature functions application to structure extraction in old newspaper. In: 2011 International Conference on Document Analysis and Recognition, pp. 493–497. IEEE (2011)

15. Iyyer, M., Manjunatha, V., Boyd-Graber, J., Daumé III, H.: Deep unordered composition rivals syntactic methods for text classification. In: Proceedings of the 53rd Annual Meeting of the Association for Computational Linguistics and the 7th International Joint Conference on Natural Language Processing (volume 1: Long papers), pp. 1681–1691 (2015)

16. Joulin, A., Grave, E., Bojanowski, P., Mikolov, T.: Bag of tricks for efficient text classification. arXiv preprint arXiv:1607.01759 (2016)

17. Krizhevsky, A., Sutskever, I., Hinton, G.E.: ImageNet classification with deep convolutional neural networks. Commun. ACM **60**(6), 84–90 (2017)

18. Le, D.S., Thoma, G.R., Wechsler, H.: Automated page orientation and skew angle detection for binary document images. Pattern Recogn. **27**(10), 1325–1344 (1994)

19. Long, J., Shelhamer, E., Darrell, T.: Fully convolutional networks for semantic segmentation. In: Proceedings of the IEEE conference on computer vision and pattern recognition, pp. 3431–3440 (2015)

20. Manjavacas, E., Fonteyn, L.: Adapting vs. pre-training language models for historical languages. J. Data Min. Digit. Humanit. 1–19 (2022)

21. Meier, B., Stadelmann, T., Stampfli, J., Arnold, M., Cieliebak, M.: Fully convolutional neural networks for newspaper article segmentation. In: 2017 14th IAPR International Conference on Document Analysis and Recognition (ICDAR), vol. 1, pp. 414–419. IEEE (2017)

22. Michael, J., Weidemann, Max, L.R., Doucet, A.: NewsEye: a digital investigator for historical newspapers (2022). www.newseye.eu/fileadmin/deliverables/NewsEye-T23-D27-ArticleSeparation-c-final-Submitted-v6.0.pdf. Accessed 26 May 2023
23. Mikolov, T., Chen, K., Corrado, G., Dean, J.: Efficient estimation of word representations in vector space. arXiv preprint arXiv:1301.3781 (2013)
24. Muehlberger, G., Hackl, G.: NewsEye / READ AS training dataset from French newspapers (19th, early 20th C.) (2021). https://doi.org/10.5281/zenodo.4600636
25. Muehlberger, G., Hackl, G.: NewsEye / READ AS training dataset from finnish newspapers (19th C.) (2021). https://doi.org/10.5281/zenodo.4600746
26. Naoum, A., Nothman, J., Curran, J.: Article segmentation in digitised newspapers with a 2D Markov model. In: 2019 International Conference on Document Analysis and Recognition (ICDAR), pp. 1007–1014. IEEE (2019)
27. Noh, H., Hong, S., Han, B.: Learning deconvolution network for semantic segmentation. In: Proceedings of the IEEE International Conference on Computer Vision, pp. 1520–1528 (2015)
28. Oberbichler, S., et al.: Integrated interdisciplinary workflows for research on historical newspapers: perspectives from humanities scholars, computer scientists, and librarians. J. Am. Soc. Inf. Sci. **73**(2), 225–239 (2022)
29. Palfray, T., Hebert, D., Nicolas, S., Tranouez, P., Paquet, T.: Logical segmentation for article extraction in digitized old newspapers. In: Proceedings of the 2012 ACM Symposium on Document Engineering, pp. 129–132 (2012)
30. Pinheiro, P., Collobert, R.: Recurrent convolutional neural networks for scene labeling. In: International Conference on Machine Learning, pp. 82–90. PMLR (2014)
31. Reimers, N., Gurevych, I.: Sentence-bert: sentence embeddings using Siamese bert-networks. arXiv preprint arXiv:1908.10084 (2019)
32. Sezgin, M., Sankur, B.l.: Survey over image thresholding techniques and quantitative performance evaluation. J. Electron. Imaging **13**(1), 146–168 (2004)
33. Yang, X., Yumer, E., Asente, P., Kraley, M., Kifer, D., Lee Giles, C.: Learning to extract semantic structure from documents using multimodal fully convolutional neural networks. In: Proceedings of the IEEE Conference on Computer Vision and Pattern Recognition, pp. 5315–5324 (2017)

Cultural Research Trends of Taiwan's Indigenous Peoples, 2000–2021

Chao-Chen Chen[1] , Yun-Fang Tu[1] , Yi-Chin Chen[1] , Aciang Iku-Silan[2] ,
and Fang-ya Chen[3(✉)]

[1] Center for General Education, College of Humanities and Education, Chung Yuan Christian
University, Taoyuan City, Taiwan
tanja.chen0411@gmail.com
[2] Graduate Institute of Applied Science and Technology, National Taiwan University of Science
and Technology, Taipei, Taiwan
[3] Graduate Institute of Library, Information and Archival, National Chengchi University, Taipei,
Taiwan

1 Introduction

The impact of socioeconomic development has led to the rapid disappearance of traditional tribes, cultures, and languages. In order to preserve the cultures of traditional ethnic groups, government agencies must not only establish protective policies and systems, but also encourage diversified and in-depth research on Indigenous peoples, which is one of the important approaches to cultural preservation and revitalization. Academic research and literature publication usually reflect the depth and trends of relevant issues, and academic literature is an objective record of knowledge—the volume of output and changes in literature directly reflect the evolution of academic knowledge and serve as an important symbol of academic development, revealing certain characteristics and laws. In recent years, scholars have frequently applied a literature analysis to analyze the long-term development of academic literature in specific fields, but few studies have focused on the long-term analysis of literature on ethnic studies. Therefore, the current study collected domestic and international journal articles and master's theses published over 22 years to establish a complete lineage and comprehensive synthesis of Indigenous ethnic studies that can guide academic research development.

2 Literature Review

A considerable amount of research on issues related to Indigenous peoples has been conducted using a literature analysis. In 2017, Clifford and Shakeshaft used 13 databases to retrieve 2,687 journal articles published between 1993 and 2014 on drug use among Indigenous peoples in Australia, New Zealand, Canada, and the United States. The study used STATA Version 13 to analyze the number of articles in each country by year and the use of alcohol, tobacco, illicit drugs, and multiple drugs during each period. Because the data were coded and quantified, the study enabled readers to quickly see the comparison of drug use among Indigenous peoples in each country. Jia Tina Du (2017) collected 166

© The Author(s), under exclusive license to Springer Nature Singapore Pte Ltd. 2023
D. H. Goh et al. (Eds.): ICADL 2023, LNCS 14457, pp. 106–115, 2023.
https://doi.org/10.1007/978-981-99-8085-7_9

articles published between 1995 and 2013 on the role of information and communication technology in Aboriginal development and reviewed the related literature. By using literature analysis, she analyzed the distribution of articles by publication era, authors, affiliations, funding sources, research methods, and other significant research issues. This review analysis demonstrated that, based on the quantity of articles published, the main research issues related to information communication technology and Indigenous people during this period were Indigenous culture and knowledge preservation, literacy education development, information communication technology interactions and applications, and the digital divide.

Climate change has also had a significant effect on Aboriginal peoples, and a long-term literature review can provide an overview of important research issues and related problems. In 2020, scholars such as Bayrak, Hsu, Hung, Tsai, and Vayayana collected domestic and international peer-reviewed literature on resilience, climate change, and climate impact in Taiwan in the 10 years after Typhoon Morakot in 2009. The peer-reviewed journals were queried by using a *Scopus* search. A search for "Indigenous" or "Indigenous people" or "Aboriginal" yielded 50 articles; "Indigenous people" (原住民 *yuán zhùmín*) or "tribes" (部落 *bùluò*) yielded 61 articles, for a total of 111 articles after excluding those not focused on climate change, climate disasters, resilience, or Indigenous peoples. The study used keyword clouds to understand the research hotspots, GIS to understand tribal and disaster sites, analysis of the number of tribes mentioned in the literature, and Aboriginal voices on climate change and disaster reconstruction. It was the beginning of a large-scale quantitative and longitudinal study on Aboriginal peoples in Taiwan. Aciang Iku-Silan's (2020) research on trends and issues in technology-supported Aboriginal language learning is the only published study on Aboriginal education issues in Taiwan based on literature analysis. The study used qualitative coding to conduct content analysis of 55 papers related to digital technology and Aboriginal language learning published in target journals between 1997 and 2019. The findings revealed that the learning outcomes affecting the target language, curriculum or content knowledge, and information and communication technology were mainly "higher-order thinking or competence", "behavior development or change", and "affective or psychological state".

3   Research Methodology

Research Questions. This study aims to examine the literature on Indigenous peoples' cultural studies in Taiwan published during the past 22 years and use a literature analysis to analyze the overall context of the development of Indigenous peoples' studies as a reference for future academic research development.

Research Methodology. In this study, we collected journal articles related to Taiwan's Aboriginal culture published between 2000 and 2021, and used the ontology to analyze the content of journal articles.

Literature Retrieval Standards. To understand the research issues and trends of Aboriginal culture in Taiwan over the past 22 years, this study queried the Index of Taiwan Periodicals and Dissertations Database for journal publications on Aboriginal culture in Taiwan published between 2000 and 2021. Two levels of search keywords were used:

1. The first level was Aboriginal-related keywords: 原住民*yuán zhùmín*, Aboriginal, Indigenous, 原住民族*yuán zhùmínzú*, Indigenous peoples, and 部落*bùluò*, tribes; 2. The second level was culture-related keywords, so as to retrieve the most complete collection of literature. We then manually checked the content of each article (including titles and abstracts) and removed duplicate, non-English, and irrelevant articles. For details, see Table 1.

Table 1. Search Criteria for Index of Taiwan Periodicals and Dissertations

Database	Index of Taiwan Periodicals and Dissertations
Field	Keywords
Language	Chinese
Literature Type	Mainly "Academic" Literature
Year of Literature Publication	January 2000 to December 2021 (over 22 years)
Keywords	
First Level Keywords	Second Level Keywords
	Culture
Aboriginal	Aboriginal and Culture (543)
Indigenous Peoples	Indigenous Peoples and Culture (159)
Tribes	Tribes and Culture (77)
Total (779)	

Data Screening Process and Final Data Sources. The Index of Taiwan Periodicals and Dissertations Database was searched for journal articles on Aboriginal cultures in Taiwan published between 2000 and 2021 by using two levels of keywords. A total of 779 articles were retrieved, and 369 articles were selected for analysis after removing duplicate and irrelevant articles.

Coding. The coding scheme of Hwang and Tsai (2011); Chang et al. (2018); and Chen et al. (2021) was used as the basis for the creation of a coding table and for the content analysis, including research subjects and research methods. In terms of the content of the research themes, we established the cultural knowledge ontology of Indigenous peoples by referring to the relevant definitions of Aboriginal culture offered by scholars and experts, then used this cultural knowledge ontology for detailed content analysis. The main content of the research conducted between 2000 and 2021 on Indigenous peoples' culture was summarized by using the first level of themes. The detailed coding scheme is explained as follows:

Research Subjects. Categorization was determined on the basis of the author's description of the research subjects' ethnic groups in the article: If an article discussed Aboriginal peoples as a whole without specifying any ethnic group, then it was included in "Aboriginal people without specified ethnic group" category; if the article specifically discussed one of the ethnic groups, then it was coded as "ethnic group (name of ethnic group)"; if the article discussed individual Aboriginal people, then it was included in the "Aboriginal people" category; research subjects were coded as "non-Aboriginal people" or "no research subjects" based on the actual situation; and where the research subjects included both Aboriginal and non-Aboriginal people, it was coded as "a mixture of two research subjects".

Research Methodology. On the basis of research by McMillan and Schumacher (2006; 2010), research methods were classified as "quantitative research method", "qualitative research method", "mixed research method", or "theoretical overview". Theoretical overview refers to the research method of interpreting, studying, and synthesizing data; using official data and documents as the main sources to explain the practices and problems surrounding the current issues; and taking theoretical analysis, historical analysis, and policy analysis as the main research cases (McMillan and Schumacher 2010). *Aboriginal Culture Research Topics.* We referenced the definitions of Taiwanese Aboriginal culture as determined by Aboriginal scholars and experts, produced an ontology of Aboriginal cultural knowledge (Huang and Huang (1990); Hitay Payan (2000); Wang Kui (2007.a); Shih (2011); Tien Che-i (2013); (Wang et al. 2016); Omaz (2017); Aciang Iku-Silan and Su Heng (2017); Aciang Iku-Silan (2018, 2020); Stevenson (1996)), and analyzed the research themes of the articles by using this ontology. The first level of this ontology of Aboriginal cultural knowledge was, in order, "Language," "Literature (mythology)", "Arts (artistry, weaving)", "Music (musical instruments, ancient rhymes, and nursery rhymes)", "Architecture", "Medicine", "Food", "Clothing", "Dreaming", "Ceremonial Rituals (rituals, shamans, and spiritualists)", "Taboos and Norms (ancient tunes)", "Sense of Identity", "Comparative Culture", and "Others". Additionally, in accordance with the research topics in the text, "Fighting for Rights" was added to this study, bringing the total to 15 items. The details are listed in Appendix 1.

4   Results of the Information Analysis

4.1   Distribution of Literature Publication Eras

As shown in Fig. 1, on the basis of the content analysis, 136 Aboriginal culture-related papers were published between 2000 and 2010, and 233 papers were published between 2011 and 2021, demonstrating an increasing trend of Aboriginal culture-related research over the years.

Only 47 studies targeted specific ethnic groups, whereas the rest did not target specific ethnic groups. Of the 47 papers that identified specific research groups, the top three discussed groups were the Amis (8 articles), the Paiwan (8 articles), and the Atayal (8 articles). Also discussed were the Bunun (6 articles), the Tsou (3 articles), the Puyuma (3 articles), and the Rukai (3 articles). Two articles categorized as "Others" discussed the Siraya people in Taiwan and the Langalanga people in the Solomon Islands respectively.

4.2   Distribution of Research Methods

More than 60% of the literature published between 2000 and 2021 used analytical methods, followed by qualitative methods (28%), mixed methods (3%), and quantitative

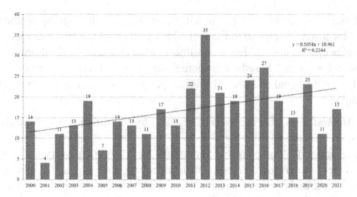

Fig. 1. Articles on Aboriginal Culture in Chinese Journals, 2000–2021

methods (3%). More than 60% of the Aboriginal cultural studies were informal academic papers, followed by more qualitative studies. The theoretical overviews were discussions of current issues with collective value based on the researchers' interpretations of facts (McMillan and Schumacher 2010). In the case of policy analysis, for example, Hsu and Tsai (2021) explored the constitutional basis of Aboriginal hunting and cultural collective rights, commenting on Justice Interpretation No. 803 with a view to positively influence the protection of Aboriginal cultural rights in Taiwan. An example of a theoretical overviews of historical analysis was Lin Han-sheng's (2020) take on the development of Taiwan's Aboriginal social work system from a historical and cultural perspective, which explored the evolution and dilemmas at each stage of development and proposed a future outlook for Aboriginal social work in Taiwan. Because most of the articles analyzed in this study were theoretical overviews and not rigorous academic papers (see Fig. 2), most were classified as "no research subject" in the research subject section.

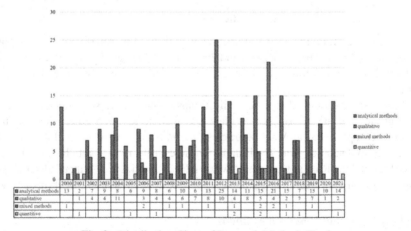

	2000	2001	2002	2003	2004	2005	2006	2007	2008	2009	2010	2011	2012	2013	2014	2015	2016	2017	2018	2019	2020	2021
analytical methods	13	2	7	9	8	6	9	8	6	10	6	13	25	14	11	15	21	15	7	15	10	14
qualitative		1	4	4	11		3	4	4	6	7	8	10	4	8	5	4	2	?	7	1	2
mixed methods	1						2		1	1		1		2	2	1		1			
quantitive		1				1			1			2		2		1	1				1

Fig. 2. Distribution Chart of Research Methods Used

4.3 Distribution of Research Topics

The distribution of research topics among relevant articles is shown in Fig. 3. This study referred to the definitions and connotations of Aboriginal traditional culture established by Aboriginal scholars and experts to develop a knowledge ontology, then used the knowledge ontology to analyze Aboriginal culture-related research. Accordingly, the most studied topics pertaining to traditional culture were Taboos and Norms (153 articles), followed by Arts (104 articles), and Sense of Identity and Ceremonial Rituals (98 articles); however, most articles (283 articles) could not be categorized as traditional culture and were placed in the Others category.

Articles based on other aspects that were less likely to be categorized as traditional culture were mostly overviews of contemporary cultural issues, such as integrating Aboriginal culture into the development of cultural products, developing cultural and creative industries, and using Aboriginal-specific traditional culture and aesthetics to promote local tourism and industrial models (Lin et al. 2011; Chen 2010; Chen et al. 2013; Huang and Lin 2006; Umav Takiludun (2010)). Other studies discussed digital collections of Aboriginal culture (Tu et al. 2006), cultural care for Aboriginal elders (Jih et al. 2019; Tsai and Chang 2018), or Aboriginal cultural differences and gender differences (Chiang 2001; Lai and Chen 2017).

Research based on the taboos and norms aspect included studies on the widely known Aboriginal traditional hunting culture. When exploring the culture and interaction of the Bihu tribe, (Hsieh and Pao 2014) learned through interviews that the role of hunter is respected and aspired to among tribesmen. Fuday Kumud Menale (Kumud and Menale 2008) attempted to understand what motivates hunters to go hunting in the mountains and interpreted the meaning of hunting culture from the perspective of hunting as a social relationship that connects with the maternal culture. Lin (2004) explored the history and social responsibility of the Katripulr clubhouse system and found that the clubhouse had a positive impact on the self-identity of the tribesmen. Hsu, Hwa-fu and Cheuk, Ya-ping (Hsu and Cho 2011) explored tribal restorative justice practices to understand the Atayal social and cultural conceptions of crimes as well as the sanctioning and mediation mechanisms exercised within the tribe, and to get a glimpse at the way the tribe tends to handle inter-tribe issues outside of the criminal justice system.

Research based on the arts aspect: Traditional Aboriginal culture does not have objects that can be called artwork, but art represents a specific expression of Aboriginal culture that combines traditional techniques, living concepts, and other unique forms. For example, Chang Wei-chi and Huang Ching-ying (2011) examined the bamboo rafts of the Amis port tribe, from material identification to raft-making procedures, reproducing the traditional raft-making process and reestablishing the connection between humans and the natural environment and culture. In addition to material culture, Chen (2009) explored modern dances created by Aboriginal peoples, using textual analysis and field research to compile the creative content of the dancers and how Aboriginal identity affects the interpretation of modern dances. The combination of cultural industry and the arts has been emphasized in many articles, with Hung (2009) and Hsu (2017) both mentioning the use of art and culture to attract and promote the development of Aboriginal cultural industries.

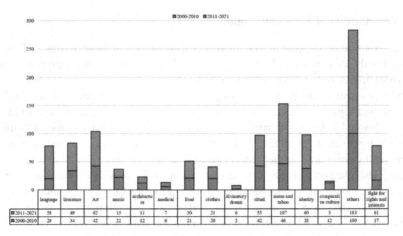

Fig. 3. Distribution of Research Topics

The chart data:

	language	literature	Art	music	architecture	medical	food	clothes	divinatory dream	ritual	norm and taboo	identity	complicative culture	others	fight for rights and interests
2011-2021	58	49	62	15	11	7	30	21	6	55	107	60	3	183	61
2000-2010	29	34	42	22	12	6	21	20	2	42	46	31	12	100	17

5   Findings and Recommendations

There was an increasing trend in the publication of Taiwanese Aboriginal cultural literature between 2000 and 2021; however, approximately 70% of the literature was not strictly academic. Most of the studies related to Taiwan's Aboriginal culture were theoretical overview articles without specific research subjects. Among the articles exploring specific ethnic groups, the Amis, Paiwan, and Atayal tribes were the most common subjects. The current study referenced the definitions and connotations of Aboriginal traditional culture established by Aboriginal scholars and experts to formulate the knowledge ontology, and then used this knowledge ontology to analyze Aboriginal culture-related research. On the basis of these findings, the most researched topics pertaining to traditional culture were taboos and norms, followed by arts, sense of identity, and ceremonial rituals; however, most of the articles (283 articles) could not be categorized as "traditional culture" and were placed in the "others" category. Articles in the "others" category mainly summarized contemporary issues of Aboriginal culture, such as how to design products with cultural connotations, how to develop cultural and creative industries, and how to use the unique traditional culture and aesthetics of Aboriginal people to promote local tourism and industries, which shows that the study of Aboriginal culture urgently seeks to break through traditional areas and connect with contemporary trends.

On the basis of the above findings, the authors of this study have the following recommendations:

- When researching Aboriginal culture, scholars and experts should utilize more rigorous methods and publish their work in Chinese so that the study of Aboriginal culture can be taken seriously.
- Although author keywords can reveal the scholars and experts' focus and the research development trends, it is not possible to judge the research situation of the overall context of traditional Aboriginal culture, so a thematic analysis based on ontology is still necessary.

- Many scholars tend to submit their rigorous research results to foreign journals; therefore, it is impossible to see the full picture of Taiwan's Aboriginal cultural studies by analyzing only Chinese literature. Researchers are advised to collect articles from *WOS* and *Scopus* as well to conduct a more comprehensive analysis.
- The respect and preservation of Aboriginal culture has become an issue of world-wide importance. Therefore, in addition to showing foreign scholars the trends of Aboriginal cultural research in Taiwan, Taiwanese scholars can reference collections of other countries' Aboriginal cultural research literature through *WOS* and *Scopus* and analyze the topics explored by scholars in other countries.

References

Aciang, I.-S.: Chūshénrùhuà: Cóng duōyuán wénhuà jiàoyù de guāndiǎn, kàn yǐngshì méi cái de yuán zhù mín wénhuà guān yǔ jiàoyù yìngyòng [Reaching Perfection: Aboriginal Cultural Perspectives and Educational Applications of Film and Television Media from the Perspective of Multicultural Education]. Dà yán guójì duōméitǐ [Dayan International Multimedia] (2018)

Aciang Iku-Silan, & Su, Heng (2017). Cóng duōyuán wénhuà jiàoyù de guāndiǎn, kàn diànyǐng 'mǎ yī nà'(Maïna) de yuán zhù mín wénhuà guān yǔ jiàoyù yìngyòng [Aboriginal Cultural Perspectives and Educational Applications of the Film *Maïna* from the Perspective of Multi-cultural Education] (Unpublished master's thesis). Guólì zhèngzhì dàxué [National Chengchi University]

Iku-Silan, A.: Kējì zhīchí yuán zhùmín yǔyán xuéxí de yánjiū qūshì yǔ yìtí:1997–2019 nián qíkān wénxiàn fēnxī [Research Trends and Issues in Technology-Supported Aboriginal Language Learning: an Analysis of Journal Literature 1997–2019]. Shùwèi xuéxí kējì qíkān [International Journal on Digital Learning Technology] **12**(4), 51–83 (2020)

Bayrak, M.-M., Hsu, Y.-Y., Hung, L.-S., Tsai, H.-M., & vayayana, tʻe. (2021). Global climate change and Indigenous peoples in Taiwan: A critical bibliometric analysis and review. *Sustainability*, *13*(1), 29. https://doi.org/10.3390/su13010029

Chang, C.Y., Lai, C.L., Hwang, G.J.: Trends and research issues of mobile learning studies in nursing education: a review of academic publications from 1971 to 2016. Comput. Educ.. Educ. **116**, 28–48 (2018)

Chang, W.-C., Huang, C.-Y.: Gǎngkǒu āměi zú de zhú fá [The bamboo raft of the port Amis]. Táiwān wénxiàn [Taiwan Literature] **62**(1), 161–188 (2011)

Chen, C., Wang, N.-C., Tu, Y.-F., Lin, H.J.: Research trends from a decade (2011–2020) for information literacy in higher education: Content and bibliometric mapping analysis (paper presentation). In: 84th ASIS&T Annual Meeting (2021)

Chen, C.-H., Li, C.-C., Chen, H.-C.: Yǐ xìtǒng dòngtài xué tàntǎo shèhuì qǐyè de wén chuàng shāngyè móshì: Yǐ bùnóng bùluò wéi lì [Exploring the Cultural and Creative Business Model of Social Enterprises with System Dynamics: The Bunun Tribe as an Example]. Táiwān qǐyè jīxiào xué kān [Taiwan Business Performance Journal] **7**(1), 25–40 (2013)

Chen, S.-C.: Yuán zhù mínzú wénhuà chuàngyì chǎnyè shìchǎng tàzhǎn fēnxī [An Analysis of Market Expansion of Cultural and Creative Industries of Indigenous Peoples]. Táiwān jīngjì yánjiū yuèkān [Taiwan Economic Research Monthly] **33**(8), 62–67 (2010)

Chen, Y.-W.: Xiàndài wǔ yǔ wénhuà rèntóng—dāngdài táiwān uan zhùmín biān wǔ zhě yánjiū [Modern Dance and Cultural Identity: A Study of Contemporary Taiwanese Aboriginal Choreographers]. Táiwān wǔdǎo yánjiū [Taiwan Dance Research Journal] **5**, 1–38 (2009)

Chiang, L.-C.: Cóng xìngbié chāyì guāndiǎn tànxī uan zhùmín nǚxìng zhī jiātíng juésè [An analysis of Aboriginal women's family roles from the perspective of gender differences]. Táiwān xìng xué xué kān [Formosan Journal of Sexology] **7**(2), 68–80 (2001)

114   C.-C. Chen et al.

Clifford, A., Shakeshaft, A.: A bibliometric review of drug and alcohol research focused on Indigenous peoples of Australia, New Zealand, Canada, and the United States. Drug Alcohol Rev. **36**, 509–522 (2017)

Du, J.T.: Research on Indigenous people and the role of information and communications technology in development: a review of the literature. J. Australian Library Inf. Assoc. **66**(4), 344–363 (2017). https://doi.org/10.1080/24750158.2017.1397857

Kumud, F., Menale‘,: Shòuliè, fēi qù bùkě?’–Āměi zú tài bā lǎng bùluò de chuántǒng, yíshì yǔ wénhuà ["You just have to go hunting, don't you?" — The traditions, rituals and culture of the Tafalong Amis tribe]. Táiwān yuán zhùmínzú yánjiū [Taiwan Journal of Indigenous Studies] **1**(4), 31–66 (2008)

Payan, H.: Tàiyǎ zú de Gaga [Gaga of the Atayas]. Xīnzhú wénxiàn [Hsinchu Literature] **3**, 65–68 (2000)

Hsieh, H.-Y., Pao, C.-H.: Huā yīdiǎn shíjiān qù rènshí bùluò': Chūtàn bì hòu bùluò wénhuà yǔ shèqū guānxì ["Take a moment to get to know the tribe": A first look at tribal culture and community relations in Bixo Tribe]. Táiwān yuán zhù mínzú yánjiū [Taiwan Journal of Indigenous Studies] **7**(2), 41–72 (2014)

Hsu, H., Cho, Y.-P.: Yuán zhù mín dìqū xiūfù shì zhèngyì zhī shíjiàn yǔ qǐfā [The Practice and Inspiration of Restorative Justice in Aboriginal Areas]. Jǐng xué cóngkān [Police Science Quarterly] **41**(5), 275–299 (2011)

Hsu, K.-T.: Wénhuà chuàngyì chǎnyè zīyuán diàochá: Yǐ yuán zhù mín pái wān zú yìshù wéi lì [A Survey of Cultural and Creative Industry Resources: An Example of Aboriginal Paiwan Art]. Rénwén zīyuán yánjiū xuébào [Journal Of Humanity Resources] **22**, 123–149 (2017)

Hsu, Y., Tsai, W.: Cóng shì zì 803 hào jiěshì tàntǎo yuán zhù mínzú shòuliè wénhuà jítǐ quán de xiànfǎ jiàngòu [The constitutional construction of the collective right of hunting culture of Indigenous peoples from the interpretation of Interpretation No. 803]. *Fǎguī yǔ zūnxún [Journal of Regulation and Compliance]* **4**(1), 1–50 (2021)

Hung, C.: Huādōng dìqū yuán zhùmínzú wénhuà chǎnyè de fāzhǎn [The development of cultural industries of Indigenous peoples in the Hualian Taitung Region]. Sūn xué yánjiū [Sunology Research] **6**, 145–171 (2009)

Huang, Kuei-chao (author), compiled by Huang, Hsuan-wei (1990). Yí wān āměi zúrén duì mèng de kànfǎ [Dreams as perceived by the Amis of Yiwan]. *Mínzú xué yánjiū suǒ zīliào huìbiān [Institute of Ethnology Academia Sinica]* **1**, 67–81

Huang, Y.-C., Lin, J.-T.: Kuà wénhuà shèjì–táiwān yuán zhù mín wénhuà de shèjì yuánsù yǔ yìngyòng [Cross-cultural Design: Design Elements and Applications of Taiwan's Aboriginal Culture]. Gōngyè shèjì [Industrial Design] **34**(2), 105–110 (2006)

Hwang, G.J., Tsai, C.C.: Research trends in mobile and ubiquitous learning: a review of publications in selected journals from 2001 to 2010. Br. J. Edu. Technol. **42**(4), E65–E70 (2011)

Jih, H., Li, H., You, S.-N.: Wénhuà zhàogù zàiyuán zhù mínzú chángqí zhàogù shàng de yìngyòng: Yǐ shèqū jí jūjiā zhínéng zhìliáo fúwù wéi lì [The Application of Cultural Care to Long-Term Care for Indigenous Peoples: An Example of Community and In-Home Functional Therapy Services]. Zhōnghuá xīnlǐ wèishēng xué kān [Mental Health Association in Taiwan] **32**(2), 209–247 (2019)

Lai, W.-F., Chen, Y.: Bùluò yuán zhùmín yǔ fēi yuán zhù mín yòu'ér xùshuō píngjià zhī yánjiū: wénhuà hé xìngbié chāyì [A study of tribal Indigenous and non-Indigenous children's narrative evaluation: cultural and gender differences]. Kèchéng yǔ jiàoxué [Curriculum and Instruction Quarterly] **20**(1), 201–227 (2017)

Lin, C.-M., Chen, C., Tung, Y.-T.: Kuà wénhuà shèjì–táiwān yuán zhùmín wénhuà de shèjì yuánsù yǔ yìngyòng [Crossultural Design: Design Elements and Applications of Taiwan's Aboriginal Culture]. Rénwén jì shèhuì kēxué qíkān [Journal of Humanities and Social Sciences] **7**(1), 25–40 (2011)

Lin, H.: Táiwān yuán zhù mínzú shèhuì gōngzuò de yángé yǔ zhǎnwàng--wénhuà guāndiǎn de lìshǐ fēnxī [The History and Prospects of Social Work for Taiwan's Indigenous Peoples—A Historical Analysis of Cultural Perspectives]. Shèqū fāzhǎn jìkān [Community Development Journal (Quarterly)] **169**, 75–89 (2020)

Lin, S.: Kǎ de bù qīngnián huì bùluò jiàoyù de lǐniàn yǔ shíjiàn [The Philosophy and Practice of Tribal Education in Katripulr Clubhouse]. Táiwān yuán zhùmínzú yánjiū [Taiwan Journal of Indigenous Studies] **9**, 143–180 (2004)

McMillan, H., Schumacher, S.J.: Research in education: Evidence-based inquiry. Pearson: MyEducationLab Series (2010)

McMillan, J., Schumacher, S.J.: Research in education (6th ed.). Pearson Education (2006)

Omaz (2017, May 8). Jiéhūn qiūqiān Tiuma de yuānyuán [The origin of the marriage swing Tiuma] (blog post). *Facebook.* facebook.com/groups/210502212772163/search/?q=結婚鞦韆%20Tiuma%20的淵源

Shih, J.-R.: Editor in Chief (2011). Táiwān yuán zhù mínzú shēngwù xué zhì yántǎo huì zhuānkān [Symposium on Biology of Indigenous Peoples in Taiwan]. Xíngzhèng yuàn yuán zhù mínzú wěiyuánhuì [Council of Indigenous Peoples, Executive Yuan]

Stevenson, M.G.: Indigenous knowledge in environmental assessment. Arctic **49**(3), 278–291 (1996)

Tien, C.: Yùshān de shǒuhù zhě: Bùnóng zú [Guardians of the Jade Mountain: The Bunun Tribe] (Second Edition). Táiwān wǔ nán túshū chūbǎn gǔfèn yǒuxiàn gōngsī [Taiwan Wunan Book Publishing Co., Ltd] (2013)

Tsai, H., Chang, Y.-L.: Xǐng sī wénhuà zhàogù zàiyuán xiāng bùluò shèqū zhàogù fúwù zhī shíjiàn—nántóu xiàn sān gè zúqún bùluò de jīngyàn [The practice of provincial cultural care in community care services for Indigenous tribes—the experience of three ethnic tribes in Nantou County]. Táiwān yuán zhùmínzú yánjiū xuébào [Journal of The Taiwan Indigenous Studies Association] **8**(4), 149–178 (2018)

Tu, L.-C., Hsiao, M.-H., Lin, J.-T.: Shùwèi diǎn zàng wénwù de wénhuà chuàngyì yìngyòng—yǐ táiwān yuán zhùmín fúshì túténg zhǎnkāi de gōngyì shèjì [Cultural and Creative Applications of Digital Collections—Craft Design with Taiwan Aboriginal Costume Totems]. Yìshù lùnwén jíkān [Collected Papers on Arts Research] **6**, 27–44 (2006)

Takiludun, U.: Cóng yǒng xù jīngyíng de guāndiǎn jiǎnshì shèqū jūmín zài dìqū xíng wénhuà zīchǎn fāzhǎn wéi guānguāng zīyuán de juésè—luóná bùluò shèngdàn jiéqìng zhī tàntǎo [Examining the role of community residents in the development of local cultural assets as tourism resources from a sustainability perspective: An exploration of the Luluna Tribe Christmas Festival]. *Měixué yǔ shìjué yìshù xuébào[International Journal of Art and Design Education]* **2**, 52–69 (2010)

Wang, K.: Běi pái wān: Sān dì mén xiāng bùluò zúqún guìzú jiāzú yuánliú [North Paiwan: The Origin of Noble Families of Tribal Groups in Sandimen Township]. Píng dōng xiàn yuán zhù mínzú wénhuà yìshù fāzhǎn xiéhuì [Pingtung County Indigenous Peoples Cultural Arts Development Association] (2007)

Wang, L., Iku-Silan, A., Mingei, Y.: Táiwān yuán zhù mínzú 'liè shǒu'xísú de xīnlíng liáo yù yīnshù—yǐ tàiyǎ zú wéi lì [Spiritual Healing Factors of "Head Hunting" Practices among Taiwan's Indigenous Peoples: The Case of the Atayal Tribe]. Shèhuì kēxué qiányán [Advances in Social Sciences] **5**(5), 775–783 (2016)

Integration Between Humanities and Technology: Using Digital Humanities Technology to Read the Gospel of Matthew

Fang-Ya Chen[1]([✉]) [iD], Chao-Chen Chen[2] [iD], Yun-Fang Tu[2] [iD], and Hsiu-Ling Huang[3] [iD]

[1] Graduate Institute of Library, Information and Archival, National Chengchi University, Taipei, Taiwan
tanja.chen0411@gmail.com
[2] Center for General Education, College of Humanities and Education, Chung Yuan Christian University, Taoyuan City, Taiwan
[3] National MiaoLi Senior High School, Miaoli City, Taiwan

1 Introduction

Given the rapid development of information technology and increasing popularity of interdisciplinary collaboration among researchers, digital humanities has become a crucial approach in humanities and social studies research. According to Hsiang and Tu (2011), digital humanities involves the use of digital materials and information technology in humanities research. According to Weng (2020), digital humanities encompasses: (a) quantifying keywords in text and explaining their meanings; (b) exploring correlations between keywords to determine the structure of an interpersonal network; (c) reproducing text by organizing and comparing textual contents to explore the deeper meanings of text, determining relationships between text, arranging events in a timeline, or using geographic information systems to convert textual information to spatial understanding and interpretation, thereby deciphering historical text while considering landscape characteristics, and (d) enabling diverse presentations and applications by using augmented reality and virtual reality technology, thereby enabling immersive content browsing of existing or new content.

To enhance proficiency in digital humanities among students, a course entitled Introduction to Digital Humanities was developed. Rather than relying on traditional teaching methods, this course used the Gospel of Matthew as a case study and encouraged students to engage in textual analysis and create visual presentations. This approach transformed students from passive to active learners. Personal meaning mapping was employed to assess whether the students, who had no prior knowledge about the Gospel of Matthew, were able to use various digital humanities techniques to interpret the Gospel of Matthew. Additionally, interviews were conducted with the students to gain further insights into their transformation throughout the course.

D. H. Goh et al. (Eds.): ICADL 2023, LNCS 14457, pp. 116–121, 2023.
https://doi.org/10.1007/978-981-99-8085-7_10

2 Using Digital Humanities to Interpret the Gospel of Matthew

The first part of the New Testament contains four gospels attributed to Matthew, Mark, Luke, and John. These gospels provide a historical account of the birth, baptism, ministry, crucifixion, resurrection, and ascension of Jesus. They also document various events related to the establishment and growth of churches between 6 B.C. and 60 A.D. In general, studying the Bible involves reading stories, historical records, and prayers. The Biblical stories involve a multitude of characters, timelines, and locations. Digital humanities technology is useful for understanding the relationships between Biblical events, themes, characters, and history. In addition to exploring the development of digital humanities, this course covers a variety of digital humanities techniques, including data analysis, data visualization, social network analysis, and the use of geographic information systems. By using these techniques, students will gain a more profound understanding of the Gospel of Matthew. Overall, the course integrates humanities and technology, examines advancements in digital archiving and digital humanities, and enhances student knowledge on this topic. The course contents are summarized in Table 1.

Table 1. *Textual analysis and other digital humanities techniques covered in course.*

Gospel of Matthew	Digital humanities instruments	Digital humanities knowledge
Textual analysis (themes, events, character dialogues, and locations)	Chinese word segmentation system CKIP Tagger, Excel, and Cohen's kappa	Textual analysis
Character emotion analysis	RAWGraphs、 Word Art	Data visualization
Analysis of active characters	UCINET	Social network analysis
Locations of relevant events	Google Earth project	Geographic information system

3 Changes in Students' Understanding of Textual Analysis and Digital Humanities

Personal meaning mapping can be used to explore changes in understanding before and after learning (Falk, 2003). The present study evaluated the learning outcomes of students to examine changes in their digital humanities knowledge and skills. Interviews were conducted to collect feedback and further clarify the cognitive and affective changes in their understanding of digital humanities.

3.1 Learning Outcomes

After one semester, the students were able to effectively use digital humanities technology to gain a deeper understanding of the events, themes, character relationships, timelines, and locations depicted in the Gospel of Matthew, despite having no prior knowledge

Table 2. Demonstration of newfound skills and knowledge of digital humanities.

Gospel of Matthew	Digital humanities instruments (example)	Demonstration of learning outcomes		
Text reading and analysis	Students actively searched for data relevant to the Gospel of Matthew, read textual content, and used Excel to create models and organize data regarding relevant events, themes, character dialogues, timelines, and locations.			
Content coding and consistency analysis	Cohen's kappa was calculated to determine the consistency of coding.	編碼者1　編碼者2 … Cohen's Kappa Coefficient = 0.889537494387068		

Cohen's Kappa Coefficient = 0.889537494387068

Coder A	Coder B			SUM
	[SPACE]	1	3	2	
[SPACE]	1	0	0	0	1
1	0	67	0	0	67
3	0	5	18	3	26
2	0	0	0	29	29
SUM	1	72	18	32	123

Keyword analysis and visualization	Word Art was used to create a keyword cloud.	

(*continued*)

Table 2. (*continued*)

Character dialogue and emotion analysis	RAWGraphs were used to depict the emotions of characters.	
Character relationship and activity analysis	UCINET was used to analyze the relative activity of characters.	
Analysis and presentation of events, timelines, and locations	Google Earth was used to show relationships between events, timelines, and locations.	

of the book and digital humanities. The students demonstrated their newfound skills and knowledge using a variety of instruments (Table 2).

3.2 Interview Responses

Interviews were conducted with 11 students (Students A–K) to determine the cognitive and affective changes in their understanding of digital humanities.

Before attending the course, the students only had a superficial understanding of digital humanities.

[Digital humanities] might have something to do with the application of computers in the arts. (B)

Based on its literal meaning, [digital humanities] is the combination of humanities and digital technology. It probably focuses on the rigorousness of data and also the requirements in humanities-related studies. (C)

I think this course is about programming.

Digital technology probably refers to consumer electronics. Humanities are like history. (H)

[This course] is probably something related to software learning. (I)

After completing the course, the students gained a profound understanding of digital humanities and demonstrated a positive attitude toward it.

At first, I thought humanities was related to the arts. Now, I think humanities are related to various aspects of everyday life. I feel that students in sociology departments should understand the concept of digital humanities, because in the future, society will be oriented toward technology. Traditional methods will no longer work... (B)

At first, I thought, from a macroscopic perspective, that digital humanities was a combination of technology and humanities; however, after seeing examples, I now understand that it is more than this. [Digital humanities] can be applied to various domains, including data processing and presentation, to help us understand textual data in a technological way... I feel that [digital humanities] is a mainstream trend. Using it to process [data] is highly convenient, and data presented in this manner are more intuitive... (J)

It is essential for humanities scholars to possess digital humanities literacy. This is extremely helpful to their research... (C)

Students in humanities departments must learn digital humanities skills to digitalize and analyze textual data and present such data in a more comprehensible manner. I believe digital humanities is important. (I)

I feel that the integration of humanities and digital technology is quite important, because interdisciplinary approaches lead to broader thinking and imagination, hence better outcome... (H)

After completing the course, the students described their views about the future application of digital humanities technology.

To me... I am currently an intern in a company's legal department. Much of the data and contract management work requires information to be digitalized and visualized before it is presented to supervisors. By possessing [digital humanities skills], we can produce reports with highly intuitive contents. (C)

I can use Google Earth to create design projects with various materials. I might also need to list some locations. It's just very useful. (D)

Using Excel functions and graphs to describe relationships between these characters is pretty cool... Graphs are an effective way of visualizing data... When I need to [explain] my code to other people at work in the future (E is a student in the computer science and information engineering department), I will not just give them the code directly or tell them how the code works. Now that I have completed this course, I know I can try to use graphs or other visualization methods to show my clients how the code works, why certain steps are performed, and the rationale behind operations. (E)

Google Earth lets you plan trips. I also learn to code and organize textual information in a way that helps others understand the information better... (H)

Visualization is helpful, because readers are usually more sensitive toward images and visualized information than they are toward text... (I)

Google Earth is useful and cool. The teacher mentioned epidemics as an example in one of the classes. He said that maps and other data can be integrated to discover various things, such as the causes of epidemics... (J)

4   Conclusion

The study found that students' cognitive and affective understanding as well as their skills in digital humanities had substantially improved after completing the course. The students described in detail how digital humanities knowledge and skills can be applied in both professional and everyday contexts. The integration of humanities and technology enables humanities students to acquire knowledge in digital technology and enables engineering students to gain a deeper understanding of the humanities. Digital humanities goes beyond conventional text reading by using data visualization to help students comprehend information more deeply. By integrating conventional reading with digital humanities technology, students become active learners who explore classical works from multiple perspectives and develop proficiency in digital technology. This approach enhances the competitiveness of humanities students in the current digital era.

References

1. Falk, J.H.: Personal meaning mapping. In: Caban, G., Scott, C., Falk, J., Dierking, L. (eds.) Museums and Creativity: A Study into the Role of Museums in Design Education, pp. 10–18. Powerhouse Publishing, Sydney, Australia (2003)
2. Hsiang, C., Tu, F.E.: Introduction—What is digital humanities. In: Hsiang, C. (ed.) From Preservation to Creation: Initiation of Digital Humanities Research, pp. 9–28. National Taiwan University Press, Taipei (2011)
3. Weng, C.A.: Introduction to the development of digital humanities. In: Su, S.P. (ed.) 2020 Almanac of Taiwan Literature, pp. 3–6. National Museum of Taiwan Literature (2020)

Social Media Analytics

Appraisal of Paradise: A Sentiment Analysis Dataset of French Tourists' Experiences in French Polynesia

Bryan Dallest[1]([✉]) [iD], Sébastien Chabrier[1] [iD], Alban Gabillon[1] [iD], and Pierre Ghewy[2]

[1] University of French Polynesia, GePaSud, Puna'auia, French Polynesia
bryan.dallest@gmail.com, {sebastien.chabrier,
alban.gabillon}@upf.pf
[2] University of French Polynesia, CETOP, Puna'auia, French Polynesia
pierre.ghewy@upf.pf

Abstract. Sentiment analysis is a significant task within the Natural Language Processing (NLP) field. It aims to identify the sentiment polarity (positive, negative, or neutral) within textual data. This paper presents the development and annotation of a specialized dataset, unprecedented in its focus on French Polynesian tourism. This corpus is composed of tourists' comments written in French concerning their experience in French Polynesia. The collated dataset comprises 1,592 comments and 10,729 sentiment-annotated triplets (aspect, opinion, sentiment), extracted from these comments. Since the issue of overlapping triplets - i.e., instances where triplets within the same comment share aspects or opinions - emerged during construction, we partitioned the original dataset into two distinct subsets: the first consists of 467 comments (2,235 triplets) devoid of overlap, while the other includes 1,125 comments (8,494 triplets) with at least one overlapping triplet. These three datasets, which enhance the availability of French NLP datasets for sentiment analysis, are accessible on the Hugging Face platform.

Keywords: NLP · Sentiment analysis · Sentiment-annotated triplets · Dataset creation

1 Introduction

In this paper, we present a sentiment analysis dataset composed of French comments extracted from TripAdvisor about hotels and guesthouses in French Polynesia from January 2001 to April 2023. To collect these comments, we used a Python-based web scraper, resulting in the acquisition of 40,391 comments. The scrapper retrieves every comment including special characters like emojis. To label these data, we associated to each comment one or more triplets (aspect, opinion, sentiment) that reflect the expressed sentiment in the comment. A triplet is composed of an aspect, an opinion, and a sentiment (positive, neutral, or negative). This labelling task was carried out by three undergraduate students, each of whom was assigned the same 2,000 comments to annotate. This was followed by a cross-validation phase conducted by us. We synthesized the results of

D. H. Goh et al. (Eds.): ICADL 2023, LNCS 14457, pp. 125–132, 2023.
https://doi.org/10.1007/978-981-99-8085-7_11

these three annotators. At the end of this cleaning phase (curation), we obtained 1,592 comments that were labeled by all three annotators, with 10,729 triplets extracted from these comments.

In the cleaned (i.e., curated) dataset, we noted several facts that should be mentioned:

- The dataset demonstrates an imbalance, as 90% of the triplets are positive.
- More than 70% of comments have at least one overlapping triplet.
- Duets (triplets without an aspect or opinion) forms constitute 8.78% of the triplets.

We subsequently derived two disjoint sub-datasets from the curated dataset:

1. A subset consisting of comments that do not have overlapping triplets at all.
2. A subset consisting of all comments with at least one overlapping triplet. This dataset was formed by selecting, from the curated dataset, all comments with a minimum of one overlapping triplet.

Out of the 1,592 comments in the curated dataset, 467 are in the first sub-dataset and the remaining 1,125 are in the second sub-dataset. These two derived sub-datasets could be used to study how overlapping affects the performance on the sentiment analysis task of French language models, such as FlauBERT [1], CamemBERT [2], or DistilCamemBERT [3]. We published the three datasets (the main dataset and the two sub-datasets) on the HuggingFace platform[1].

The structure of this paper is as follows: Sect. 2 briefly explains the Polynesian context and the reason for creating this dataset. Section 3 introduces the notion of triplet, the annotation of the data and the validation process to produce the dataset. Section 4 presents the dataset produced with its distinctive features such as the presence of imbalance in the dataset, duets and overlapping triplets. Section 5 delves into the curated dataset and the derived sub-datasets. Section 6 describes the data format we used. Section 7 discusses the possible future work. Section 8 concludes this paper. Finally, Sect. 9 enumerates the limitations of our dataset.

2 Context of the Dataset

French Polynesia's economy heavily leans on tourism, with tourists regularly sharing experiences on various online platforms. To better understand these experiences, a project was launched in 2019 by the Ministry of Tourism, requiring sentiment analysis of these comments. Given the high volume of reviews, an automated sentiment analysis model becomes crucial. Platforms like TripAdvisor serve as reliable sources for valuable feedback about French Polynesia. This platform has been used as a reliable source for other datasets[2,3] concerning other countries.

We created a dataset of French comments extracted from TripAdvisor, each annotated accurately with triplets (aspect, opinion, sentiment). In a future work, we shall use this dataset to analyze the experiences of tourists in French Polynesia. In this paper, we simply present this dataset and make it available to the research community.

---

[1] https://huggingface.co/datasets/GePaSud/TROPICAL.

[2] https://github.com/devina-ekawati/absa-indonesia.

[3] https://github.com/Bouaskaoun/Aspect-Based-Sentiment-Analysis-of-Marrakesh-hotel-rev iews.

3 Dataset Presentation

Amongst the array of online platforms, TripAdvisor distinguishes itself by hosting the most abundant collection of reviews concerning tourist accommodations in French Polynesia, hence it was selected as the primary data source.

3.1 Triplets

Our dataset adopts a triplets-based structure. This structure comprises an 'aspect', an 'opinion', and a 'sentiment' inferred from the aspect and opinion. This format has been effectively employed in numerous research works [4–17] analogous to the Aspect Sentiment Triplet Extraction (ASTE) task [18], a sub-task of the Aspect Based Sentiment Analysis (ABSA) task [19, 20].

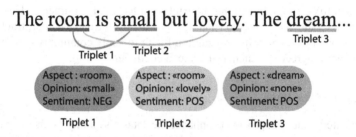

Fig. 1. Illustration of overlapping and duet structure. In the first sentence, the green underlined word is the aspect, and the blue and orange underlined words are the opinions. While the second sentence contains a duet, a variation of the triplet structure.

An aspect is a specific subject or entity being discussed, such as 'room' in the first triplet of Fig. 1. An opinion is the author's sentiment towards the aspect, such as 'small' expressing negative sentiment towards the 'room' as shown in the first triplet of Fig. 1. Multiple aspects can be associated to the same opinion and vice versa, resulting in 'overlapping' triplets. Overlapping refers to a scenario where different triplets extracted from the same text share an aspect or an opinion, such as two triplets sharing the 'room' aspect with distinct opinions 'small' and 'lovely' as shown in Fig. 1.

During the dataset creation, sentiments were categorized into three broad classes: positive, negative, and neutral, following established practices in the field [18]. However, the dataset can be further improved by including nuanced emotions. Furthermore, we also encounter 'duets' - a triplet without an aspect or opinion. For instance, sentences like 'The view!' or 'Delicious!' are considered as duets with a positive sentiment, without explicit aspects or opinions. The third extraction from the Fig. 1 illustrates a duet.

3.2 Data Preprocessing

In our preprocessing phase, we removed punctuation from comments, treating words with apostrophes as single words, adhering to French language conventions. This process is crucial for the extraction and annotation of triplets, since it ensures accurate word indexing for our annotation tool. We only considered textual data, aligning with the text-centric approach presented in the literature [18] as the cornerstone for our triplet structure (see Sect. 3.1).

3.3 Data Annotation

Our database comprises 40,391 raw TripAdvisor comments in French. For the annotation process, we engaged three undergraduate students over two months, utilizing our internally developed Python tool, TLI-ASTE (Triplet Labelling Interface-Aspect Sentiment Triplet Extraction). The students annotated 2,000 pre-processed comments following the procedures outlined in Sect. 3.2, extracting and annotating relevant triplets. To mitigate bias, the students worked independently. From the comments annotated by all three, 1,592 were chosen for the dataset, excluding the rest due to the lack of annotation by all three students. It is important to underline that the annotators were tasked with both identifying and annotating the triplets in terms of sentiments. This posed a challenge in assessing the annotation quality. Specifically, the data was constructed gradually over a span of two-months, making it difficult to apply commonly used measures of inter-annotator agreement such as the kappa coefficient.

3.4 Curation of the Data

We implemented a curation process to enhance the dataset's quality by ensuring accurate annotation of triplets in terms of aspect, opinion, and sentiment. The need for curation arose from potential inconsistencies, contradictions, and omissions in the students' initial annotations. To address these, we developed a TLI-ASTE tool variant for data curation, enabling corrections, extraction of missed triplets, and validation of initial annotations. This approach resulted in 10,729 validated triplets across the 1,592 annotated comments.

4 Dataset Features

Our curated dataset has unique features such as overlapping and duets that could affect the training of a model. Out of the 10,729 triplets, 943 are duets: 692 lack an aspect and 251 lack an opinion. As for comments, 1,125 (70.6%) of those exhibit overlapping triplets. In terms of data distribution during the curation process, the majority of sentiment triplets were positive, which is a total of 9,889 triplets (92.2%) in our comments. Those comments were randomly selected from various hotels and guesthouses. Negative and neutral triplets are less common in the dataset, with 734 (6.84%) and 106 (0.98%) instances, respectively. This distribution reflects the overall sentiment of our source database. Despite the challenge of obtaining more negative or neutral comments, these 1,592 comments could be used to train a sentiment analysis model. Following such model's evaluation, we might achieve a more balanced extraction from the remaining 38,391 comments.

Table 1. Overview of the two sub-datasets

		Dataset ø overlapping	Dataset with overlapping
Comments		467	1,125
Triplets	Total	2,235	8,494
	ø aspect	242	450
	ø opinion	107	144
Sentiment of triplets	Positive	2,032	7,857
	Negative	184	550
	Neutral	19	87

5 Created Datasets

In the previous section, we acknowledged that the dataset included comments with overlapping triplets. We opted to create two additional disjoint sub-datasets from the original dataset:

- The first exclusively contains comments with non-overlapping triplets.
- The second solely incorporates comments with at least one instance of overlapping triplets.

Each of these datasets manifests the imbalance discussed in Sect. 4. Table 1 presents the characteristics of the two disjoint subsets. The three datasets could be used to observe a model's performance and behavior when it is trained or fine-tuned on this data. This could potentially reveal the influence of the presence or absence of overlap within the dataset on the quality of triplet sentiment detection and evaluation. While some ASTE-related research [8, 13, 18] occasionally mentions overlapping instances, only a handful of studies have endeavored to address or consider this effect [10, 15–17].

6 Data Format

Our curated dataset and its subsets, accessible on HuggingFace1 and described in Sect. 5 are organized in a standardized JSON format. Each entry features a comment ID, word array, triplet list, and an overall sentiment ("general_polarity"). Each triplet, contained in a dictionary, includes the aspect and opinion words - both arrays - and their respective positions in the word array (with absent entity in a duet noted as "-1" for the index and labeled "non-existent aspect" or "non-existent opinion"). In the dictionary, "polarity" is the key representing the sentiment of the triplet.

7 Future Work

In collaboration with the Ministry of Tourism, we aim to analyze tourist comments to provide a practical application in a real-world context. First, we intend to manually annotate the remaining 38,391 remaining comments -a labor-intensive process. This approach could yield a balanced and diverse dataset, thereby improving the accuracy of sentiment analysis. Second, we plan to leverage the GPT-4 API for automated annotation. Preliminary experiments have shown us that GPT-4 can successfully extracts triplets. Recent studies [21–24] have highlighted the capabilities of GPT models, such as GPT 3.5 or GPT 4, in NLP tasks. Our approach will involve submitting zero-shot prompts to the GPT-4 API for each comment, considering various emotional nuances. This approach could enrich the diversity of our dataset and potentially balance sentiment distribution. It would also be interesting to compare the performance of GPT-4 in labialization tasks with that of human annotators.

8   Conclusion

In this paper, we presented a unique sentiment analysis dataset, the first of its kind focusing specifically on French Polynesian tourism. This corpus drawn from French tourist reviews on TripAdvisor consists of 1,592 comments and 10,729 triplets, can help in developing a sentiment analysis model fine-tuned for analyzing tourists' sentiments. Despite its utility, our dataset exhibits a skewness towards positive sentiments - a limitation that may influence the performance of sentiment classification models. To further facilitate research, we created two disjoint subsets from the original dataset; one free of overlapping triplets and the other with comments containing at least one overlapping triplet. These subsets, along with the full dataset, are available on HuggingFace1 for research purposes. The publication of this dataset contributes to the growth of French NLP resources and lays the groundwork for analysis of tourism experiences in French Polynesia, offering potential insights into the evolution of sentiments over time.

9   Limitations

Although our dataset paves the way for the development of a sentiment classification model specialized in tourists' comments in French, it is not without its shortcomings.

As mentioned, the uneven distribution of sentiments, resulting in a majority of positive sentiments in triplets, may bias a model. The dataset's size is another restriction, given its limited number of annotated comments. Extending the dataset by annotating the remaining 38,391 comments of our database would be beneficial - either manually or by using GPT-4. Furthermore, the dataset currently lacks nuanced or mixed sentiment classification.

References

1. Le, H., et al.: FlauBERT: Unsupervised language model pre-training for French. In: Proceedings of the Twelfth Language Resources and Evaluation Conference. Eu-ropean Language Resources Association, Marseille, France, pp 2479–2490 (2020)
2. Martin L, et al.: CamemBERT: a tasty French language model. In: Proceedings of the 58th Annual Meeting of the Association for Computational Linguistics. Association for Computational Linguistics, Online, pp. 7203–7219 (2020)

3. Delestre, C., Amar, A.: DistilCamemBERT: a distillation of the French model CamemBERT. In: CAp (Conférence sur l'Apprentissage automatique). Vannes, France (2022)

4. Xu, L., Chia, Y.K., Bing, L.: Learning span-level interactions for aspect sentiment triplet extraction. In: Proceedings of the 59th Annual Meeting of the Association for Computational Linguistics and the 11th International Joint Conference on Natural Language Processing (Volume 1: Long Papers). Association for Computational Linguistics, Online, pp. 4755–4766 (2021)

5. Liu, S., Li, K., Li, Z.: A Robustly optimized BMRC for aspect sentiment triplet extraction. In: Proceedings of the 2022 Conference of the North American Chapter of the Association for Computational Linguistics: Human Language Technologies. Association for Computational Linguistics, Seattle, United States, pp. 272–278 (2022)

6. Xu, K., Li, F., Xie, D., Ji, D.: Revisiting aspect-sentiment-opinion triplet extraction: detailed analyses towards a simple and effective span-based model. IEEE/ACM Trans. Audio Speech Lang. Process **30**, 2918–2927 (2022). https://doi.org/10.1109/TASLP.2022.3202122

7. Wang, F., Li, Y., Zhong, S., Yin, C., He, Y.: Aspect-sentiment-multiple-opinion triplet extraction. Computing Research Repository, arXiv:211007303 Version 1 (2021). https://doi.org/10.48550/arXiv.2110.07303

8. Mao, Y., Shen, Y., Yu, C., Cai, L.: A joint training dual-MRC framework for aspect based sentiment analysis. In: Proceedings of the AAAI Conference on Artificial Intelligence. Online, pp. 13543–13551 (2021)

9. Chen, S., Wang, Y., Liu, J., Wang, Y.: Bidirectional machine reading comprehension for aspect sentiment triplet extraction. In: Proceedings of the AAAI Conference on Artificial Intelligence, pp. 12666–12674 (2021)

10. Chen, F., Yang, Z., Huang, Y.: A multi-task learning framework for end-to-end aspect sentiment triplet extraction. Neurocomputing **479**, 12–21 (2022). https://doi.org/10.1016/j.neucom.2022.01.021

11. Chen, Y., Keming, C., Sun, X., Zhang, Z.: A span-level bidirectional network for aspect sentiment triplet extraction. In: Proceedings of the 2022 Conference on Empirical Methods in Natural Language Processing. Association for Computational Linguistics, Abu Dhabi, United Arab Emirates, pp. 4300–4309 (2022)

12. Chen, Z., Huang, H., Liu, B., Shi, X., Jin, H.: Semantic and syntactic enhanced aspect sentiment triplet extraction. In: Findings of the Association for Computational Linguistics: ACL-IJCNLP 2021. Association for Computational Linguistics, Online, pp. 1474–1483 (2021)

13. Xu, L., Li, H., Lu, W., Bing, L.: Position-aware tagging for aspect sentiment triplet extraction. In: Proceedings of the 2020 Conference on Empirical Methods in Natural Language Processing (EMNLP). Association for Computational Linguistics, Online, pp. 2339–2349 (2020)

14. Li, Y., Wang, F., Zhang, W., Zhong, S., Yin, C., He, Y.: A more fine-grained aspect-sentiment-opinion triplet extraction task. Computing Research Repository, arXiv:210315255 Version 5 (2021). https://doi.org/10.48550/arXiv.2103.15255

15. Fei, H., Ren, Y., Zhang, Y., Ji, D.: Nonautoregressive encoder-decoder neural framework for end-to-end aspect-based sentiment triplet extraction. IEEE Trans. Neural Netw. Learn. Syst. 1–13 (2021). https://doi.org/10.1109/TNNLS.2021.3129483

16. Mukherjee, R., Nayak, T., Butala, Y., Bhattacharya, S., Goyal, P.: PASTE: a tagging-free decoding framework using pointer networks for aspect sentiment triplet ex-traction. In: Proceedings of the 2021 Conference on Empirical Methods in Natural Language Processing. Association for Computational Linguistics, Online and Punta Cana, Dominican Republic, pp. 9279–9291 (2021)

17. Zhao, S., Chen, W., Wang, T.: Learning cooperative interactions for multi-overlap aspect sentiment triplet extraction. In: Findings of the Association for Computational Lin-guistics: EMNLP 2022. Association for Computational Linguistics, Abu Dhabi, United Arab Emirates, pp. 3337–3347 (2022)
18. Peng, H., Xu, L., Bing, L., Huang, F., Lu, W., Si, L.: Knowing what, how and why: a near complete solution for aspect-based sentiment analysis. In: Proceedings of the AAAI Conference on Artificial Intelligence, pp. 8600–8607 (2020)
19. Pontiki, M., et al.: SemEval-2016 Task 5: aspect based sentiment analysis. In: Proceedings of the 10th International Work-shop on Semantic Evaluation (SemEval-2016). Association for Computational Linguistics, San Diego, California, pp. 19–30 (2016)
20. Bing, L.: Sentiment Analysis and Opinion Mining. Springer, Cham (2012). https://doi.org/10.1007/978-3-031-02145-9
21. Wang, S., Liu, Y., Xu, Y., Zhu, C., Zeng, M.: Want to reduce labeling cost? GPT-3 can help. In: Findings of the Association for Computational Linguistics: EMNLP 2021. Association for Computational Linguistics, Punta Cana, Dominican Republic, pp. 4195–4205 (2021)
22. Ding, B., Qin, C., Liu, L., Joty, S., Lidong, B., Li, B.: Is GPT-3 a good data annotator? Comput. Res. Repository, arXiv:221210450 Version 2 (2022). https://doi.org/10.48550/arXiv.2212.10450
23. Törnberg, P.: ChatGPT-4 outperforms experts and crowd workers in annotating political twitter messages with zero-shot learning. Comput. Res. Repos. arXiv:230406588 Version 1 (2023). https://doi.org/10.48550/arXiv.2304.06588
24. Gilardi, F., Alizadeh, M., Kubli, M.: ChatGPT outperforms crowd-workers for text-annotation tasks. Comput. Res. Repos., arXiv:230315056 Version 1 (2023). https://doi.org/10.48550/arXiv.2303.15056

SLHCat: Mapping Wikipedia Categories and Lists to DBpedia by Leveraging Semantic, Lexical, and Hierarchical Features

Zhaoyi Wang[1], Zhenyang Zhang[1], Jiaxin Qin[1,2P], and Mizuho Iwaihara[1(✉)]

[1] Graduate School of Information, Production, and Systems, Waseda University,
Kitakyushu 808-0135, Japan
wangzy-joey@akane.waseda.jp, {zhangzhenyang,
jiaxinqin}@fuji.waseda.jp, iwaihara@waseda.jp
[2] United Automotive Electronic Systems Co., Ltd., Beijing, China

Abstract. Wikipedia articles are hierarchically organized through categories and lists, providing one of the most comprehensive and universal taxonomy, but its open creation is causing redundancies and inconsistencies. Assigning DBPedia classes to Wikipedia categories and lists can alleviate the problem, realizing a large knowledge graph which is essential for categorizing digital contents through entity linking and typing. However, the existing approach of CaLiGraph is producing incomplete and non-fine grained mappings. In this paper, we tackle the problem as ontology alignment, where structural information of knowledge graphs and lexical and semantic features of ontology class names are utilized to discover confident mappings, which are in turn utilized for finetuing pretrained language models in a distant supervision fashion. Our method SLHCat consists of two main parts: 1) Automatically generating training data by leveraging knowledge graph structure, semantic similarities, and named entity typing. 2) Finetuning and prompt-tuning of the pre-trained language model BERT are carried out over the training data, to capture semantic and syntactic properties of class names. Our model SLHCat is evaluated over a benchmark dataset constructed by annotating 3000 fine-grained CaLiGraph-DBpedia mapping pairs. SLHCat is outperforming the baseline model by a large margin of 25% in accuracy, offering a practical solution for large-scale ontology mapping.

Keywords: Knowledge graph · Ontology alignment · Wikipedia categories and lists · DBpedia · CaLiGraph · Distant supervision

1 Introduction

Categorizing concepts and entities into a taxonomy is a fundamental task of digital libraries. A universal entity categorization system is desirable for various tasks such as entity disambiguation, entity linking, and text classification. For such a universal taxonomy, Wikipedia serves as an indispensable knowledge resource, because it is the largest online encyclopedia containing a wide range of articles on vast topics. Most of

D. H. Goh et al. (Eds.): ICADL 2023, LNCS 14457, pp. 133–148, 2023.
https://doi.org/10.1007/978-981-99-8085-7_12

its entries (i.e., Wikipedia articles) can be considered as (semi-structured) representations of entities. For grouping related articles, Wikipedia provides three complementary mechanisms: Categories, lists and navigation templates, based on shared characteristics or topics of articles [18]. Categories are organized in a hierarchy and each Wikipedia article is assigned to at least one category. Lists provide a mean for manual categorization of articles and can include entities that do not have a Wikipedia page yet. Lists are more difficult to process automatically due to informal construction.

Although lists and categories of Wikipedia provide rich resources for universal taxonomy, their vastness and open creation introduce wildness such as irregularities and redundancies, causing difficulties in automating categorization of new entities. DBpedia [21] is a project aiming at extracting structured information from Wikipedia and organizing into a large knowledge graph. The DBpedia ontology is the heart of DBpedia, currently enlisting 788 classes, and around 4.8 million instances, on which a subsumption hierarchy is formed.

An ontology is a structured representation of knowledge that models a collection of concepts within a particular domain, along with their interrelationships [8]. However, independent development of ontologies often results in heterogeneous knowledge representations with varying categorizations and naming schemes. Ontology alignment is a vital solution to the semantic heterogeneity problem, which aims to establish the relation between semantically related entities in heterogeneous ontologies.

CaLiGraph [5–7] is a large semantic knowledge graph with a rich ontology compiled from the DBpedia ontology and Wikipedia categories and list pages, as depicted in Fig. 1(a). CaLiGraph expands the DBpedia ontology classes with fine-grained value restrictions to more than one million classes and over 200,000 restrictions by Cat2Ax [7] approach, which extracts entities from Wikipedia listings through a combination of the ontological information, axioms, and transformer-based extractors.

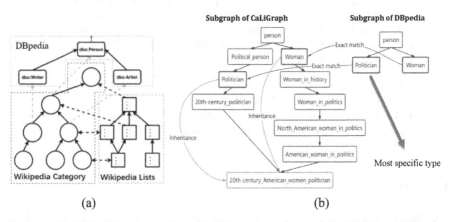

(a)   (b)

Fig. 1. (a) CaLiGraph ontology schema [5] (b) A mapping between CaLiGraph and DBPedia

Figure 1(b) shows an example of mapping CaLiGraph classes to DBPedia classes. Suppose we intend to find a DBPedia class for the CaLiGraph class "20th-century_Americal_women_politician." The word "politician" indicates the possibility of mapping the class to "Politician" in DBPeida, which can be done by lexical analysis. We also notice that the ancestors of the class also include "Politician," where class inheritance can be considered. However, the class "Woman" is also a candidate because of the word match, where multiple inheritance to the same class is occurring. In this case, "Politician" can be chosen as the most specific class because this is less populated than class "Woman."

Although the objective of CaLiGraph occupies a vital role in utilizing Wikipedia as a universal taxonomy, the quality of precise categorization on Wikipedia entities still needs improvement. In this paper, we propose an effective method for finding the most specific and accurate DBpedia class for a given Wikipedia list or category.

Our method includes the following parts: (1) A mapping method by lexical properties, which includes root phrase matching between class names of CaLiGraph and DBPedia, part-of-speech (POS) tagging, and inheritance in the class hierarchies. These mappings are then used for finetuning the pretrained language model (PLM) BERT [1]. Also, class name embeddings generated by SimCSE [4] are used to find semantically similar class names. We further utilize named entity typing on article titles of a target Wikipedia list or category, to find majority types in these listings. These approaches are combined to build CaLiGraph-DBpedia class pairs. (2) Finetuning of the pre-trained language model BERT, with the distantly supervised samples from the previous step. Here we also try to finetune BERT using a simple prompt-tuning strategy [10]. To reflect hierarchical properties of ontologies in prompt-based tuning, we use hierarchical classification such that ancestor class names are appended into prompt templates to enrich contextual information.

For evaluating the correctness of the generated mappings, we construct a manually annotated benchmark dataset, which consists of 3000 fine-grained CaLiGraph-DBpedia mapping pairs annotated by three annotators. We evaluate our model SLHCat on the CaLiGraph-DBpedia mapping task, by macro and micro F1-scores, and accuracy. Our proposed model outperforms the baseline model Cat2Ax by all the evaluation metrics by a large margin.

2 Related Work

2.1 Ontology Alignment

Lexical matching serves as the foundation for traditional ontology mapping solutions, which is often combined with structural matching. This gave rise to various existing systems such as Cat2Ax [7]. Their lexical matching approach, however, only focuses on the text's surface form, such as overlapping sub-strings and sharing a textual pattern, which is unable to capture word semantics. Lexical and structural matchings have recently been suggested to be replaced by machine learning; for instance, DeepAlignment [9] and OntoEmma [16] use word embeddings to represent classes and compute the similarity of two classes according to the Euclidean distance between their word vectors. However, these approaches either require extensive feature engineering that is ad-hoc and relies on great amounts of annotated examples for training, or they use classic non-contextual word embedding models like Word2Vec [11], which only learns a global (context-free) embedding for each word.

2.2 CaLiGraph and Cat2Ax

CaLiGraph is a large semantic knowledge graph that incorporates a rich ontology compiled from the DBpedia ontology and Wikipedia categories and list pages [6]. The ontology is enriched with fine-grained value restrictions on its classes that are discovered with the Cat2Ax approach. CaLiGraph covers over 1 million classes and over 200,000 restrictions, containing information of 15 million entities, as shown in Table 1.

Table 1. Statistics of DBpedia and CaLiGraph

	Classes	Instances
DBpedia	788	4,828,418
CaLiGraph	1,061,597	15,230,974

The following four major steps are used in Cat2Ax for allocating a DBPedia class to Wikipedia lists and categories: (1) Identify candidate category sets that share a textual pattern. (2) Find characteristic properties and types for candidate sets and combine them to patterns. (3) Apply patterns to all categories to extract axioms. (4) Apply axioms to their respective categories to extract assertions. The estimated mapping accuracy of Cat2AX reported in [7] is 96.8%. However, the authors' independent examinations on the mappings generated by Cat2Ax, reported in Sect. 5.1, reveals that 50% of mappings are either onto very general DBpedia types, mapping to a wrong type, or no DBpedia type is given. One example is that the CaLiGraph class "Male actor from Saskatchewan" is mapped to DBpedia class "Person" by Cat2Ax, but in this case "Actor" is more specific and appropriate.

2.3 Distant Supervision

Most of machine learning and deep learning techniques require a large amount of training samples for training a model for the target task. Manual labeling of training data requires considerable time and cost. An alternative approach to annotating training data is distant supervision [12], in which training samples are labeled automatically based on certain rules, suitable for situations where training data construction is costly.

Distant supervision for semantic typing is an extension of the paradigm used by [15] for utilizing WordNet to uncover hypernym (is-a) relations between entities, and is analogous to the application of poorly labeled data in bioinformatics [1, 13], and in relation extraction which has no labeled data [12]. A typical distant supervision's assumption for relation typing is that any statement that contains two entities that are involved in a relationship may refer to that relationship [12].

In our work, we introduce distant supervision rules for discovering mappings between CaLiGraph classes and DBpedia classes, where the rules are based on textual and semantic similarities between class names, knowledge graph structures, and the lexical database WordNet on semantic relations.

2.4 Prompt-Based Learning

Prompt-based learning [15] is a new paradigm for finetuning PLMs for specific tasks by providing task-specific prompts, which has attracted attentions in the NLP field. In prompt learning, downstream tasks are formalized as equivalent cloze-style tasks by adding some pieces of text as a prompt, and the PLM is asked to handle these cloze-style tasks instead of original tasks. In contrast to the traditional finetuning methods, prompt-based learning does not require extra neural layers and bridges the objective form gap between pre-training and finetuning.

3 Problem Definition and Overview

In this paper, we focus on finding the most specific and matching DBpedia class for each of Wikipedia category and list names included in CaLiGraph. This task can be formulated as a multi-class classification problem.

Ontologies are often composed of statements in the form of triples (subject, predicate, object) in the Web Ontology Language OWL. Here, we denote by O and O' the two ontologies of CaLiGraph and DBpedia, respectively. The named class set O (resp. O') is denoted as C (resp. C'). The set of articles assigned to a class $c \in C$ is denoted as as $e_c \in E_c$.

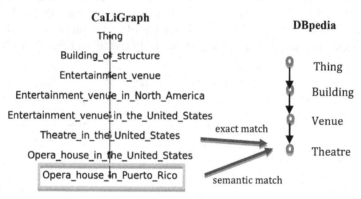

Fig. 2. Matching by exact and semantic match on root phrases

The goal of this paper is to find a mapping that maps each class $c \in C$ to a target class $c' \in C'$, where the target class c' should represent the minimum concept that subsumes c. In other words, our goal is to find the most specific named class c' of DBpedia for each CaLiGraph class c.

Figure 2 shows an example of the task of mapping CaLiGraph classes to DBPedia classes. Suppose that "Opera_house_in_Puerto_Rico" is the target CaLiGraph class. Lexical analysis of the class name indicates the *root phrase*, which is the phrase located at the root of its dependency tree. The phrases "house," "opera house," "house in Puerto rico" are also root phrases. Using this root phrase set, we can search the DBPedia classes. However, since there is no exactly matching class in DBpedia, we need to consider semantic similarities between class names. DBPedia classes "Venue" and "Theatre" are semantically close to "opera house." For evaluating semantic similarities, we can utilize contextualized representations of texts generated by PLMs, such as SimCSE [4] and BERT [2]. "Theartre" turns out to be most specific and semantically close to the target, so "Theartre" will be selected.

An alternative approach to the above is utilizing inheritance on the class hierarchies. The target class has an ancestor "Theatre_in_the_United_States." The root phrase of this class name is also matching with "Theatre." We can propagate this class mapping to its descendants. The approach of hierarchical classification [15] can be applied here. One another approach is utilizing named entity typing. Existing part-of- speech (POS) tagging tools can provide named entity typing. Although the results of the typing are general, such as "house" is typed as "building," this extra information can assist semantic matching by PLMs.

4   Methodology

4.1   Model Architecture

In this paper, we propose a novel ontology mapping method **SLHCat**, which exploits the hierarchical structures of DBpedia and CaLiGraph, as well as lexical and semantic similarities between class names. Then a hierarchical classifier based on pre-trained language model BERT is finetuned by distantly-supervised samples. Figure 3 shows the overall structure of SLHCat. Our method consists of two main parts: (1) Generating distantly-supervised training samples. (2) Finetuning pretrained language models.

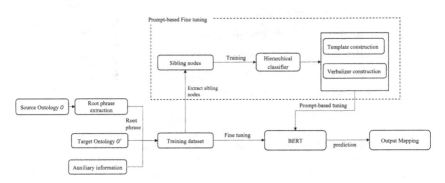

Fig. 3. Overall structure of our proposed model SLHCat.

4.2   Root Phrase Extraction

A DBPedia class node in the hierarchy of DBPedia may have an exactly identical class name in the hierarchy of CaLiGraph. As shown in Fig. 1(a), CaLiGraph uses DBPedia as an upper-level taxonomy and categorizes these rather general types in DBPedia into more specific types, although the mapping is not accurate enough. We check an exactly matching CaLiGraph node in the hierarchy for every DBPedia node. For example, "Joan Baez compilation album" is a CaLiGraph node, which contains "album" as a part of the class name, which is also found in DBpedia. So, it is likely that "Joan Baez compilation album" is mapped to "Album". Such matching pairs can be utilized as confident samples for distant supervision.

More generally, we define the *root word* as a single noun word which represents the subject information of the whole sentence. For a long noun phrase, the root word holds the most basic meaning of the whole phrase. However, considering only the root word may not be sufficient to find matching class names. The root word needs to be extended to a phrase by adding part of words that are modifying the root word. A *root phrase* is a phrase consisting of a root word and its modifying components. Figure 4(a) shows an example of part-of-speech (POS) tagging and Fig. 4(b) shows an example of dependency parsing for class name "American football team in Finland". Here, the phrase "football team" is more specific than the root word "team," which could be matched with DBPedia class "SportTeam." But the most specific DBPedia type for this CaLiGraph class is "AmericanFootballTeam." Also, the phrase "team in Finland" can be a candidate of matching class names. This example indicates that we need to extract a candidate set of root phrases from a given class name, and then select the root phrase that matches with the most specific and semantically consistent and DBpedia class.

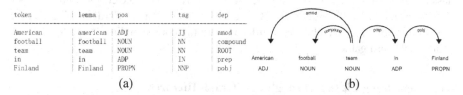

(a)   (b)

Fig. 4. (a) "American football team in Finland" after POS tagging (b) dependency parsing

We extract a root phrase candidate set for each CaLiGraph class as follows:

Step 1. Perform POS tagging and dependency parsing on the CaLiGraph class names. Extract root words and append them to the root phrase set.

Step 2. In the dependency parse tree, enumerate the left and right subtrees of the root word, and add the phrase corresponding to each subtree to the root phrase set.

Step 3. If the subtree node is a preposition, append the preposition and its descendant nodes to the root word, and add the corresponding phrase to the root phrase set.

In the example of "American football team in Finland," we obtain the root phrase candidate set consisting of "team", "American team", "football team", "American football team" and "team in Finland."

SpaCy [20] is a tool for advanced natural language processing, which provides modules for POS tagging and dependency parsing. In this paper, we utilize these two modules to analyze the dependency structure of sentences and extract root words and root phrases.

4.3 Sentence Embedding for Matching by Semantic Similarities

Sentence embedding can capture semantic and contextual features of texts and the embedding can be mapped onto a shared vector space, on which semantic similarities can be measured by certain distance metrics over the vector space. In this paper, we use unsupervised SimCSE [4] to embed each root phrase v_{root_phrase} in the root phrase candidate set V_{root_phrase}, where $v_{root\_phrase} \in V_{root\_phrase}$, and DBpedia class names V_{DBO}. We utilize the cosine similarity to calculate the distance between each root phrase from the root phrase candidate set and DBpedia class names as follows:

$$sim(v_{root\_phrase}, V_{DBO}) = \cos(v_{root\_phrase}, V_{DBO}) = \frac{\overrightarrow{v_{root\_phrase}} \times \overrightarrow{V_{DBO}}}{|\overrightarrow{v_{root\_phrase}}| \times |\overrightarrow{V_{DBO}}|}$$

We choose the pair of a root phrase and DBpedia class which has the highest cosine value as a confident sample for BERT finetuning under distant supervision. In the previous example, the cosine value of the root phrase "American football team" and DBpedia class "AmericanFootballTeam" achieves the highest, which is close to 1, so we assign "AmericanFootballTeam" to CaLiGraph class "American football team in Finland."

There may exist multiple pairs whose cosine values are close to 1. In such cases, we choose the DBpedia class which has the longest word matching to the CaLiGraph class name. For the CaLiGraph class "Collectible card game", the cosine values of root phrases "game" and DBpedia class "Game", "card game" and "CardGame" are close to 1. In this situation, we choose "CardGame" as the corresponding DBpedia class of "Collectible card game".

4.4 Propagating Classes Through CaLiGraph Hierarchy

The subsumption hierarchies of CaLiGraph and DBpedia can be utilized for class inference. Suppose that a confident mapping that maps a CaLiGraph class $c \in C$ to a DBPedia class $c\prime \in C\prime$. Then we can extend the mapping to the descendants of c as type inheritance. Regarding the example of Fig. 2, CaLiGraph class "Theatre_in_the_United_States" can be mapped "Theatre", thorough matching on the root phrase. Then by class inheritance, "Opera_house_in_Puerto_Rico" can be also mapped to "Theatre." Class inheritance is useful when no corresponding DBpedia class is found for a descendant of However, the hierarchies of Wikipedia lists and categories allow one class having multiple parents, causing multiple inheritance, as we saw in Fig. 1(b). To resolve multiple inheritance and choose one target class, we utilize the BERT classifier.

We call nodes sharing the same parent as sibling nodes. We observe that sibling nodes sharing the same root phrase are likely to have the same DBpedia type, thus propagating types to such sibling nodes is possible. Sibling nodes can be searched from each CaLiGraph node in the current confident labeled dataset. In Fig. 5, the classes "Penn State Lady Lions basketball player", "Virginia Tech Hokies women's basketball player" and "Virginia Tech Hokies women's basketball player" are the children of "College women's basketball player in the United States," and share the same root phrase "basketball player." These class names can be added to the confident dataset. This can be viewed as a form of class inheritance, but sharing a root phrase between the parent and siblings is a strong indicator that they belong to the same class, giving a higher priority when resolving multiply assigned classes.

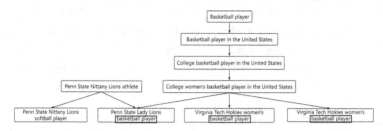

Fig. 5. Propagating classes to sibling nodes sharing a common root phrase

4.5 Named Entity Typing on Wikipedia Article Titles

Wikipedia articles included in the same category or list are supposed to share the same theme or subject. Thus, we can assume that in a given Wikipedia category or list, its member articles share a common aspect or attribute, from which we can infer the DBpedia class of the list or category.

Pages in category "American football teams in Finland"

The following 7 pages are in this category, out of 7 total. This list may not reflect recent changes.

H
- Helsinki 69ers
- Helsinki Roosters
- Helsinki Wolverines

K
- Kuopio Steelers

S
- Seinäjoki Crocodiles

T
- Tampere Saints
- Turku Trojans

Fig. 6. Wikipedia pages in category "American football teams in Finland"

Figure 6 shows the Wikipedia articles belong to CaLiGraph class "American football team in Finland," on which several entities can be linked to American football players. To infer the DBpedia type of each member article, we utilize the technique of named entity typing on the article titles, where each article is regarded as representing a Wikipedia entity. Here we use the named entity recognition tool of SpaCy to identify the types of articles. The type of "Helsinki Roosters" is "ORG", which refers to companies, agencies, institutions, etc. We adopt a criterion such that we select the type that appears for more than half of the occurrences to reduce the potential errors in named entity recognition or the presence of multiple entity types within a single category or list.

Since the named entity types predicted by SpaCy do not exactly match with DBpedia classes, we map the types to DBpedia classes based on their descriptions. Table 2 shows the named entity types, their descriptions, and the mapped DBpedia classes.

This method can be effective when member article titles indicate entity types such as person names, which can complement the approaches based on ontology hierarchies and class names. However, the resulting DBpedia classes shown in Table 2 are rather

Table 2. The mapping from named entity types to DBpedia class

Named entity type	Description	DBpedia class
PERSON	People, including fictional	Person
NORP	Nationalities or religious or political groups	Organization
ORG	Companies, agencies, institutions, etc	
FAC	Buildings, airports, highways, bridges, etc	ArchitecturalStructure
GPE	Countries, cities, states	Place
LOC	Non-GPE locations, mountain ranges, bodies of water	
PRODUCT	Objects, vehicles, foods, etc. (Not services.)	Thing
EVENT	Named hurricanes, battles, wars, sports events, etc	Event
WORK_OF_ART	Titles of books, songs, etc	Work

general, locating around the top level of DBpedia. To find more specific and precise DBpedia classes, we need to search descendants of these classes.

Similarly to named entity typing on classes names, we can utilize the external lexical database WordNet for typing root words. WordNet provides semantic relations between words and sets of cognitive synonyms (synsets), as well as POS tags having suffix (POS.suffix), such as *noun.person* and *noun.animal*, from which we can extract candidate DBpedia classes. For example, the root word of CaLiGraph class "Recipient of French pardons" is "recipient", and the corresponding POS.suffix is noun.person. The POS tags and lexical name can further give us hints of labeling. However, as the POS tags from WordNet are either too general, or not fitting well with DBpedia classes, in this work we only consider the types *noun.person* and *noun.group*. If the root word of a CaLiGraph class name belongs to *noun.person*, it is highly likely that the CaLiGraph class belongs to DBpedia class "Person" or its descendants.

4.6 Resolving Results Predicted by Multiple Methods

In the step of Sect. 4.3 for obtaining vector representations using SimCSE, there can exist multiple vector pairs with similarity close to 1, which means that CaLiGraph classes have a nearly exact match to certain DBpedia classes. We regard such CaLiGraph-DBpedia pairs as having high confidence, and use these pairs for distant supervision. For those whose similarity is significantly less than 1, we use the candidate types obtained in the previous steps, and select a DBpedia class according to the following rules:

Rule 1: If the WordNet POS.suffix of the root word is *noun.person* or *noun.group* we only consider the types under person or group, respectively.

Rule 2: Suppose the DBpedia classes predicted by 1) named entity typing, 2) CaLiGraph hierarchy, and 3) sentence similarity with similarity score higher than 0.75 form a directed path in the DBpedia hierarchy. Then we choose the DBpedia class that is deepest in the path.

Rule 3: If two or more methods predict one identical class, the class is selected.

Rule 4: If none of the above rules are met, the class given by named entity typing is selected.

4.7 BERT Finetuning

BERT Finetuning. Given sets of CaLiGraph-DBpedia pairs generating from previous steps, we finetune a pre-trained BERT model along with a downstream binary classifier on the cross-entropy loss. We limit the inputs length of BERT to 256. The classifier consists of a linear layer which takes as input the embedding of [CLS] token from BERT's last-layer outputs and apply to the output softmax layer. The optimization is done by Adam algorithm. The final output is the probability distribution over the DBpedia classes for the given CaLiGraph class.

Prompt-Based Tuning. In our prompt-based learning, for each DBpedia class $c' \in C'$, we define a supplemental word set $S_{c'} = \{\omega_1, \omega_2, \ldots, \omega_m\}$, where $S_{c'}$ is a subset of the vocabulary of BERT. A prompt template $T(\cdot)$ wraps the input $c \in C$ (the input is CaLiGraph class) into a prompt input $T(c)$ by adding additional tokens, and a [MASK] token is added. The classification task is transformed into a masked language modeling (MLM) problem, that is to predict the missing word in [MASK] [3].

Verbalizer. The verbalizer is a significant part of prompt-tuned classification task, which projects the words that predicted at [MASK] to our label set. We use related words [19] to expand the DBpedia classes. Specifically, we chose the top-10 related words for each class in DBpedia as the supplemental word set of the class.

For MLM, we use the confidence scores of all the words in $S_{c'} = \{\omega_1, \omega_2, \ldots, \omega_m\}$ to construct the final score of each DBpedia class.

$$P\left(c' | c\right) = \frac{1}{m} \sum_{j}^{m} \lambda_j P([MASK] = \omega | T(c))$$

where m is the number of top-ranked related words, ω is a related word for DBpedia class $c\prime$, and λ_j is a parameter indicating the importance of the current word ω_j.

Template. Template wraps the inputs with textual or soft-encoding sequence. Here, we utilize the soft-encoding templates, which can continuously optimize in a vector space. Soft-encoding strategy introducing special tokens $[P_1], \ldots, [P_l]$ as the templates. The template becomes:

$$T_1(c) = [P_1] \ldots [P_n] Category [P_{n+1}] \ldots [P_l].c.$$

Hierarchical Classification as Hint for Prompt-Based Learning. Hierarchical classification [14] is an effective approach for classification when the target classes are organized in a tree structure. As we discussed in Sect. 1, we can proceed hierarchical classification according to the hierarchy of the DBpedia ontology, where the classification result at a class is utilized as a hint H or bias at its child classes. The template that utilizes the result of hierarchical classification is realized by:

$$T_2(c) = [P_1] \ldots [P_n] Category [P_{n+1}] \ldots [P_l].c.H.$$

5 Experiments

5.1 Benchmark Dataset Construction

To evaluate the accuracy of the mappings of the proposed method, the authors constructed a benchmark dataset that consists of 3,000 mappings from CaLiGraph classes to DBpedia classes. The benchmark dataset construction was done as follows: 3,000 classes were randomly sampled from CaLiGraph. For each CaLiGraph class, one corresponding DBpedia class was selected by three annotators, where the most specific and valid class was instructed to be chosen. The mappings were cross-checked by the three annotators and one DBpedia class was selected after reaching agreement.

We compare the mappings generated by Cat2Ax and our benchmark dataset. Table 3 shows the results of comparison. We find that 49.2% of the mappings generated by Cat2Ax are identical to our manual mappings, which we judge as correct. On the other hand, the remaining 17.8% are judged as wrong, in which 437 mappings are not specific enough. The remaining 32.9% classes have assigned no DBpedia class, meaning that Cat2Ax failed to find a class. Overall, 50% of CaLiGraph classes have not been assigned appropriate DBpedia classes, leaving room for improvement.

Table 3. Evaluation of Cat2Ax mappings by the benchmark dataset

Cat2Ax mapping		Benchmark dataset	Percentage
Correct		1476	49.2%
Wrong	Not specific	437	17.8%
	Others	97	
Missing		986	32.9%
Total		3000	100%

For finetuing the PLM, we generated another 3,000 mappings by the distant supervision method described in Sect. 4, as follows: 3,000 CaLiGraph classes were randomly sampled, where the classes are disjoint from the 3000 classes used for the benchmark dataset. Then the method of Sect. 4 was used to assign DBpedia classes to construct 3,000 mappings. The training dataset is divided into 90% for the training set and 10% for the validation set. Then the training dataset was augmented into 12,700 classes, by propagation on sibling nodes described in Sect. 4.4. Table 4 shows the statistics of the benchmark dataset.

5.2 Experimental Settings

Our proposed model SLHCat, for mapping CaLiGraph classes to DBpedia classes, is evaluated over the benchmark dataset. SLHCat is compared against the baseline model Cat2Ax. We evaluate effectiveness of each proposed component, by comparing seven different configurations (a) – (g), where each configuration is shown in Table 5. Each

Table 4. Statistics of datasets

Dataset	Training data		Augmented set	Benchmark dataset
	Training set	Validation set		
CaLiGraph-DBpedia	2700	300	12700	3000

symbol means that: (**Dist**) No PLM classifier, and only distant supervision rules are used. (**BERT**) BERT finetuning. (**Prompt**) Prompt-based tuning. The distant supervision rules are divided as: (**Root Phase**) Root phrase set. (**NER**) Name entity typing on entities in Wikipedia member pages. (**Inherit**) Class inheritance. (**Lex**) Lexical typing by WordNet. (**Hier**) Hierarchical classification approach in prompt tuning.

The evaluation metrics of the experiments are {Macro, Micro}-{Precision, Recall, F1 score} and Accuracy. For BERT finetuing, we use vanilla finetuning. We choose early stopping to monitor the training process and determine the early training stop when the performance on the validation set starts to deteriorate. In the training, when the validation loss no longer decreases for 7 consecutive times, the model is considered to have converged, and the training is stopped. The training batch size is equal to 16, the input max length is 256 and learning rate is 1e-5 for both vanilla finetuning and prompt-based tuning.

5.3 Results and Discussions

Table 5 shows the results of the evaluation. The overall results demonstrate that our proposed method SCHCat achieved higher scores in all the seven metrics than the baseline model Cat2Ax. Within the seven configurations, using BERT finetuning for final classification is prevailing over the models (a) using only the distant supervision rules, and (f, g) prompt-based tuning. Full-finetuning of BERT achieves higher performance than the prompt-based approach, which is explained as prompt-based tuning is training only prompt-related parameters, although it is cost effective.

NER (c) is improving Micro and Macro F1 scores by 0.015 and 0.081, respectively, over the model (b) using only **Root Phrase**. **Inherit** (d) shows improvement over (c) on Micro-F1 score and accuracy, while **Lex** (e) shows improvement over (d) on Macro-F1 score. Macro-F1 score assigns equal weights on both populated and minority classes in averaging, indicating that **Lex** is showing effectiveness on minority classes. Same trends are observed between **Hier** (g) and without **Hier** (f) on the prompt-based models. In terms of accuracy, the prominent configuration of SCHCat is (d) **BERT + Root Phrase + NER + Inherit + Lex**, improving the accuracy of Cat2Ax by 0.251.

Table 5. Results of mapping categories and lists to DBpedia classes by SLHCat and baseline

Model	Macro-Pre	Macro-Recall	Macro-F1	Micro-Pre	Micro-Recall	Micro-F1	Accuracy
Cat2Ax	0.342	0.335	0.321	0.528	0.492	0.509	0.492
SLHCat							
a) Dist + Root Phrase + NER + Inherit + Lex	0.623	0.567	0.562	0.670	0.662	0.666	0.662
b) BERT + Root Phrase	0.607	**0.667**	0.598	0.699	0.642	0.669	0.642
c) BERT + Root Phrase + NER	**0.646**	0.647	0.613	0.746	0.723	0.734	0.723
d) BERT + Root Phrase + NER + Inherit	0.625	0.658	0.608	**0.774**	**0.743**	**0.758**	**0.743**
e) BERT + Root Phrase + NER + Inherit + Lex	0.636	0.663	**0.618**	0.753	0.723	0.728	0.723
f) Prompt + Root Phrase + NER + Inherit + Lex	0.601	0.623	0.578	0.748	0.712	0.729	0.712
g) Prompt + Root Phrase + NER + Inherit + Lex + Hier	0.644	0.627	0.607	0.741	0.703	0.721	0.703

6 Conclusion and Future work

In this paper, we proposed a novel approach for ontology alignment that utilizes distant supervision to automatically generate confident mappings, for finetuning a pretrained language model. Our approach covers textual, semantic, lexical, and structural features of ontologies. We employ two different training strategies, namely prompt-based tuning and finetuning on the pre-trained language model BERT. Hierarchical classification is employed to give guiding signals in prompt-based tuning. To evaluate the correctness of mappings, we constructed a benchmark dataset consisting of 3,000 labeled mappings, through manual annotation. Our proposed method outperforms the baseline Cat2Ax by a wide margin of 0.25 in accuracy.

While category and list structures of Wikipedia are considered as an important source for finding valid mappings, considerable noises are also introduced due to not well-maintained link structures. In future work, we shall consider denoising mechanisms to improve correctness, and consider utilization of large language models, for augmenting class names.

References

1. Craven, M., Kumlien, J.: Constructing biological knowledge bases by extracting information from text sources. In: ISMB, vol. 1999, pp. 77–86 (1999)
2. Devlin, J., Chang, M.W., Lee, K., et al.: BERT: pre-training of deep bidirectional transformers for language understanding. In: Proceedings of the NAACL 2019, Minneapolis, June 2019, pp. 4171–4186 (2019)
3. Ding, N., Hu, S., Zhao, W., et al.: OpenPrompt: an open-source framework for prompt-learning. Proc. ACL **2022**, 105–113 (2021)
4. Gao, T., Yao, X., Chen, D.: SimCSE: simple contrastive learning of sentence embedding. In: Proceedings of the EMNLP 2021, pp. 6894–6910 (2021)
5. Heist, N., Paulheim, H.: Entity extraction from Wikipedia list pages. In: The Semantic Web: 17th International Conference, ESWC 2020, Heraklion, Crete, 2020, pp. 327–342 (2020)
6. Heist, N., Paulheim H.: The CaLiGraph ontology as a challenge for OWL reasoners. In: Proceedings of the Semantic Reasoning Evaluation Challenge (SemREC 2021) (2021)
7. Heist, Nicolas, Paulheim, Heiko: Uncovering the semantics of Wikipedia categories. In: Ghidini, C., et al. (eds.) ISWC 2019. LNCS, vol. 11778, pp. 219–236. Springer, Cham (2019). https://doi.org/10.1007/978-3-030-30793-6_13
8. Jeong, J.-W., Hong, H.-K., Lee, D.-H.: Ontology-based automatic video annotation technique in smart TV environment. IEEE Trans. Consumer Electron. **57**(4), 1830–1836 (2011)
9. Kolyvakis, P., Kalousis, A., Kiritsis, D.: Deepalignment: unsupervised ontology matching with refined word vectors. In: Proceedings of the 2018 Conference on North American Chapter of the Association for Computational Linguistics: Human Language Technologies, vol. 1, pp. 787–798 (2018)
10. Liu, P., Yuan, W., Fu, J., et al.: Pre-train, prompt, and predict: a systematic survey of prompting methods in natural language processing. ACM Comput. Surv. **55**(9), 1–35 (2023)
11. Mikolov, T., et al.: Efficient estimation of word representations in vector space. arXiv preprint arXiv:1301.3781 (2013)
12. Mintz, M., Bills, S., Snow, R., Jurafsky, D.: Distant supervision for relation extraction without labeled data. Proc. ACL-IJCNLP **2009**, 1003–1011 (2009)

13. Morgan, A.A., Hirschman, L., Colosimo, M., Yeh, A.S., Colombe, J.B.: Gene name identification and normalization using a model organism database. J. Biomed. Inform. **37**(6), 396–410 (2004)
14. Silla, C.N., Freitas, A.A.: A survey of hierarchical classification across different application domains. Data Min. Knowl. Disc. **22**, 31–72 (2011)
15. Snow, R., Jurafsky, D., Ng, A.: Learning syntactic patterns for automatic hypernym discovery. In: Advances in Neural Information Processing Systems, vol. 17 (2004)
16. Wang, L.L., Bhagavatula, C., Neumann, M., et al.: Ontology alignment in the biomedical domain using entity definitions and context. In: Proceedings of the BioNLP 2018 Workshop, pp. 47–55 (2018)
17. http://CaLiGraph.org/statistics.html
18. https://en.wikipedia.org/
19. https://relatedwords.org/
20. https://spacy.io/usage/processing-pipelines
21. https://www.DBpedia.org/resources/ontology/

Quantitative Analysis of Scholarly References on YouTube

Focusing on Their Research Fields and Contributors

Jiro Kikkawa[✉][ID], Masao Takaku[ID], and Fuyuki Yoshikane

University of Tsukuba, Ibaraki, Japan
{jiro,masao,fuyuki}@slis.tsukuba.ac.jp

Abstract. Scholarly communication through video by various people and institutions has spread more and more in recent years and impacts the dissemination of scholarly knowledge and people's daily lives. However, most of the previous works were conducted to measure the impacts of these research outputs as Altmetrics studies; little is known about characteristics and trends of scholarly articles and their associated videos. E.g., how many of these articles and videos are available since when?, and who has been publishing these videos? Hence, we analyzed 410,101 articles with 228,192 unique DOIs referenced in 137,629 videos uploaded by 39,416 channels, using data provided by Altmetric.com. As a result, the total number of scholarly references on YouTube has increased rapidly since 2016 and has continued to grow. The top research fields of scholarly articles were Clinical Medicine and Multidisciplinary consistently. The most common channels in the number of videos associated with scholarly references were hosted by publishers and academic societies, SciShow, and other individuals/organizations.

Keywords: YouTube · Scholarly Communication · Bibliometrics · Altmetrics

1 Introduction

Along with the mass digitization of scholarly articles, their rapid dissemination on social media has been expanding. In addition, scholarly communication through video by various people and institutions has spread more and more in recent years. Compared to citations between scholarly articles, these non-traditional mentions have been focused on as a new source to measure the impact of research on society in general. A number of research to measure these new impacts have been conducted as the research of Altmetrics, which stands for alternative metrics. Besides, researchers are increasingly supplementing scholarly articles with video summaries to bridge the gap with society and enhance engagement with a broader audience. YouTube, the largest online video platform is used to share various videos including content related to these kinds of scholarly knowledge.

D. H. Goh et al. (Eds.): ICADL 2023, LNCS 14457, pp. 149–158, 2023.
https://doi.org/10.1007/978-981-99-8085-7_13

Understanding these trends in the videos related to research articles is essential from the perspective of distributing scholarly information in the future and their impacts on various people and society in general. However, little is known about the relationship between scholarly articles and videos associated with them [2,22]. For instance, Shaikh et al. [19] revealed that the most common research fields of scholarly articles referenced on YouTube videos are medicine and biochemistry, but it is unknown whether the most common research fields have been changing over the years. Moreover, more details of the research fields and topics are unknown. Bonnevie et al. [7] pointed out that video abstracts, which summarize each research provided by researchers and publishers as short videos, contribute to an increase in the number of views of research outcomes through a case study of the New England Journal of Medicine. They indicated that video abstracts could earn a small increase in citations and social attention. However, there is a lack of investigations on the following aspects of scholarly articles and their associated videos. For instance, how many of these articles and videos are available since when? and who has been publishing these videos?

As described above, various videos associated with scholarly content have been available in online communities. These videos play an important role in diffusing scholarly knowledge to a diverse audience, and it is possible to influence their daily lives. Considering this background, we clarify the characteristics of scholarly references and their videos through analyses of (1) Temporal changes in the number of scholarly references and the videos and channels associated with them, (2) Trends in research fields of scholarly references and characteristics of the most common channels for uploading videos associated with these references by answering the following research questions (hereinafter, referred to as RQs).

RQ1 How do the numbers of scholarly references and the associated videos and channels transition over time?

RQ2 Do the highly referenced research fields of scholarly references change over time?

RQ3 What kind of YouTube channels (contributors) are the most common in the number of scholarly references and videos?

2   Related Work

Scholarly References on YouTube Videos. In a review of the research on the scholarly usage of social media and Altmetrics, Sugimoto et al. [22] pointed out that limited studies specifically focus on video-sharing platforms. As one of the few such studies, Shaikh et al. [19] analyzed scholarly articles referenced on YouTube videos using the data obtained from Altmetric.com, a well-known service and data provider for Altmetrics. Their findings revealed that the most common research fields of scholarly articles referenced in YouTube videos were medicine and biochemistry, based on Scopus categories, regardless of the publication year of the articles. They have contributed valuable insights on scholarly references on YouTube, but further investigations are needed to understand the characteristics in more detail. Thus, we analyze scholarly references on YouTube to reveal time-series changes in the most common research fields based on the published date of each video, and more detailed topics of each field.

Video Abstracts and Their Impact on Citations and Presence. With the digitization of scholarly information, there is a movement to create and publish video abstracts. Spicer [20] defined the video abstract as "a video presentation corresponding to a specific science research article, which typically communicates the background of a study, methods used, study results and potential implications through the use of images, audio, video clips, and text." The Journal of Visualized Experiments (JoVE) [15], launched in 2006, is a pioneering journal that adopted video abstracts. After that, multiple journals adopted video abstracts, and research on these videos has been conducted in bibliometrics communities mainly to determine whether video abstracts increase citations and boost social attention, but no consensus has been reached [1, 7, 20, 23]. Moreover, Spicer [20] suggested that YouTube would work as a reasonable channel to outreach scholarly articles to a wider audience. However, little is known about how many video abstracts are available on YouTube and which publishers hosted them. Thus, we analyze video abstracts and their channels on YouTube in this study.

3   Materials and Methods

We built the dataset through the following four steps.

In step 1, we collected scholarly references on YouTube via Altmetric Explorer [3,4] provided by Altmetric.com. Specifically, we used the search conditions where the target is "all mentions," and the source type is "Videos" on April 10th, 2023, and obtained 457,453 scholarly references on 153,398 YouTube videos. This data includes identifiers of scholarly articles such as DOI, PubMed ID, and PubMed Central ID derived from the values directly written in the video description text or those values converted from the other URIs written in the description by Altmetric.com. The first author manually confirmed and added the corresponding DOI values to the dataset based on the PubMed ID and PubMed Central ID when the DOI values were empty. If we got no DOI information, we excluded the data.

In step 2, we obtained Crossref metadata [10] for each DOI via the Crossref REST API [11] and extracted ISSN numbers for retrieving research field information at the step 3. We excluded the data if the Crossref metadata did not include ISSN numbers.

In step 3, we associated the research fields of the Essential Science Indicators (ESI) and the Web of Science categories with each DOI by matching ISSN numbers to the ESI journal list [8] and the Web of Science journal list [9], respectively. The ESI journal list represents journal names, research fields consisting of 22 categories, and ISSN numbers. As for the Web of Science journal list, we collected the Science Citation Index Expanded (SCIE), Social Sciences Citation

Index (SSCI), Arts & Humanities Citation Index (AHCI), and Emerging Sources Citation Index (ESCI). These lists represent journal names, research fields consisting of 260 categories, and ISSN numbers. We converted these data into pairs of ISSN numbers and research fields, and associated with each DOI. We excluded the data if the ISSN numbers did not match the ESI categories.

In step 4, we obtained each YouTube video and channel data included in the dataset by using YouTube Data API [14]. We omitted the data if the video and channel metadata were unavailable via YouTube Data API or the video length was zero as an error.

We removed a total of 47,352 records out of 457,453 scholarly references obtained from Altmetric Explorer by applying the conditions above.

4 Results and Discussion

4.1 Temporal Changes in the Number of Scholarly References and the Videos and Channels Associated with Them

RQ1 How do the numbers of scholarly references and the associated videos and channels transition over time?

Table 1. Number of scholarly references and the videos and channels associated with them for each year based on the published date of each video

Year	# of total DOIs	# of unique DOIs	# of unique Videos	# of unique Channels
2006	18	17	8	7
2007	173	105	115	42
2008	526	311	330	136
2009	897	587	701	329
2010	1,962	1,130	1,536	447
2011	2,411	1,716	1,746	703
2012	4,706	3,272	3,613	1,305
2013	6,343	4,984	4,642	1,586
2014	8,861	7,072	6,022	2,079
2015	9,972	8,518	6,177	1,834
2016	15,829	12,747	7,046	2,731
2017	31,548	22,382	12,049	4,830
2018	42,595	31,637	14,364	5,842
2019	49,921	35,908	14,042	5,650
2020	44,984	33,878	11,677	5,518
2021	73,546	51,808	19,160	7,522
2022	87,392	60,717	27,041	7,258
2023	28,417	20,147	7,360	2,861
Overall	410,101	228,192	137,629	39,416

Table 1 shows the total and unique numbers of DOIs referenced on YouTube videos based on the published date of each video, as well as the unique numbers of the corresponding videos and their channels for each year. We note that the data in 2023 was not one year but three months. As a whole, 410,101 scholarly articles corresponding to 228,192 unique DOIs were referenced on 137,629 videos uploaded by 39,416 channels. The total and unique DOIs, unique videos, and unique channels have been growing over the years. Regarding the total and unique numbers of DOIs, they were small, from a few dozen to several hundred in 2006–2009; they exceeded 1,000 and 10,000 in 2010 and 2016, respectively; and their size has continued to grow since 2017. Focusing on the gap between the total and unique number of DOIs each year, the same DOIs tend to be referenced across multiple years rather than in the same year.

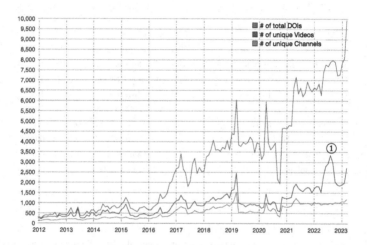

Fig. 1. Monthly plot of the time-series transitions for the scholarly references and the videos and channels associated with them since January 2012 based on the published date of each video. Dashed lines show the month of January for each year.

Figure 1 shows the monthly plot of the time-series transition for scholarly references, videos, and channels since 2012 based on the published date of each video. The transition from 2006 to 2011 is not shown because their size is small and due to space limitations. The size of DOIs has increased rapidly since 2016, with a more significant gap compared to the size of videos and channels. As for videos, it has remained over 500 per month since 2016 and over 1,000 per month since 2021. The spike seen in 2022 (① in Fig. 1) was caused by uploading more than 1,000 videos per month by the "JoVE (Journal of Visualized Experiments)" channel. As we described in Sect. 2, JoVE is a peer-reviewed scientific video journal. According to the description texts of these videos, they are preview versions, and full versions of video abstracts are provided on the publisher's website for the subscribers. As for channels, it has been stable at around 500 per month since 2017 and around 1,000 per month since 2021.

4.2 Trends in Research Fields of Scholarly References and Characteristics of the Most Common Channels for Uploading Videos Associated with These References

RQ2 Do the highly referenced research fields of scholarly references change over time?

Table 2. Distribution of the ESI categories corresponding to unique DOIs (n=187,102)

#	ESI category		#	ESI category	
1	Clinical Medicine	28.94%	12	Environment/Ecology	1.99%
2	Multidisciplinary	14.50%	13	Chemistry	1.95%
3	Biology & Biochemistry	7.60%	14	Microbiology	1.87%
4	Neuroscience & Behavior	6.61%	15	Geosciences	1.86%
5	Psychiatry/Psychology	6.17%	16	Space Science	1.50%
6	Agricultural Sciences	5.36%	17	Physics	1.38%
7	Social Sciences, General	4.23%	18	Engineering	1.02%
8	Pharmacology & Toxicology	3.98%	19	Materials Science	0.76%
9	Molecular Biology & Genetics	3.90%	20	Economics & Business	0.69%
10	Plant & Animal Science	3.04%	21	Computer Science	0.35%
11	Immunology	2.17%	22	Mathematics	0.15%

Table 3. Top 2 ESI categories corresponding to scholarly references since 2012 based on the published date of each video

Year	Total	1st category		2nd category	
2012	3,795	Multidisciplinary	19.10%	Clinical Medicine	16.15%
2013	4,636	Clinical Medicine	20.90%	Multidisciplinary	20.51%
2014	7,071	Clinical Medicine	22.84%	Multidisciplinary	18.78%
2015	7,893	Clinical Medicine	24.62%	Multidisciplinary	19.33%
2016	12,813	Clinical Medicine	32.92%	Multidisciplinary	14.42%
2017	25,913	Clinical Medicine	35.57%	Multidisciplinary	13.05%
2018	35,013	Clinical Medicine	35.16%	Multidisciplinary	11.45%
2019	42,227	Clinical Medicine	37.22%	Biology & Biochemistry	9.70%
2020	37,535	Clinical Medicine	34.93%	Multidisciplinary	9.48%
2021	61,444	Clinical Medicine	36.52%	Multidisciplinary	9.29%
2022	74,060	Clinical Medicine	34.71%	Multidisciplinary	16.19%
2023	23,634	Clinical Medicine	35.21%	Multidisciplinary	9.53%

Table 2 shows the distributions of the ESI categories corresponding to unique DOIs. Of 228,192 unique DOIs on the dataset, 187,099 DOIs (88.19%) were matched to the ESI categories based on their ISSN numbers, while 41,093

(18.01%) were excluded because of not matched to the categories. Out of 187,099 DOIs with the ESI categories, 187,096 DOIs were matched to one category, and 3 DOIs were matched to two categories. As a result, the total number of the ESI categories corresponding to 187,099 DOIs was 187,102. The most common ESI category was Clinical Medicine at 28.94% ($= 54,151/187,102 * 100$), followed by Multidisciplinary (14.50%) and Biology & Biochemistry (7.60%).

Table 3 shows the top 2 ESI categories corresponding to scholarly references for each year since 2012. The top 2 categories for each year were Clinical Medicine, Multidisciplinary, and Biology & Biochemistry. These categories were the same as the top categories shown in Table 2. With the exception of 2012, Clinical Medicine accounted for the highest percentage in all years. In addition, while the percentage of Clinical Medicine in 2013–2015 was 20 percent level, it has been 30 percent level since 2016, indicating that the content with references to scholarly articles in this field has been increasing over the years. The 2nd most common category was Multidisciplinary, with the exception of 2012 and 2019. Thus, we observed that the highly referenced research fields of scholarly references do not change over time.

Regarding the more detailed research fields, out of 187,099 unique DOIs matched to the ESI categories, 186,555 were matched to at least one category of the Web of Science based on their ISSN numbers. The most common category was "Nutrition & Dietetics" at 23.64% ($44,106/186,555 * 100$), followed by "Multidisciplinary Sciences," "Sport Sciences," "Medicine, General & Internal," and "Endocrinology & Metabolism" (22.05%, 13.80%, 11.25%, and 10.50%, respectively).

RQ3 What kind of YouTube channels (contributors) are the most common in the number of scholarly references and videos?

Table 4. Top 12 channels for the number of videos associated with scholarly references. Channels are classified into three groups by highlighted color as follows. Yellow shows the publisher and academic societies, green shows the SciShow series channels, and blue shows the channels hosted by news media.

#	Videos associated with scholarly references		Total DOIs	Unique DOIs	Channel ID	Title
1	6,730	78.02%	6,750	6,612	@jovejournal	JoVE
2	2,287	69.18%	12,898	12,506	@scishow	SciShow
3	1,640	86.00%	1,677	1,623	@researchsquare	Research Square
4	1,234	20.99%	1,235	1,235	@sciencevio	ScienceVio
5	1,114	44.42%	1,114	1,041	@dovemedicalpress	Dove Medical Press
6	1,055	26.53%	1,413	1,392	@seeker	Seeker
7	772	33.02%	5,782	3,754	@thomasdelauerofficial	Thomas DeLauer
8	696	21.96%	1,091	1,039	@whatdamath	Anton Petrov
9	696	44.73%	717	700	@cellvideoabstracts	Cell Press
10	673	16.69%	703	567	@springervideos	SpringerVideos
11	636	15.13%	636	632	@theofficialacm	ACM
12	593	29.98%	2,793	5	@vikadiamante4k	Vika Diamante

Table 4 shows the top 12 channels for the number of videos associated with scholarly references. For instance, JoVE is the 1st ranked channel in the number of videos associated with scholarly references. Out of 8,626 videos uploaded by this channel, 6,730 videos (78.02%) contain scholarly references in their description text; a total of 6,750 DOIs and unique 6,612 DOIs correspond to these references.

Of the channels, #1, #3, #5, #9, #10, and #11 in Table 4 were hosted by the publishers and academic societies. JoVE (#1) uploaded the preview versions of video abstracts in the Journal of Visualized Experiments as described in Sect. 4.1. Research Square (#3) is a preprint platform; this channel uploaded 1,640 videos with 1,677 DOIs; 654 and 523 out of these 1,677 DOIs were scholarly articles published in the "Microbiome" and the "Communication and Signaling," respectively. These journals adopted video abstracts called the Video Bytes [16], which are one or two minutes video summaries provided via Research Square [5,6]. SpringerVideos (#10) is the channel of SpringerNature; they adopted Video Bytes [21] and published them on their own channel. As for Dove Medical Press (#5) and Cell Press (#9), their journals have the option to submit video abstracts and encourage submitting them along with the research papers [12,13]. Thus, the majority of the videos published by these channels were video abstracts. As for ACM (Association for Computing Machinery, #11), they uploaded videos referring to their international conference proceedings papers. For the percentage of videos with scholarly references of these channels, JoVE and Research Square are high at more than 70%, but SpringerVideos and ACM are low at less than 20%.

SciShow (#2 in Table 4) is the channel uploading videos related to scientific subjects such as science, news, history, particle physics, chemistry, biology, and psychology [17,18]. Seeker (#6) is the channel hosted by Verge, which is American technology news media. As for other channels, i.e., #4, #7–8, and #12 in Table 4 were hosted by other individuals and organizations.

5   Conclusion

We analyzed scholarly references on YouTube using the data provided by Altmteric.com. As a result, 410,101 articles corresponding to 228,192 unique DOIs were referenced on 137,629 videos uploaded by 39,416 channels as of April 10th, 2023. The total number of scholarly references on YouTube has increased rapidly since 2016 and has continued to grow. The top research fields of scholarly articles were Clinical Medicine and Multidisciplinary, regardless of the year of each video published. The most common channels in the number of videos associated with scholarly references were hosted by publishers and academic societies, SciShow, and other individuals/organizations.

As the limitations of this study, we were unable to analyze the scholarly references on YouTube not covered by Altmetric.com. In particular, YouTube channels tracked by Altmetric.com are curated, so even if videos with scholarly references exist, they could not be included in the dataset [3]. In addition, target scholarly references are limited to the ones written in the description text of the videos with identifiers such as DOI and PubMed ID. We will develop a methodology to capture more comprehensive YouTube videos with scholarly references and analyze them as future work.

Acknowledgments. This work was partially supported by JSPS KAKENHI Grant Numbers JP22K18147, JP21K12592, and JP23K11761. We are grateful to Altmetric.com (https://www.altmetric.com/) for providing valuable data through the researcher data access program.

References

1. Aggarwal, V.: Visual abstracts do not increase some impact scores more than conventional abstracts of clinical research: a retrospective cohort study. Health Inf. Lib. J. **38**(4), 259–267 (2021). https://doi.org/10.1111/hir.12376
2. Allgaier, J.: Science and medicine on YouTube. In: Hunsinger, J., Allen, M.M., Klastrup, L. (eds.) Second International Handbook of Internet Research, pp. 7–27. Springer, Dordrecht (2020). https://doi.org/10.1007/978-94-024-1555-1_1
3. Altmetric: YouTube tracking : Altmetric (2020). https://help.altmetric.com/support/solutions/articles/6000236682-youtube
4. Altmetric: Introduction to the Altmetric Explorer (2023). https://help.altmetric.com/support/solutions/articles/6000240622-introduction-to-the-altmetric-explorer
5. BioMed Central: Cell Communication and Signaling | Submission guidelines (2023). https://biosignaling.biomedcentral.com/submission-guidelines
6. BioMed Central: Microbiome | Submission guidelines (2023). https://microbiomejournal.biomedcentral.com/submission-guidelines
7. Bonnevie, T., et al.: Video abstracts are associated with an increase in research reports citations, views and social attention: a cross-sectional study. Scientometrics (2023). https://doi.org/10.1007/s11192-023-04675-9
8. Clarivate: ESI Journal List (2023). https://esi.help.clarivate.com/Content/journal-list.htm
9. Clarivate: Web of Science Master Journal List - Collection List Downloads (2023). https://mjl.clarivate.com/collection-list-downloads
10. Crossref: Crossref Metadata API JSON Format (2023). https://github.com/CrossRef/rest-api-doc/blob/master/api_format.md
11. Crossref: Crossref REST API (2023). https://api.crossref.org/
12. Dove Press: Medical Research Papers Preparation & Submission Guidelines | Dove Press | Dove Press Author guidelines (2023). https://www.dovepress.com/author-guidelines
13. Elsevier: Video guidelines: Cell Press (2023). https://www.cell.com/video-guidelines
14. Google for Developers: YouTube Data API (2023). https://developers.google.com/youtube/v3
15. MyJoVE Corporation: JoVE Journal (2023). https://www.jove.com/journal
16. Research Square: Research Promotion | Research Square (2023). https://www.researchsquare.com/researchers/promotion
17. SciShow: Channels - SciShow (2023). https://www.scishow.com/channels/
18. SciShow: SciShow (2023). https://www.scishow.com/

19. Shaikh, A.R., Alhoori, H., Sun, M.: YouTube and science: models for research impact. Scientometrics **128**(2), 933–955 (2023). https://doi.org/10.1007/s11192-022-04574-5

20. Spicer, S.: Exploring Video Abstracts in Science Journals: An Overview and Case Study. J. Librarianship Schol. Commun. **2**(22) (2014). https://doi.org/10.7710/2162-3309.1110

21. SpringerNature: Promote your publication | For Researchers | Springer Nature (2023). https://www.springernature.com/gp/researchers/publication-promotion

22. Sugimoto, C.R., Work, S., Larivière, V., Haustein, S.: Scholarly use of social media and altmetrics: a review of the literature. J. Am. Soc. Inf. Sci. **68**(9), 2037–2062 (2017). https://doi.org/10.1002/asi.23833

23. Zong, Q., Xie, Y., Tuo, R., Huang, J., Yang, Y.: The impact of video abstract on citation counts: evidence from a retrospective cohort study of New Journal of Physics. Scientometrics **119**(3), 1715–1727 (2019). https://doi.org/10.1007/s11192-019-03108-w

TweetVi: A Tweet Visualisation Dashboard for Automatic Topic Classification and Sentiment Analysis

Matthew Laurence William Graham[1(✉)], Huilan Zhu[1(✉)],
Hamzah Osop[2(✉)] (iD), Basem Suleiman[1,3(✉)] (iD), Yixuan Zhang[1(✉)],
Ruoxia Wang[1], and Xiaoyu Xu[1(✉)]

[1] School of Computer Science, University of Sydney, Camperdown, Australia
{mgra6502,hzhu4249,yzha7679,rwan0849,xixu7003}@uni.sydney.edu.au,
basem.suleiman@sydney.edu.au
[2] Wee Kim Wee School of Communication and Information, Nanyang Technological
University, Singapore, Singapore
hamzah.osop@ntu.edu.sg
[3] School of Computer Science and Engineering, University of New South Wales,
Kensington, Australia

Abstract. Social media has witnessed a remarkable surge in popularity, serving as a platform where individuals express their views on crucial subjects, including politics, infectious diseases, social movements, and security issues. This profusion of readily accessible information empowers decision-makers and stakeholders to shape policies and strategies grounded in statistical insights into societal dynamics. To facilitate an in-depth collaborative analysis of social trends and public sentiment, we developed TweetVi - an interactive dashboard. Within the interactive dashboard, we've developed a pipeline encompassing three machine-learning components: language detection, spam detection, and sentiment analysis. This collaborative platform further provides analytical results on topical sentiments and trends, fostering a deeper understanding of the social landscape. The TweetVi application empowers users to gain valuable insights into evolving social narratives and sentiments, facilitating evidence-based decision-making in a dynamic online environment.

Keywords: Visualisation dashboard · Language detection · Sentiment detection · Topic modeling · Spam detection

1 Introduction

The advent of social media platforms has changed the way we connect, communicate, and access news and current events in the digital age [1]. Among them, Twitter aims to help people share and discover news, information, and interests with the world and has gradually become one of the essential tools for our communication and information sharing. However, every second, Twitter generates massive amounts of data, including tweets, user interactions, trends, and

D. H. Goh et al. (Eds.): ICADL 2023, LNCS 14457, pp. 159–166, 2023.
https://doi.org/10.1007/978-981-99-8085-7_14

engagement metrics, which is difficult to monitor and analyse [2]. Therefore, Twitter's interactive dashboard has become an indispensable tool for identifying and displaying feeds of emerging events in real-time and allowing users to gain insights.

The project aims to present valuable summaries of events in a visually appealing and easy-to-understand form through techniques of data analysis, visualisation of trends, sentiment analysis, and real-time updates. This process entails extracting data from Twitter, performing preprocessing tasks, and storing the obtained information securely. Additionally, we employ unsupervised learning to identify emerging themes in the collected data, display temporal analysis and perform sentiment analysis on said themes.

2   TweetVi Conceptualisation

TweetVi is constructed in data and analysis focused parts. Deployed with Django, Postgresql, Nginx, Redis and React, TweetVi provided a three-step approach comprised of (i) *Filtering*, (ii) *Embedding* and (iii) *Clustering* (see Fig. 1). TweetVi provided users with increasingly informative statistics, metrics and visualisations after every stage to guide them through the analytic process.

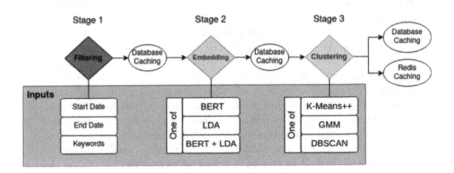

Fig. 1. User Analytic Workflow

2.1   Data Collection and Preprocessing

Approximately 3.3 million tweets were collected over eleven weeks using the Twitter Streaming API [3]. Streaming rules were created to avoid tweets containing common explicit phrases and spam phrases as identified by Burns [4], and those officially marked as advertisements or retweets. Tweets were processed using techniques employed by Osop [5] including URL removal, tokenisation and parts of speech tagging to isolate relevant information. These processed tweets were passed to a pipeline that filtered out tweets identified as non-English or spam using machine learning models. Both sentiment scores and BERT embedding of each tweet were calculated and stored in the database.

2.2   Filtering

Language Detection. A novel vectorisation technique, *Inclusive Term Document Frequency* (ITDF), was developed as a part of a pipeline that also includes Standard Scaler (SS), Cosine Kernel Principal Component Analysis (CKPCA) and Support Vector Machine (SVM) with Radial Basis Function (RBF) Kernel to filter English tweets among all collected tweets. The ITDF vectorisation technique is inspired by Bag of Words (BoW) [6] and TF-IDF [7]. This ITDF vectorisation technique is formalised as

$$w_{i,j} = \begin{cases} 0 & tf_{i,j} = 0 \\ \frac{df_i}{N} & tf_{i,j} \neq 0 \end{cases}$$

where:

$w_{i,j}$ = the weight of term i in document j
$tf_{i,j}$ = the number of occurrences of term i in document j
df_i = the number of documents containing term i
N = number of documents

This vectorisation was applied to tweets from the *TweetLID* [8] and *Tweet Retriever* [9] datasets. CKPCA was applied to the vectorisation to improve separability of classes in sparse vectorisations [10] before training a SVM with RBF kernel. After fine-tuning with the ITDF using two-fold cross validation, the language detection model's best performance was achieved by the SVM pipeline with our novel ITDF vectoriser, SS, CKPCA and outlier regularisation parameter 'C' value of 0.75, with 95.3% accuracy.

Spam Detection. TF-IDF Vectorisation was applied to one-gram and two-gram tokenisations of sms data from the *SMS Spam Collection* dataset [11]. The Spam Detection pipeline includes TF-IDF vectorisation and Linear SVM. The dataset was split into 80% training and 20% testing sets for the best model determination. Grid search with five-fold cross-validation was used to select the optimal pipeline for spam detection. Therefore, the optimised hyperparameters were a combination of one and two grams for TF-IDF, followed by a cost value of '1' for the linear SVM model, achieving a weighted F1-score of 0.983.

2.3   Topic Modeling

Latent Dirichlet Allocation (LDA) and Bidirectional Encoder Representations from Transformers (BERT) models were applied to the tweets to generate an embedding in vector space. Additionally, LDA and BERT embeddings were used in combination to maintain textual information and produce contextual topic identification [5]. A two-dimensional linear PCA model was applied to the embedding output for visual inference and data storage considerations. Next, unsupervised learning algorithms, including K-Means++, Gaussian Mixture Models (GMM), and Density-Based Spatial Clustering of Applications with

Noise (DBSCAN), were used to identify clusters in the dataset based on the computed embedding. Silhouette Scores and the Calinski-Harabasz Score were calculated to evaluate clustering quality. For users to select the best clustering method.

See Fig. 2 for model overview.

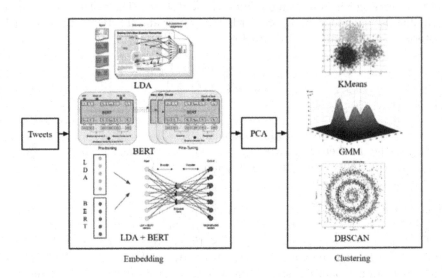

Fig. 2. Topic modelling flowchart

Sentiment Analysis. A RoBERTa model trained on 58 million tweets [12] was used as the base for sentiment analysis. While the original model was trained to classify sentiment as positive, negative or neutral, the output layer was altered to output binary results of positive and negative results.

A sample of 10,000 tweets was taken from the *Sentinment 140* dataset [13] to train the slightly altered model using transfer learning. The binary classification had softmax applied to produce a continuous real valued output $S_T \in [-1, 1]$.

The sentiment of 1,000 collected tweets was manually annotated for the test set. The performance of the different vectorisers and classifiers such as Naive Bayes, SVM, *VaderSentiment*, and *RoBERTa* were evaluated on the validation set. It was observed that employing a transfer learning approach to train the RoBERTa model on downstream tasks, based on RoBERTa with a hidden layer size of 192 and a learning rate of 1e−5, resulted in improved performance (see Table 1).

Table 1. Sentiment Analysis Results

Model	BoW + CKPCA + SVM	BoW + CKPCA + Gaussian Naive Bayes	VaderSentiment	RoBerTa
Training time	1173.52 s	306.65 s	0 s	0 s
Testing time	367.07 s	26.17 s	0.52 s	1031.01 s
Accuracy	0.48	0.57	0.66	0.85
Precision	0.54	0.54	0.73	0.85
Recall	0.48	0.57	0.66	0.85
F1	0.45	0.45	0.65	0.85
MCC	0.05	0.03	0.40	0.70

3   TweetVi Demonstration

An interactive dashboard was developed for users to filter tweets, define custom topics of interest, and conduct popularity and sentiment analysis through informative visualisations. As an illustrative example, a case study was conducted using the keywords "twitter", "elon", "musk", and "trump" between the 20th and 27th of October 2022.

Users began by selecting the desired embedding settings, between LDA with a dimensionality range from 2 to 9, or BERT with a dimensionality of 384 or 768. For LDA, a dimensionality of 2 would result in two topics being generated. While for BERT, the dimensionality referred to the size of embeddings. The dimensionality of 384 is light-weight and carries less semantic meaning. Subsequently, users would choose the clustering parameters between KMeans++ suited for homogeneous circular clusters, GMM for elliptical clusters, and DBSCAN for irregularly shaped clusters. In this case, the clustering results were based on DBSCAN with an epsilon of 0.05 and 5 min neighbours (see Fig. 3).

Fig. 3. User Input Panels for Embedding (left) and Clustering (right) Settings

After each stage of user input, the dashboard displayed progressive visualisations showcasing the performance of the selected parameters (see Fig. 4). The principal component scatter-plot assists users in selecting clustering settings after the embedding process. Subsequently, word clouds are used to showcase trending keywords and sentiment analysis results for the identified topics.

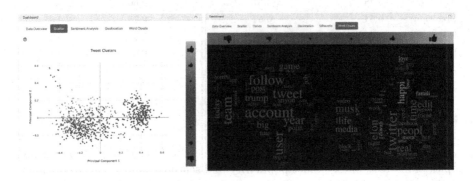

Fig. 4. Graphics Following the Embedding (left) and Clustering (right) Settings

In addition, sentiment trends were depicted using a line chart organised by topic cluster. Users explored an interactive table to view associated tweets, arranged by their assigned clusters, along with other relevant details (see Fig. 5).

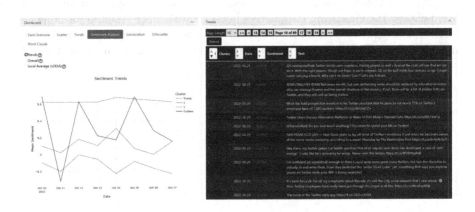

Fig. 5. Sentiment Trends by Topic Cluster

A local minimum was observed on October 21st, 2022 for the numbered '1' cluster sentiment trend-line. This dip could be correlated with the Washington Post article on Musk's plan to reduce the Twitter workforce by 75%, indicating public dissatisfaction regarding the layoffs. The table in Fig. 5 showed supporting evidence for this hypothesis with several tweets discussing the incident.

Accompanied by over 3 million tweets collected over 44 days from September to October 2022, this intuitive and interactive dashboard adopts similar models as in previous research and vastly improves efficiency in model selection and evaluation for tweet topic modeling. This is achieved by enabling the collection, filtering, topic modeling, and visualization of vast user-generated tweet content, allowing investigations into user perceptions to be analyzed by topics. Furthermore, the dashboard also allows users to collaborate remotely and in real-time, with the potential to crowdsource topic labeling and quality assessment for enhanced insights and analysis.

The following website provides access to the datasets, model implementation, dashboard, and detailed experimental results of the work presented in this paper: https://topstop.info:8080.

References

1. Keogh, S.: Social media: a guide for researchers. Record. Manag. J. **21** (2011). https://doi.org/10.1108/09565691111152134
2. Sarker, A., Malone, D., Gonzalez, G.: Authors' reply to jouanjus and colleagues' comment on "social media mining for toxicovigilance: automatic monitoring of prescription medication abuse from twitter". Drug Saf. **40** (2017). https://doi.org/10.1007/s40264-016-0498-6
3. Developer Platform. Getting started with the twitter API. developer platform (2022). https://developer.twitter.com/en/docs/twitter-api/getting-started/about-twitter-api
4. Burns, R.: 188 spam words to avoid: how to stay out of spam email filters. active campaign (2022). https://www.activecampaign.com/blog/spam-words
5. Osop, H., Suleiman, B., Lakhdari, A.: 14 days later: temporal topical shifts in COVID-19 related tweets after pandemic declaration. In: Meiselwitz, G. (ed.) HCII 2022. LNCS, vol. 13315, pp. 358–369. Springer, Cham (2022). https://doi.org/10.1007/978-3-031-05061-9_26
6. Harris, Z.S.: Distributional Structure. In: Hiz, H. (ed.) Papers on Syntax, pp. 3–22. Springer, Dordrecht (1981). https://doi.org/10.1007/978-94-009-8467-7_1 ISBN 978-94-009-8467-7
7. Sparck Jones, K.: A statistical interpretation of term specificity and its application in retrieval, pp. 132–142. Taylor Graham Publishing, GBR (1988). ISBN 0947568212
8. Zubiaga, A., et al.: Tweetlid: a benchmark for tweet language identification. Lang. Resour. Eval. **50**, 729–766 (2016). https://doi.org/10.1007/s10579-015-9317-4
9. Mozetič, I., Grčar, M., Smailović, J.: Multilingual twitter sentiment classification: the role of human annotators. PLoS ONE **11**, 729–766 (2016). https://doi.org/10.1371/journal.pone.0155036
10. Liu, Z., Xu, H.: Kernel parameter selection for support vector machine classification. J. Algorithms Comput. Technol. **8**(2), 163–177 (2014). https://doi.org/10.1260/1748-3018.8.2.163
11. Almeida, T., Hidalgo,J.: SMS Spam Collection. UCI Machine Learning Repository (2012). https://doi.org/10.24432/C5CC84

12. Barbieri, F., Saggion, H.: Automatic detection of irony and humour in twitter. In International Conference on Innovative Computing and Cloud Computing (2014). https://api.semanticscholar.org/CorpusID:2139885
13. Go, A., Bhayani, R., Huang, L.: Twitter sentiment classification using distant supervision. CS224N Project Report (2009)

Health Information Encountering: Topic Modelling and Sentiment Analysis of Pre- and Current-COVID-19 Tweets

Hamzah Osop[(⊠)] [iD], Jie Yang Wong, Shwe Waddy Lwin, and Chei Sian Lee

Wee Kim Wee School of Communication and Information, Nanyang Technological University, Singapore, Singapore

{hamzah.osop,leecs}@ntu.edu.sg, {jwong157,shwe0016}@e.ntu.edu.sg

Abstract. Twitter has become a platform for online health information seeking and sharing, especially during the COVID-19 pandemic. Prior studies revealed evidence of health information topics in Twitter discussions, but the analysis was primarily on tweets made before or during the pandemic. This research investigated tweets made pre- and current-COVID era for health information content and information encountering. *COVD19-* and *COVD23 +* datasets containing 13,667 and 9,855 tweets were analysed and clustered into four health-related topics using Convolutional Neural Network. We compared the tweet distribution and tweet emotions for content and sentiment analysis. We found a higher proportion of tweets in the *Medication & Treatment* topic and greater *Negative* and *Ambiguous* emotions in the *COVD23 +* dataset, with tweet discussions focusing more on diabetes and its relationship with COVID-19. Elements of information encountering exist based on Panahi's and Jiang's IE model, with a decrease in encountering diabetes prevention and management information during the pandemic.

Keywords: Information Encountering · Topic Modelling · Sentiment Analysis · Emotion Analysis · COVID-19 · Diabetes

1 Introduction

The COVID-19 pandemic brought huge adverse social and health impacts to the massive global population. Many countries implemented strict movement and safe distancing controls to hinder the spread of infection, limiting physical socialisation and communication activities, disrupting access to healthcare resources, and increasing the risk of other health outcomes [1]. Fortunately, accessibility to social media tools aided users' need for health information seeking and sharing [2] and facilitated information encountering [3]. Evidently, a significant increase in tweets related to COVID-19 was observed right after the pandemic declaration [4], suggesting a continued endeavour to share information.

Twitter plays a significant role in health information sharing, allowing for quick and easy dissemination of information to large and diverse audiences [5]. Through Twitter, healthcare organisations, government agencies and individuals can share health-related news and information [6] and engage patients in conversations [7, 8]. This fills the need

D. H. Goh et al. (Eds.): ICADL 2023, LNCS 14457, pp. 167–177, 2023.
https://doi.org/10.1007/978-981-99-8085-7_15

for health information and provides emotional support to other patients and caregivers with similar challenges [7, 9].

Many studies have uncovered evolving public discussion themes and sentiments during the COVID-19 pandemic [10–12]. Understanding the sentiment in health-related tweets helps researchers and public health organisations gain insights into public opinion on various health issues. [28] found emotions of *Fear* and *Sadness* exhibited more during the pandemic, whereby not many studies have collectively considered the possible differences in these discussion themes and sentiments before and during the pandemic. Such studies can reveal the impact of a pandemic on users' sentiments and information encountering. Therefore, this study conducts sentiment analysis to shed light on the information encountered by users searching for diabetes tweets before and during the COVID-19 pandemic to address the following research questions:

- What insights were gained from analysing social media data regarding the public's views and attitudes towards diabetes?
- How has the public discourse on social media regarding diabetes changed over time, and what factors may have influenced these changes?
- What are the trends of diabetes-related information over time, and how do these trends correlate with shifts in sentiments?

2   Related Works

2.1   Eliciting Health-Related Information

Understanding health information from vast user-generated content like Twitter is tedious. Several studies proposed approaches such as Content Analysis [13, 14] and Sentiment Analysis [15, 16]. Content analysis gains insights into people's attitudes, behaviours, and perceptions, thereby explaining how Twitter could be an effective communication tool [14]. Sentiment refers to subjective information measured on a categorical or continuous polarity scale [18].

During the COVID-19 pandemic, people's negative outlook toward COVID-19 was discovered through sentiment analysis [16]. Topic Modelling [17] has been increasingly used to analyse and interpret content and identify underlying themes. Topic modelling is a machine learning technique that automatically clusters textual corpus containing similar themes together. [19, 20] demonstrated the capability of the Support Vector Machine (SVM) model in classifying topics from Twitter content. [21, 22] shared the use of Convolutional Neural Networks (CNN) to model health-related topics from Twitter and social healthcare networks. Topic modelling was used to identify relevant topics in COVID-19 related tweets, by accurately depicting the Covid-related flow of information with little misinformation [15] and successfully identifying similar topics from two temporal tweet datasets [23]. Hence, topic modelling simplifies the understanding of huge tweet content by classifying them into meaningful categories [24].

2.2   Information Encountering

Information encountering (IE) has been defined as the "accidental" discovery of information while seeking or browsing for something else [3] or a serendipitous acquisition of information with low or no involvement of others [29]. IE allows one to acquire information that is not planned or anticipated. This is true with content generated on Twitter, which can be easily shared, accessed and consumed at any time.

According to [29], social interaction, such as networking and problem-solving, is the underlying activity where users encounter information. Social media platforms are information-intensive environments and, through social interaction, promote purposefully or accidentally the use and exchange of information. Two prominent factors that influence information encountering are user-related and information-related factors. User-related factors such as emotions, attitudes and curiosity are characteristics that contribute to the occurrence of information encountering. Positive emotions are said to favour encountering, while negative emotions hinder it. Some information-related factors are information features that depict relevance and quality. The quality of information covers information accuracy, authenticity, and timeliness.

[3] identified six themes that facilitate information encountering on social media. Through these themes, users can potentially access existing knowledge and information efficiently, leading to the formation and sharing of tacit knowledge.

(I) Broadcasting and publicising information to a wider audience focuses on the ability to circulate knowledge to large populations worldwide, impacting the pace and reach of information. *(II) Faster dissemination of information* refers to the ability to increase the probability of discovering novel concepts and data. *(III) Personalised and filtered information feed* refers to the capabilities of social media to assist individuals in determining the most valuable and relevant information to read based on others' viewpoints, akin to peer review. *(IV) Keeping up-to-date* is having the capacity to stay current on the newest occurrences and developments that impact the practice of industry or what is happening globally. *(V) Documentation of knowledge and experiences* refers to social media as permanent archival storage for tacit knowledge where information is indefinitely available to a wider audience. It enables users to reread, evaluate and share information repeatedly. *(VI) Retrievability* is the ease with which information preserved can be accessed.

In our study, we will consider these IE perspectives and use them to analyse tweet sentiments suggesting evidence of IE.

3   Methodology

3.1   Data Collection

Two datasets containing publicly available tweets were used for this study (i) 2019 pre-COVID-19 tweets (*COVD19-*) and (ii) 2023 current COVID-19 era tweets (*COVD23* +) for tweet sentiment and information encountering comparisons. Both datasets contained full tweet details such as full tweet text, user screen name, user location, hashtag, retweeted, and favorited.

The *COVD19-* dataset was obtained from a previous study by [24], with a total of 13,667 tweets collected from February 4 to February 14, 2019, using the keyword '*#diabetes*'. The *COVD23* + was collected from February 4 to February 26, 2023. The keywords used for this dataset were expanded to include other diabetes-related terms such as '*blood sugar, insulin, glucose, type 1 diabetes, type 2 diabetes, HbA1c, DKA,*

CGM, neuropathy, retinopathy, kidney disease, hyperglycaemia, hypoglycaemia'. A total of 38,000 tweets were initially collected, and after duplicates, retweets, non-English and non-ASCII characters and hashtags were removed, it resulted in a final *COVD23* + dataset of 9,855 for analysis.

COVD19- dataset served as a baseline obtained from a previous study. Considering the scarcity and evolving nature of recent data, we collected *COVD23* + data over three weeks to enable a thorough examination between the two time periods to ensure a robust and relevant dataset for our comparative research.

3.2 Topic Modelling and Sentiment Analysis

We adopted the same categories to identify categories to cluster diabetes-related tweets for health information. Our analysis identified four tweet categories: *'Medication and Treatment'* (MT), *'Prevention and Management'* (PM), *'Risk Factor, Symptom and Complication'* (RSC), and *'Spam and Others'* (SO), excluding *'News'* (NW). We used a semi-supervised clustering approach in a five-step process: (i) manual labelling, (ii) machine classification, (iii) label correction, (iv) enhanced training, and (v) model application.

We manually labelled 1,048 random *COVD19-* tweets for machine training, ensuring inter-coder reliability (138 MT, 147 PM, 117 RSC, and 646 SO). A label agreement index of at least 0.67 (2 out of 3 coders) was required to ensure intercoder reliability. We employed SVM and CNN models to classify the remaining 12,619 unlabelled *COVD19-* tweets. A 2,524-tweet sample evaluated model performance (Table 1).

The machine learning classifications performed indifferently (Table 1i) compared to the initial manual classification. Inaccurately classified tweets were further rectified manually, and the finalised distribution is illustrated in Table 1ii.

Table 1. Classification of tweets by SVM and CNN model, and after classification rectification

Categories	(i) Before label rectification		(ii) After label rectification
	SVM	CNN	
MT	124 (4.9%)	152 (6.0%)	192 (7.6%)
PM	153 (6.1%)	227 (9.0%)	237 (9.4%)
RSC	132 (5.2%)	206 (8.2%)	203 (8.0%)
SO	2,115 (83.8%)	1,936 (76.8%)	1,892 (75.0%)

CNN was the best-performing model with a recall rate of 73.57 compared to SVM at 70.84, based on the clustered *COVD19-* sample. Several studies have also indicated CNN performs well in topic modelling on highly imbalanced social media datasets [25, 26].

Next, we reinforced the initial training data with the improved labelled data of 2,524 tweets, bringing the total to 3,572 labelled tweets. The CNN model was retrained with the new training data and applied to the original *COVD19-* dataset using reinforcement learning with the human feedback approach.

A similar approach was used for the *COVD23* + dataset, where 690 tweets were randomly labelled. These were integrated into the existing training data, totalling 4,262 newly labelled tweets. The CNN model also received additional training, incorporating the human feedback approach. This has resulted in a higher accuracy in the model's performance (Table 2).

Table 2. SVM and CNN Recall rate on two samples of tweets

Model	*COVD19- sample; n = 2,524*			*COVD23- sample; n = 1,883*		
	Recall	TP	FP	Recall	TP	FP
SVM	70.84	1,788	736	–	–	–
CNN	73.57	1,857	667	80.96	1,484	349

Note: TP - True Positives; FN - False Negatives

Insights into the tweets gathered before and during the COVID-19 era were gained using distribution analysis and Prado Emotion analysis. The Prado Emotions analysis was performed using PRADO, a sequence projection model architecture, and Google GoEmotions, a comprehensive human-annotated dataset, to predict the wide range of emotions expressed in the tweets obtained from the dataset. Google GoEmotions is the largest documented fine-grained emotion dataset in English, with 28 emotion categories [27]. For every tweet, 28 emotion categories were generated, and the emotions ranked based on their sentiment score. The scores were then used for several of our analyses of emotions or sentiments.

4   Results

4.1   Topic Modelling Results

We observed an overall decrease in the proportion of tweets for all categories from *COVD23* + compared with *COVD19-*, except for *MT,* which showed a considerable increase of 35.3%, as illustrated in Table 3. *SO* topic exhibited the most significant decrease (21.3%) in the proportion of tweets in *COVD23* + compared to *COVD19-*. Both *PM* and *RSC* topics displayed a reduction in the proportion of tweets of less than 10%.

The differences potentially suggested that efforts to reduce spam or irrelevant information dissemination might have been practical. It was also plausible that information sharing had shifted to other more meaningful topics from 2019 to 2023. However, the noteworthy rise indicated a heightened interest among individuals seeking information about different medications and treatments for specific ailments during 2023.

In Fig. 1i and 1ii, we analysed the distribution of tweets in each topic by date for any observable evidence to explain the frequency of tweets generated. We observed an increasing distribution of tweets for *PM* and *RSC* topics in *COVD19-* and for all topics in *COVD23* +, as illustrated by the regressed lines. We also observed that the rate of tweets generated in PM and RSC in *COVD23* + was consistent with *COVD19-*, where the *PM* regressed line was above *RSC*.

Table 3. Distribution of tweets according to topics for COVD19- and COVD23 + dataset

Categories	Description	COVD19-	COVD23 +
MT	Tweets encompassing information regarding various medications, therapies, and medical interventions used to address and improve the overall well-being of diabetes patients	747 (5.5%)	4,018 (40.8%)
PM	Tweets possessing content related to preventive measures and strategies to manage diabetes effectively	1,303 (9.5%)	109 (1.1%)
RSC	Tweets that offer insights on warning signs connected to diabetes, common indicators that may suggest a likelihood of diabetes and issues that result from neglect or improper management of the condition	1,087 (8.0%)	226 (2.3%)
SO	Tweets that cannot be classified into all other categories and those that contain non-relevant information	10,530 (77.1%)	5,502 (55.8%)

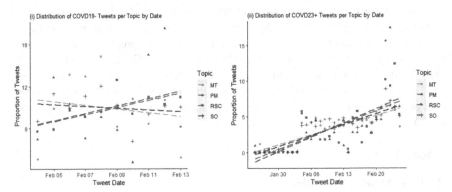

Fig. 1. Tweet Distribution by Date per Topic in (i) *COVD19-* and (ii) *COVD23 +* dataset. *Note: We omitted the distribution of tweets on the last day of COVD19- as it was significantly different from other days.*

4.2   Sentiment Analysis Results

Tweet Emotion Overall Analysis. We calculated the total sentiment scores for all 28 emotions from the two datasets and plotted the distribution of each emotion. Both datasets exhibited similar categories for the top three tweet emotions detected. *Neutral* emotion held the largest distribution, at 29.42% in 2019 and 29.53% in 2023. *Annoyance* was the second most frequently expressed emotion in 2019 at 13.39% and in 2023 at 13.58%. The third was *Curiosity,* with 11.9% and 8.51%, respectively. Beyond this, the emotions detected differed between the datasets. For *COVD19-*, a similar distribution was noted for *Sadness, Caring, Admiration, Disapproval* and *Approval*. For *COVD23 +*, emotions detected were *Admiration, Approval, Confusion, Anger, Excitement* and *Disapproval*. It was interesting to note in *COVD19-*, the fourth emotion detected was negative compared to in *COVD23 +*.

We noted that the major prevalence of *Neutral* emotions could suggest a lack of any charged sentiments. Therefore, we stressed the importance of analysing non-neutral emotions for deeper insights into the evolving emotional landscape of social media discourse.

Top Emotions. This analysis only considered the emotions with the highest sentiment score from each tweet. The total sentiment score of all top emotions from each dataset was calculated, and its distribution is illustrated in Fig. 2i and 2ii. *Neutral* was still the most prevalent category in both years (81.86% in 2019, 82.94% in 2023), indicating predominantly emotionally neutral tweets. This was consistent with PRADO's multi-model emotion analysis, where the 28 emotions could be broadly classified into three categories [27], excluding *Neutral*. Subsequently, we observed *Positive* tweets decreased from 13.59% in 2019 to 11.05% in 2023, suggesting a decline in positive emotions during COVID-19. *Ambiguous* and *Negative* tweets increased slightly in 2023, reflecting potential ambiguity or unhappiness. This aligned with [30] study on negative emotions during the COVID-19 outbreak.

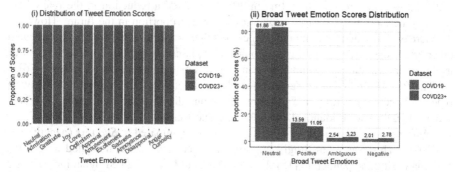

Fig. 2. (i) Distribution of Emotion based on Sentiment scores, and (ii) Redistribution of Emotions into 4 broad categories.

Emotions Topical Analysis. Utilising the multi-model emotions, we analysed the proportion of emotions belonging to each topic for insights into health information encountering surrounding diabetes. In each topic, we considered only the six highest-scoring emotions of each tweet and generated the sentiment score proportion of emotions. For instance, the sentiment score proportion of *Neutral* emotion in *MT* topic was calculated by aggregating only the top *Neutral* sentiment scores in *MT*, divided by the summation of aggregated top *Neutral* emotion sentiment scores from *MT*, *PM* and *RSC*.

We excluded the *SO* topic and focused on the three highly relevant health-related topics. We witnessed a compelling shift in the display of top emotions in tweets from *RSC* and *PM* topics in *COVD19-* to *MT* in *COVD23 +*. In Fig. 2i, we noted the increase in tweets categorised as *Curiosity* in 2023 compared to 2019. When considering the classification of tweets into the three topics, most of the *Curiosity* tweets in *COVD23 +* were in the *MT* topic, whereas in *COVD19-*, they were associated more with *RSC* and *PM* topics. This shift in dominant topics suggested changing opinions and interests among the users over time.

5 Discussion

The two distinct datasets collected during different periods provided a basis for comparison. We noted the slight differences in the distribution of tweets clustered into the four health-related categories for *COVD19-* and *COVD23 +* (Table 1). The significantly higher proportion of tweets in *MT* for *COVD23 +*, indicated an increase in user-generated content, relating to medication and treatment information. This was also seen in the distribution of tweets generated by day (Fig. 1), where the rate of tweets generated in *MT* in 2023 showed an upward trend compared to 2019. It was also evident in higher proportions of emotions identified in *MT* in 2023 than in 2019. Considering the continuing uncertainties surrounding possible health risks attributed to the COVID-19 pandemic, it was unsurprising to notice more information being shared about it. The noteworthy rise could also suggest a heightened interest among individuals seeking information about different medications and treatments during 2023. It could also be attributed to changing opinions and interests over time.

The other notable difference was the reduction in the proportion of *SO* tweets for *COVD23 +*. A decreasing trendline in 2019 suggested a reduction in the rate of *SO* tweets generated, thus possibly explaining a lower proportion in the future. However, the increasing trend in 2023 should suggest a higher proportion, but the results indicated otherwise. Possibly, the differences could be explained by efforts to reduce spam or irrelevant information dissemination using various machine-learning techniques [36].

The PRADO multi-model emotion analysis effectively identified specific emotion types in tweets. Generally, the top three emotions displayed in tweets for *COVD19-* and *COVD23 +* were identical. Interestingly, the fourth top emotion for *COVD23 +* was *Admiration*, categorically a positive sentiment, compared to *Sadness* (negative) in *COVD19-*. This was interestingly opposite to other studies that indicated a negative emotion during the pandemic [16]. Perhaps this could be explained by an increasingly positive global perception towards vaccination or other treatment protocols [32].

We noticed slight but meaningful differences using the tweet sentiment scores to evaluate prominent emotions and categorised them into broad emotions. Even though our sentiment analysis findings did not indicate many differences in the distribution of broad emotions, the results were much different when analysing the emotions from the perspective of individual topics of interest. Before summarising broad emotions, there was a significant increase in tweets on *MT* topic and emotions such as *Admiration*, *Curiosity, Annoyance, Anger* and *Approval* being displayed in *COVD23 +*, which suggested the impact of COVID-19 on users' need for information seeking and sharing. When generalising to broad emotions, we found fewer *Positive* and more *Negative* and *Ambiguous* emotions in *COVD23 +*. A decline in *Positive* emotions and more *Negative* emotions seemed to be aligned with most studies like [15, 16, 32] during the COVID-19 outbreak and user-related factors in [29] social interaction promoting IE.

Our following analysis results also indicated evidence of selected themes from Panahi's IE framework, suggesting that Twitter can be a platform for health information seeking. We identified four out of the five IE themes from our data analysis.

We found that using diabetes-related hashtags as keywords facilitated the extraction of associated tweets. This accessibility allowed users to revisit and review shared information, making it a valuable resource for research and knowledge generation, therefore aligning with a collective intelligence that emphasises the power of collaboration over individual efforts. The semi-supervised topic modelling approach enabled the classification of tweets into four health-related topics, contextualising the vast collection of tweets and indicating the existence of tacit knowledge and valuable information. These aligned with the themes of *Personalised and Filtered Information Feed, Documentation of Knowledge and Experiences* and *Retrievability*. The decline in tweets clustered in *PM* and *RSC* topics in 2023 indicated possible changing viewpoints and what users deemed "valuable and relevant information." Similarly, a significant increase in positive emotions (*Admiration, Curiosity, Approval*) suggested the availability of "valuable and relevant information".

In *Keeping Up-To-Date,* the increase in the proportion of tweets for *MT* topic in 2023 (Table 3) could explain Twitter's rapid dissemination of innovative knowledge and exposure to more up-to-date material pertaining to medication and treatment, increasing the opportunity to chance upon new information. Tweet emotions suggested users showed higher *Admiration* and *Curiosity* emotions, possibly attributed to increased information-seeking behaviours during the pandemic. A decrease in tweets about diabetes as the pandemic spread indicated a shift in attention to COVID-19-related subjects. It highlighted how the pandemic had affected discussions surrounding diabetes on social media. This observation could potentially be helpful to physicians in gaining new insights, enhancing clinical practice, and providing better care to COVID-19 patients.

6 Conclusion

Investigating diabetes-related tweets before and after the COVID-19 pandemic declaration provided insight into health information encountering during different healthcare contexts and periods. Our analysis revealed several interesting findings, specifically a decrease in encountering diabetes prevention and management information during the pandemic. There was increased Twitter activity and engagement with COVID-19 and diabetes-related content after the pandemic declaration and the influence of the pandemic on social media conversations. Notably, individuals showed heightened information-seeking and curiosity emotions towards diabetes medication, potentially due to limited healthcare resources and COVID-19-related fears. Our study highlighted the impact of external factors, such as a global pandemic, on the quality and quantity of information available to support health information encountering and seeking behaviours.

References

1. Douglas, M., Katikireddi, S. V., Taulbut, M., McKee, M., McCartney, G.: Mitigating the wider health effects of COVID-19 pandemic response. BMJ **369**, m1557 (2020). https://doi.org/10.1136/bmj.m1557
2. Jaidka, K., Eichstaedt, J., Salvatore Giorgi, H., Schwartz, A., Ungar, L.H.: Information-seeking vs. sharing: which explains regional health? an analysis of Google search and Twitter trends. Telematics Inform. **59**, 101540 (2021). https://doi.org/10.1016/j.tele.2020.101540
3. Panahi, S., Watson, J., Partridge, H.: Information encountering on social media and tacit knowledge sharing. J. Inf. Sci. **42**(4), 539–550 (2016). https://doi.org/10.1177/0165551515598883

4. Project, G.: Visualising Twitter's evolution 2012–2020 and how tweeting is changing in the COVID-19 era (2020). https://blog.gdeltproject.org/visualizing-twitters-evolution-2012-2020-and-how-tweeting-is-changing-in-the-covid-19-era/

5. Chew, C., Eysenbach, G.: Pandemics in the age of Twitter: content analysis of tweets during the 2009 H1N1 outbreak. PLoS ONE **5**(11), e14118 (2010). https://doi.org/10.1371/journal.pone.0014118

6. Herrera-Peco, I., Jiménez-Gómez, B., Peña Deudero, J.J., Benitez De Gracia, E., Ruiz-Núñez, C.: Healthcare professionals' role in social media public health campaigns: analysis of Spanish pro vaccination campaign on Twitter. Healthcare **9**(6), 662 (2021)

7. Markham, M.J., Gentile, D., Graham, D.L.: Social media for networking, professional development, and patient engagement. Am. Soc. Clin. Oncol. Educ. Book **37**, 782–787 (2017)

8. Sinnenberg, L., Buttenheim, A.M., Padrez, K., Mancheno, C., Ungar, L., Merchant, R.M.: Twitter as a tool for health research: a systematic review. Am. J. Public Health **107**(1), e1–e8 (2017). https://doi.org/10.2105/AJPH.2016.303512

9. Zhao, Y., Zhang, J.: Consumer health information seeking in social media: a literature review. Health Info. Libr. J. **34**(4), 268–283 (2017)

10. Xue, J., et al.: Twitter discussions and emotions about the COVID-19 pandemic: machine learning approach. J. Med. Internet Res. **22**(11), e20550 (2020)

11. Lwin, M.O., et al.: Global sentiments surrounding the COVID-19 pandemic on Twitter: analysis of Twitter trends. JMIR Public Health Surveill. **6**(2), e19447 (2020)

12. Priyadarshini, I., Mohanty, P., Kumar, R., Sharma, R., Puri, V., Singh, P.K.: A study on the sentiments and psychology of twitter users during COVID-19 lockdown period. Multimedia Tools Appl. **81**(19), 27009–27031 (2022)

13. Krippendorff, K. (2018). Content analysis: An introduction to its methodology. Sage publications

14. Rufai, S.R., Bunce, C.: World leaders' usage of Twitter in response to the COVID-19 pandemic: a content analysis. J. Public Health **42**(3), 510–516 (2020)

15. Corti, L., Zanetti, M., Tricella, G., Bonati, M.: Social media analysis of Twitter tweets related to ASD in 2019–2020, with particular attention to COVID-19: topic modelling and sentiment analysis. J. Big Data **9**(1), 113 (2022)

16. Boon-Itt, S., Skunkan, Y.: Public perception of the COVID-19 pandemic on Twitter: sentiment analysis and topic modeling study. JMIR Public Health Surveill. **6**(4), e21978 (2020)

17. Curiskis, S.A., Drake, B., Osborn, T.R., Kennedy, P.J.: An evaluation of document clustering and topic modelling in two online social networks: Twitter and Reddit. Inf. Process. Manage. **57**(2), 102034 (2020)

18. Mejova, Y.: Sentiment Analysis: An overview. University of Iowa, Computer Science Department (2009)

19. Cahyani, D.E., Putra, A.W.: Relevance classification of trending topic and Twitter content using support vector machine. Int. Semin. Appl. Technol. Inf. Commun. (ISemantic) **2021**, 87–90 (2021). https://doi.org/10.1109/iSemantic52711.2021.9573243

20. Telnoni, P.A., Budiawan, R., Qana'a, M.: Comparison of machine learning classification method on text-based case in twitter. In: 2019 International Conference on ICT for Smart Society (ICISS), vol. 7, pp. 1–5 (2019). https://doi.org/10.1109/ICISS48059.2019.8969850

21. Asghari, M., Sierra-Sosa, D., Elmaghraby, A.: Trends on health in social media: analysis using twitter topic modeling. IEEE Int. Symp. Sig. Process. Inf. Technol. (ISSPIT) **2018**, 558–563 (2018). https://doi.org/10.1109/ISSPIT.2018.8642679

22. Lavanya, P., Sasikala, E.: Deep learning techniques on text classification using natural language processing (NLP) in social healthcare network: a comprehensive survey. In: 2021 3rd International Conference on Signal Processing and Communication (ICPSC), pp. 603–609 (2021). https://doi.org/10.1109/ICSPC51351.2021.9451752

23. Prabhakar Kaila, D.R., Prasad, D.A.V.: Informational flow on Twitter–Corona virus outbreak–topic modelling approach. Int. J. Adv. Res. Eng. Technol. (IJARET) **11**(3), 128–134 (2020)

24. Osop, H., Hasan, R., Lee, C.S., Neo, C.Y., Foo, C.K., Saurabh, A.: Diabetweets: analysis of tweets for health-related information. In: Stephanidis, C., Antona, M., Ntoa, S. (eds.) HCII 2020. CCIS, vol. 1294, pp. 500–508. Springer, Cham (2020). https://doi.org/10.1007/978-3-030-60703-6_65

25. Du, J., et al.: Public perception analysis of tweets during the 2015 measles outbreak: comparative study using convolutional neural network models. J. Med. Internet Res. **20**(7), e236 (2018)

26. Yu, M., Huang, Q., Qin, H., Scheele, C., Yang, C.: Deep learning for real-time social media text classification for situation awareness – using Hurricanes Sandy, Harvey, and Irma as case studies. Int. J. Digit. Earth **12**(11), 1230–1247 (2019). https://doi.org/10.1080/17538947.2019.1574316

27. Alon, D., Ko, J.: GoEmotions: a dataset for fine-grained emotion classification (2021). https://ai.googleblog.com/2021/10/goemotions-dataset-for-fine-grained.html

28. Wilson, E.K.: A smart pill for insulin? Engineering **5**(4), 603–604 (2019). https://doi.org/10.1016/j.eng.2019.07.008

29. Kwan, A.C., Ebinger, J.E., Botting, P., Navarrette, J., Claggett, B., Cheng, S.: Association of COVID-19 vaccination with risk for incident diabetes after COVID-19 infection. JAMA Netw. Open **6**(2), e2255965–e2255965 (2023). https://doi.org/10.1001/jamanetworkopen.2022.55965

30. Moreira-Lucas, S.T., et al.: Effect of vitamin D supplementation on oral glucose tolerance in individuals with low vitamin D status and increased risk for developing type 2 diabetes (EVIDENCE): a double-blind, randomised, placebo-controlled clinical trial. Diabetes Obes. Metab. **19**(1), 133–141 (2016). https://doi.org/10.1111/dom.12794

31. Hussain, A., Bhowmik, B., do Vale Moreira, N.C.: COVID-19 and diabetes: Knowledge in progress. Diabetes Res. Clin. Pract. **162**, 108142 (2020). https://doi.org/10.1016/j.diabres.2020.108142

32. Li, J., Zheng, H.: Online information seeking and disease prevention intent during COVID-19 outbreak. Journalism Mass Commun. Q. **99**(1), 69–88 (2020). https://doi.org/10.1177/1077699020961518

33. Diabetes Times UK.: Good insulin pump self-management improves HbA1c, evidence demonstrates. The Diabetes Times (2023). https://diabetestimes.co.uk/good-insulin-pump-self-management-improves-hba1c-evidence-demonstrates/

34. Savolainen, R.: Information need as trigger and driver of information seeking: a conceptual analysis. Aslib J. Inf. Manag. **69**(1), 2–21 (2017). https://doi.org/10.1108/AJIM-08-2016-0139

Information Retrieval

Analyzing Web Search Queries of Before and After Purchase on e-Commerce Site

Yuka Kawada[1], Takehiro Yamamoto[1](✉), Hiroaki Ohshima[1],
Yuki Yanagida[2], Makoto P. Kato[2], and Sumio Fujita[3]

[1] University of Hyogo, Kobe, Japan
ad221019@gsis.u-hyogo.ac.jp, t.yamamoto@sis.u-hyogo.ac.jp,
ohshima@ai.u-hyogo.ac.jp
[2] University of Tsukuba, Tsukuba, Japan
ynagi2@klis.tsukuba.ac.jp, mpkato@acm.org
[3] Yahoo Japan Corporation, Tokyo, Japan
sufujita@yahoo-corp.jp

Abstract. In this study, we investigated how Web search queries change before and after purchasing a product. We focused on the Web searchers who purchased cameras from an e-commerce site. First, we manually classified the words that characteristically appear during pre-purchase and post-purchase searches with cameras. From the manual classification, we found 14 intents. The intents include model number, evaluation, shipping, and accessory, etc. Based on these classified intents, we then analyzed when the words in each intent were used in queries before/after the purchase. Our analyses revealed that the users narrowed the search space with respect to the product as the user nears purchase.

Keywords: Web search · Consumer behavior · Behavior analysis

1 Introduction

Numerous users search the Web to obtain information about a product. Market research firm Survata conducted a survey to investigate which websites users in the US in searching for products [4]. Survata reported that 35.5% of users utilize Web search as their first step in purchasing a product, and 45.5% of users search the Web when they have not decided which specific product to buy.

Web search queries of users change depending on their interests in the product [3]. Analyzing the changes in Web search queries over time can help us understand the purchasing behavior of users. For example, a user searches the Web issuing the query *"camera types"* to look for suitable cameras for purchase. At this time, the user still has not yet decided which product to purchase. The user also searches the Web issuing the query *"canon kiss x10 price"* when trying to find the price of the Canon Kiss X10 camera model. This time, the user is searching for a specific product and is likely to purchase the same. Understanding the purchasing behavior process based on Web search queries enables

© The Author(s), under exclusive license to Springer Nature Singapore Pte Ltd. 2023
D. H. Goh et al. (Eds.): ICADL 2023, LNCS 14457, pp. 181–187, 2023.
https://doi.org/10.1007/978-981-99-8085-7_16

us to support users, by customizing advertisements to be shown to the users or, by presenting search results that are customized to the user's information needs [1,5].

In this study, we analyze the change in Web search queries before and after purchasing a camera using the Web search logs of a commercial Web search engine and purchase data from an online e-commerce site. We address the following research questions in this study.

RQ1: What types of words are used in Web search queries before and after a purchase?

RQ2: How do the words identified in RQ1 change when users approach a purchase and after the purchase?

2 Data

We used the Web search logs provided by Yahoo! Search and purchase data from Yahoo! Shopping. We used Web search logs for 13 months between October 1, 2016 and October 31, 2017 provided by Yahoo! Search. We used the search logs of users who performed at least 10 searches per month to target users who use Web search engines on a daily basis. As for the purchase data, we analyzed the logs of users who purchased cameras between October 1, 2016 and October 31, 2017 from Yahoo! Shopping. The cameras include digital cameras and digital SLR cameras.

In this study, we focused on cameras since we believe that users who purchase cameras tend to use a Web search engine to gather information before making a purchase. Thus, it is important to understand the search behaviors of users with respect to these products. In this study, we analyzed 5,508 users who bought cameras.

3 Extraction of Characteristic Words Used During Pre- And Post-purchase Queries and Their Classification into Query Intents

We investigate the query types before and after purchases by identifying characteristic words and categorizing them into **query intents**. For instance, users search **price** information before buying and **accessories** after purchasing. In this study, we aim to identify the intent of queries issued before and after a purchase.

We prepared product-related queries for the 72 h before and after a purchase. For pre-purchase queries, we extracted sessions with product-related queries in 30-minute inactivity intervals [2]. Post-purchase queries were also extracted. The list of product names was prepared based on the purchase data and data from kakaku.com[1].

---

[1] https://kakaku.com/.

We trained a classifier using logistic regression to determine pre-purchase and post-purchase queries, employing tf-idf weighted words. We analyzed queries from 5,508 users related to cameras, resulting in an accuracy and an F1 score of 0.65 and 0.64. Furthermore, we extracted the top 100 words with the largest (absolute) regression coefficient for both positive and negative coefficients, leading to the extraction of 200 words in total.

We then manually classified the characteristic words into query intents, which represent the types of information the users searched for. To prepare query intents, we first refer to the taxonomy from the previous study [6] that analyzed the relationship between search behavior and satisfaction related to product search. By referring to their taxonomy and sampling queries, we first prepared the initial query intents as **category**, **manufacture**, **series**, **model number**, **evaluation**, **sales method**, **store**, **price**, and **function & feature**. Three authors of this paper manually classified the characteristic words into the query intents based on this taxonomy. As a result, we determined 14 query intents.

Table 1 lists these 14 query intents and presents example characteristic words assigned to each query intent prepared in our study. The query intents **accessory**, **shipping**, **how to use**, and **new & used** are the newly prepared query intents based on our study. From this classification process, we obtained the query intents that could be issued after purchasing a product. For example, users search for information regarding product shipping by issuing queries containing words such as "*tracking*". Moreover, users search for information regarding product usage by issuing queries containing words such as "*treatment*." These query intents are expected to be issued after a purchase. The queries related to these intents may not be issued on an e-commerce site, but rather on a Web search engine. We believe that these intents could be revealed by analyzing queries on a Web search engine. The identification of these intents suggests that it is important for the system to not only recommend products related to the purchased product (such as accessories) but also to recommend information regarding usage and guarantees to support the users' purchasing process. In this next section, we will analyze how these query intents occur and change before and after a purchase.

4   Time Series Analysis of Queries Based on Query Intents

In this section, we analyze how users' Web search queries changed as they were about to make a purchase and as after making a purchase. By understanding these changes, we can understand when the users make a purchase, and what information they search for after the purchase. First, we analyzed the changes in queries on a 24 h basis. Next, we analyzed the changes in queries on a query basis.

To analyze the queries, we classified them into the query intents prepared in Sect. 3. A query is classified into a query intent if it contains a word that belongs to the query intent.

Table 1. List of query intents, definitions, and example words to be assigned for each intent prepared in our study.

Query intent	Definition	Words
Category	A type of the product	digital cameras
Manufacturer	A manufacturer of the product	Casio
Series	A series name of the product	ixy
Model number	A model number of the product	g800
Function & feature	A function or a feature of the product	pixels
Store	A store name	Kitamura
Price	Price of the product	price
Guarantee	Product registration and guarantee	customer registration
Evaluation	A reputation of the product	comparison
Sales method	Selling and payment method for the product	on sale
Accessory	Another product to be used with the product	sd card
Shipping	Shipping of the product	tracking
How to use	Information on how to use the product	treatment
New & used	A condition of the product	used
Other	Do not fit into any of these categories	–

4.1 Occurrences of Query Intents per 24 h

We analyzed the frequency of query intents at each 24 h interval in the time period between one week before and one week after making a purchase. Table 2 presents the ratio of the frequency of queries for each query intent. The value in the table is computed based on the ratio of the number of queries in a certain period divided by the total number of queries issued in two weeks. For example, in Table 2 the value of query intent **price** in the interval $(-24\,h, 0]$ is 0.18. This means that 18% of queries that are classified as **price** were issued in the period between 24 h before the purchase and immediately before the purchase.

First, we describe the trend of change in queries before the purchase. As the purchase time approaches, the frequency of **category**, **manufacturer**, **series**, and **model number** gradually increases. In addition, the largest proportions of **category**, **manufacturer**, **series**, **model number**, **function & feature**, **store**, **price**, and **evaluation** appear in the time period between 24 h before the purchase and immediately before purchase. These results suggest that many users perform Web searches in the 24 h period before purchasing a camera.

Next, we describe the trend of change in queries after the purchase. The highest number of queries from the query intents **accessory** and **how to use** are issued after purchasing cameras. Moreover, the query intent **shipping** is issued the most after a purchase. It is worth noting that products bought from e-commerce are typically shipped immediately, arriving within 24 to 48 h.

We observe that information regarding **accessory** of the camera is searched just after the purchase $((0\,h, 24\,h])$. This indicates that users who purchased a camera search for the related products immediately after the purchase. Information regarding **shipping** of the product $((24\,h, 48\,h])$ is then searched, followed by information regarding **how to use** of the product $((48\,h, 72\,h])$. These results suggest that the users search for a variety of information after purchasing a product, and

the timing of when this information is searched varies depending on the information type.

Table 2. Frequency of queries for each intent analyzed in 24 h intervals between one
week before and after the purchase.

Query intent	pre-purchase							post-purchase						
	(-168h, -144h]	(-144h, -120h]	(-120h, -96h]	(-96h, -72h]	(-72h, -48h]	(-48h, -24h]	(-24h, 0h]	(0h, 24h]	(24h, 48h]	(48h, 72h]	(72h, 96h]	(96h, 120h]	(120h, 144h]	(144h, 168h]
Category	0.05	0.05	0.06	0.07	0.09	0.11	0.25	0.08	0.05	0.05	0.04	0.04	0.03	0.03
Manufacturer	0.05	0.05	0.05	0.06	0.07	0.09	0.21	0.10	0.07	0.06	0.05	0.04	0.04	0.04
Series	0.03	0.05	0.05	0.05	0.07	0.10	0.37	0.09	0.05	0.04	0.04	0.02	0.02	0.02
Model number	0.04	0.04	0.05	0.06	0.07	0.09	0.25	0.11	0.07	0.06	0.05	0.04	0.04	0.03
Function & feature	0.07	0.06	0.07	0.07	0.07	0.09	0.16	0.08	0.06	0.06	0.05	0.05	0.05	0.05
Store	0.06	0.06	0.06	0.07	0.08	0.10	0.20	0.08	0.06	0.05	0.05	0.05	0.04	0.04
Price	0.07	0.07	0.06	0.07	0.08	0.09	0.18	0.08	0.06	0.05	0.05	0.05	0.05	0.05
Guarantee	0.05	0.05	0.04	0.06	0.06	0.08	0.27	0.07	0.06	0.08	0.06	0.05	0.05	0.04
Evaluation	0.07	0.07	0.07	0.07	0.08	0.09	0.15	0.08	0.06	0.05	0.05	0.05	0.05	0.05
Sales method	0.06	0.07	0.06	0.06	0.07	0.09	0.17	0.10	0.06	0.05	0.06	0.05	0.05	0.06
Accessory	0.04	0.04	0.04	0.04	0.05	0.06	0.14	0.16	0.10	0.10	0.07	0.06	0.06	0.05
Shipping	0.04	0.04	0.04	0.04	0.04	0.04	0.04	0.11	0.19	0.12	0.10	0.08	0.06	0.06
How to use	0.05	0.05	0.05	0.06	0.05	0.06	0.07	0.09	0.10	0.10	0.09	0.08	0.08	0.07
New & used	0.06	0.07	0.07	0.07	0.08	0.10	0.17	0.08	0.06	0.05	0.05	0.05	0.05	0.05

4.2   Occurrence of Query Intents per Query

In this section, we analyze the changes on a query basis in a more fine-grained
way. First, we extract queries from users who have issued exactly five queries that
contain any of the characteristic words presented in Sect. 3 before and after their
purchases. We then analyze the changes in query intents in the issued queries
when users approach the purchase and after the purchase.

Table 3 presents the changes in the occurrence of query intents before and
after the purchase. For example, the value of the query intent **model number** in
the $n = 1$ of "The n-th query pre-purchase" column is 0.30. Therefore, 30% of the
queries that contain model names occurred just before the purchase. Similarly,
the value of query intents **model number** in the $n = 1$ of "The n-th query pre-
purchase" column is 0.21. This shows that 21% of the queries that contain model
names occurred just after the purchase. The query intents for which the total
frequency of queries was 50 or less were excluded from the analysis (denoted as
– in the table) because it was difficult to find reliable trends for these intents.

As for the query intents when the purchase approaches, we can observe
that the frequency of some query intents increases as the purchase approaches
while that of the some other query intents decreases. The occurrences of query
intents **series** and **model number** in issued queries increase as the purchase
approaches. Conversely, the occurrence of the query intent **evaluation** gradually

decreases as the purchase approaches[2]. These findings suggest that the users first search for information on a broad scope by looking for recommended products and then gradually narrow down the scope by issuing a specific model name of a product in their query.

As for the query intents after purchase, we can observe that the frequencies of **category**, **manufacturer**, **series** and **model number** decrease with increasing time after the purchase. This suggests that users search for information related to a product immediately after making a purchase.

Table 3. Frequency of queries for each query intent for users who conducted five searches related to product purchases before and after the purchase.

Query intent	The n-th query pre-purchase					The n-th query post-purchase				
	n=5	n=4	n=3	n=2	n=1	n=1	n=2	n=3	n=4	n=5
Category	0.18	0.20	0.22	0.21	0.19	0.20	0.21	0.22	0.20	0.17
Manufacturer	0.17	0.18	0.21	0.22	0.22	0.19	0.22	0.21	0.20	0.18
Serie	0.10	0.13	0.18	0.25	0.34	0.25	0.25	0.20	0.16	0.14
Model number	0.12	0.15	0.19	0.24	0.30	0.21	0.21	0.21	0.20	0.17
Function & feature	0.21	0.18	0.23	0.20	0.18	0.17	0.21	0.23	0.18	0.21
Store	0.19	0.21	0.19	0.19	0.21	0.22	0.20	0.21	0.19	0.19
Price	0.17	0.19	0.21	0.22	0.22	0.21	0.20	0.21	0.19	0.19
Guarantee	–	–	–	–	–	0.14	0.14	0.20	0.23	0.20
Evaluation	0.22	0.24	0.21	0.19	0.14	0.20	0.19	0.19	0.20	0.21
Sales method	0.21	0.18	0.16	0.21	0.24	0.23	0.19	0.18	0.15	0.25
Accessory	0.19	0.18	0.20	0.21	0.23	0.21	0.20	0.20	0.19	0.20
Shipping	0.19	0.22	0.21	0.21	0.17	0.21	0.22	0.19	0.20	0.18
How to use	0.21	0.27	0.17	0.20	0.15	0.16	0.18	0.20	0.20	0.25
New & used	0.22	0.19	0.18	0.19	0.22	0.15	0.20	0.20	0.23	0.22

5   Conclusion

In this study, we investigated how words used in Web search queries change over time from the pre-purchase to the post-purchase phase with respect to users who purchased a camera from an e-commerce site.

We classified pre- and post-purchase queries based on distinctive words found through manual categorization using a logistic regression. Our study shows that users search for diverse information both before and after making purchases.

Before making a purchase, **evaluation** searches decreased while **manufacturer** and **series** searches increased, revealing the product selection process. After making a purchase, users search **shipping**, **accessory**, and **how to use** information.

---

[2] Due to the space limitation, we only report the results related to users who issued five queries. We observed a similar trend with respect to users who issued six queries.

The findings of this study will help in understanding how users reach the point of purchase via Web search and their post-purchase information needs. In the future, we aim to explore search behavior variations based on user characteristics.

Acknowledgment. This work was supported in part by JSPS KAKENHI Grant Numbers JP21H03774, JP21H03775, JP22H03905.

References

1. Ashkan, A., Clarke, C.L.: Characterizing commercial intent. In: Proceedings of the 18th ACM Conference on Information and Knowledge Management, pp. 67–76 (2009)
2. Huang, J., Efthimiadis, E.N.: Analyzing and evaluating query reformulation strategies in web search logs. In: Proceedings of the 18th ACM Conference on Information and Knowledge Management, pp. 77–86 (2009)
3. Jansen, B., Simone, S.: Bidding on the buying funnel for sponsored search and keyword advertising. J. Electron. Commer. Res. **12**(1), 1 (2011)
4. Murga, G.: Amazon Takes 49 Percent of Consumers' First Product Search, But Search Engines Rebound. https://blog.survata.com/amazon-takes-49-percent-of-consumers-first-product-search-but-search-engines-rebound
5. Sondhi, P., Sharma, M., Kolari, P., Zhai, C.: A taxonomy of queries for e-commerce search. In: Proceedings of the 41st International ACM SIGIR Conference on Research & Development in Information Retrieval, pp. 1245–1248 (2018)
6. Su, N., He, J., Liu, Y., Zhang, M., Ma, S.: User intent, behaviour, and perceived satisfaction in product search. In: Proceedings of the 11th ACM International Conference on Web Search and Data Mining, pp. 547–555 (2018)

Web Page Evaluation and Opinion Formation on Controversial Search Topics

Ryo Hagiwara and Takehiro Yamamoto$^{(\boxtimes)}$ [ID]

University of Hyogo, Kobe, Japan
ad23t050@guh.u-hyogo.ac.jp, t.yamamoto@sis.u-hyogo.ac.jp

Abstract. This study investigates the types of web pages people find useful regarding controversial topics and how these pages affect people's opinion formation capacity. An experiment was conducted involving participants who were asked to decide whether they agreed or disagreed with a given topic. During the study, information on the types of web pages participants found useful and the reasons for their opinions were collected to analyze how and why individuals formulated their opinions. Analysis of the results revealed the following. In the homework task, participants found that useful web pages included those that contained information and opinions from multiple viewpoints, as well as evidence-based information. In the vaccine task, many participants found that useful web pages included those that contained evidence-based information. Moreover, opinion formation was categorized into seven types, including damage minimization, merit-oriented, demerit-oriented, credibility-oriented, majority, single-page, and prior beliefs.

Keywords: Information retrieval · Controversial topics · Search behavior analysis

1 Introduction

Currently, web search engines are used for various purposes. One is to help formulate opinions on a particular topic. According to a survey by Moz, 46% of the respondents answered that they often use Google to make important medical decisions [14].

Regarding health information searchers, studies have been conducted on the quality of health information available on the Web [5,19] as well as the criteria for credible web pages [12,13,18]. However, limited studies have been conducted on controversial search topics, such as "Should I become a vegetarian?" and "Is homework necessary for elementary school students?" In this study, controversial topics were defined as those in which the truth was unclear, resulting in arguments for and against them. Such controversial topics require careful opinion formation from various information sources because the answers remain unknown. A better understanding of how people search the Web for answers regarding controversial topics, what information they find useful, and how they

D. H. Goh et al. (Eds.): ICADL 2023, LNCS 14457, pp. 188–203, 2023.
https://doi.org/10.1007/978-981-99-8085-7_17

finally form their opinions is crucial in the development of reliable web search engines.

To this end, the following research questions were investigated.

RQ1: What kind of web pages do people find useful when they search on controversial topics?

RQ2: How do people form their opinions after searching?

In the user study, 12 participants were asked to use a web search engine to formulate their opinions on controversial topics, such as "Is homework necessary for elementary school students?" and "Should children receive the COVID-19 vaccine?" After completing the search task, the participants were then asked to assess the usefulness of the web pages they viewed during the search task, their opinions on the topic, and the reasons in formulating them. By analyzing the data, it can be clarified what web pages people found helpful and how people formulated their opinions on controversial topics.

To answer RQ1, the web pages, which evaluate data obtained from the post-task questionnaire and interview content, were analyzed. Specifically, labels based on previous studies of highly rated web pages were assigned [18]. The labeling results revealed that in the homework task, useful web pages included those that contained evidence-based information, such as experimental results, and those that contained information and opinions from multiple perspectives. Meanwhile, in the vaccine task, useful web pages included those that contained evidence-based information.

To answer RQ2, opinion formation data obtained from the posttask questionnaire and interview content were analyzed. Specifically, descriptions of the reasons for opinion formation given by the participants were classified into seven types: damage minimization, merit-oriented, demerit-oriented, credibility-oriented, majority decision, single-page belief, and prior belief.

2 Related Work

This section discusses the related studies on controversial topics, search behavior analysis, and opinion formation analysis.

2.1 Controversial Topics

There are studies conducted to identify whether or not a query is controversial [3,10] and studies focusing on search results and user search behavior [1,7,9]. For example, Gyllstrom et al. found that it is possible to identify whether or not a search query is controversial by checking Google's query completion function [10]. Meanwhile, Gezici et al. found that search results for queries related to controversial topics tend to be biased [9].

Research has also been conducted on search systems that can provide both supporting and opposing views on controversial topics [4,6,17]. Stab et al. developed and demonstrated the usefulness of a search system called ArgumenText that visualizes supporting and opposing views on a controversial topic [17].

However, few studies have clarified what types of web pages are referred to and how opinions are formulated. Therefore, this study focuses on the analysis of these two aspects.

2.2   Search Behavior

Research has been conducted to reveal user web search behavior [16,21,22]. Yamamoto et al. defined "verification attitude" as the attitude toward behavior that is necessary to obtain reliable information through web searches and clarified the relationship between verification attitude and actual web search behavior [22]. Moreover, Pothirattanachaikul et al. found that when users read documents containing opinions contrary to their preexisting beliefs before conducting a search, they tend to exert more effort during the search process and are more likely to change their initial beliefs after the search [16].

2.3   Opinion Formation

Studies have also been conducted on how searchers formulate their opinions when they search for health information. For instance, White et al. found that for yes-no type queries in health information, searchers tend to view web pages with positive results on the search engine results page and avoid those with negative results [20]. A search engine manipulation effect (SEME) is also known to occur when using web search engines to form opinions. SEME refers to intentionally biasing search results in favor of one opinion or the other to influence the opinion formation of searchers [2,15]. Pogacar et al. found that biasing search results with correct information tends to result in accurate opinion formation, while biasing results with incorrect information tends to result in inaccurate opinion formation [15].

3   Methods

This section first describes the user study procedure and then thoroughly describes the participants and the selection of topics for the search task. Finally, the pretask questionnaire, search task, posttask questionnaire, and interviews conducted in the user study are described in detail.

3.1   Procedure

Figure 1 shows the flow of the user study. First, the participants were informed as to what data will be collected during the experiment and that these data would be used for academic purposes. Only participants who agreed were involved, who were then asked to sign a consent form.

Next, a training task was conducted for the participants to get familiarized with the search system developed by the authors. In the training task, they were asked to search for the following topic: "Should they become a vegetarian?".

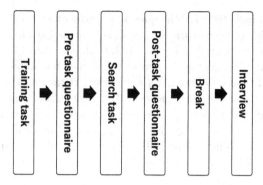

Fig. 1. Flow of the user study.

After completing the training task, the participants were asked to answer a pretask questionnaire that examines their level of interest in the search topic, prior knowledge, and prior thoughts about the search topic (Sect. 3.3). After answering the pretask questionnaire, the participants were asked to perform a search task described in Sect. 3.4. After completing the search task, they were asked to answer a posttask questionnaire, wherein they expressed their opinions regarding the topic and the reasons for their opinions. In addition, they were asked to evaluate whether the web pages they viewed during the search task were helpful or not in formulating their opinions (Sect. 3.5). Finally, the user study concluded with an oral interview to further investigate the posttask questionnaire content.

3.2 Topics

Topics were selected from the list provided in ProCon.org[1], a website that presents various controversial topics. The two selected topics are the following: "Is homework necessary for elementary school students?" "Should children receive the COVID-19 vaccine?" The former and the latter topics will be referred as the "homework task" and "vaccine task," respectively.

3.3 Pretask Questionnaire

Before performing the search task, the participants answered a pretask questionnaire, wherein they were asked about their interest, prior knowledge, and prior thoughts about the search topic.

In the homework task, participants were asked about their level of interest in the topic with the question, "How interested are you in the necessity of homework for elementary school students?" The response options were measured using a 5-point Likert scale (1, not interested at all; 2, not very interested; 3, neutral; 4, somewhat interested; 5, very interested). Meanwhile, participants were asked

---

[1] https://www.procon.org/.

regarding prior knowledge with the question, "How much do you think you know about the necessity of homework for elementary school students?" The response options were also measured using a 5-point Likert scale (1, no knowledge at all; 2, not very knowledgeable; 3, neutral; 4, somewhat knowledgeable; 5, very knowledgeable). Finally, participants were asked regarding their prior thoughts about the search topic with the question, "Do you think homework is necessary for elementary school students?" The response options were measured using a 5-point Likert scale (1, strongly disagree; 2, somewhat disagree; 3, neutral; 4, somewhat agree; 5: strongly agree). The same questions were framed in context with the vaccine task.

3.4   Search Task

After completing the pretask questionnaire, the participants were asked to perform the search task. They were instructed to read the task description before engaging in it. The following description was presented to the homework task participants:

> In this search task, the target was limited to elementary school students, and homework was defined as an assignment that is mandatorily assigned by a teacher. You recently watched a TV program discussing homework. Today, a new homework method called AI Drill is spreading, while some schools are doing away with homework.
> In this task, you are free to use a web search to investigate whether homework is necessary for elementary school students.

Participants were given a maximum of 30 min to complete the search task and were allowed to stop searching if they felt satisfied with their search even before the 30-min duration. A 30-min duration allowed the participants to have a sufficient time searching. If they had not completed the search after 28 min, they were instructed to, "Please finish the search in about two minutes."

Figures 2 and 3 show the actual search system interface used in the user study. Participants were allowed to use only this search system. The search system uses the Microsoft Bing Web Search API[2] to retrieve and return search results to the participants. The participants were allowed to issue any queries, click the search results, and visit the web pages.

---

[2] https://www.microsoft.com/en-us/bing/apis/bing-web-search-api.

Fig. 2. Search task.

Fig. 3. Search results page interface.

3.5 Posttask Questionnaire

After the search task, a posttask questionnaire was administered to investigate participants' opinions about the search topic and their evaluation of the web pages they viewed during the search task.

Participants' Opinions on the Topic After the Search. The posttask questionnaire was used to explore the opinions of participants following the search task.

From a list of options, the participants were asked to choose what opinion they held about the topic and to describe the reasons for their opinion in a form of a free text. Specifically, in the homework task, the first question asked their opinion about the searched topic: "Did you think that homework was necessary for elementary school students?". The participants could select from three options: "Yes," "No," or "I couldn't determine from the search." They were also asked to provide the reason for choosing one of the options in the free-response section. After providing opinions about the search topic, the participants were then asked about the reasons as to why their opinions on the topic were not opposed. For example, the following response was given to participants who answered that homework was necessary for elementary school students were asked: "Please give any reason you can think of why you did not agree that homework is not necessary for elementary school students." The same questions were framed in context with the vaccine task.

Web Page Evaluations. The participants were asked to evaluate all the web pages they viewed during the search task to investigate what kinds of web pages searchers found helpful. Table 1 lists the five questions from Q1 to Q5. A 5-point Likert scale was used for the answers (1, not at all; 2, not very much; 3, undecided; 4, a little; 5, a lot). Q1 asked, "To what extent did you view the web pages you visited?" Participants who answered "not at all" were asked to answer, "Please select this option if you chose "not at all" in Q1 for Q2, Q3, and Q4, and Q5: "Nothing in particular." Q2 asked, "Did the web pages you visited mention whether elementary school students need to do their homework?" The

Table 1. Content of posttask questionnaire.

ID	Questions
Q1	To what extent did you view the web pages you visited?
Q2	Did the web page you viewed mention whether homework is required?
Q3	Which of the following applies to the content of the web pages you viewed?
Q4	How helpful were the web pages you viewed in forming your opinion?
Q5	Please tell us why you made the choices you did in Q4

response options were "mentioned" or "did not mention." Q3 asked, "Which of the following applies to the content of the web pages you viewed? The response options included "expressed agreement with the task", "expressed disagreement with the task", "expressed both agreement and disagreement with the task", or "was unrelated to the task." Q4 asked, "To what extent did the web pages you viewed help you to form your own opinions?" A 7-point Likert scale was used for the answers (1, not helpful at all; 2, not very helpful; 3, somewhat helpful; 4, undecided; 5, somewhat unhelpful; 6, very helpful; 7, extremely helpful). Finally, Q5 asked, "Please tell us why you made the choices you made in Q4." Participants were then asked to answer by writing freely.

3.6   Interview

After the participants completed the posttask questionnaire and took a 5-min break, semistructured interviews were conducted to thoroughly investigate what they had answered in the posttask questionnaire. During the interview, questions were asked while reading their respective posttask questionnaire answers and evaluation of the web pages they viewed. All interview contents were recorded. The two questions were prepared in advance and varied according to the participants' responses. The first question focused on the reasons for opinion formation. Specifically, the participants were asked, "Could you please explain why you formed the opinion after viewing various web pages?" The second question focused on the reason for completing the search. Specifically, the participants were asked, "Could you explain what information you found that led you to end your search?" Participants who had searched for 30 min were asked, "Was your search satisfactory enough through searching for a long time?" Moreover, they were asked about their evaluation of the web pages and the reasons for their answers. For example, a participant may indicate that a particular page was very useful, or he/she may write in the free-response section of the questionnaire that the page was useful since it included both advantage and disadvantages. In this case, they were asked, "Why do you find it helpful to have both positive and negative aspects of a topic presented?" For each question, additional questions were asked depending on the participant's responses.

Table 2. Labels for annotating web page evaluation.

Label	Definition
Expertise	Whether the author has sufficient knowledge to handle the information properly
Authoritative	Whether the organization providing the information is socially credible
Objectivity	Whether the information is based on facts without personal ideas or commercial intentions
Popularity	Whether or not the information is popular
Detail	Whether the information is detailed or not
Double-sided presentation	Whether the information states both advantages and disadvantages
Comprehensibility	Whether the information is broad- based
Opinion	Whether the advantages and disadvantages are clearly stated
Example	Whether the information is based on actual experience
Viewpoint	Whether the information is from the viewpoints of the various stakeholders
Knowledge Acquisition	Whether or not the user learned information they did not know
Other	Those that do not fit into the above labels are evaluated according to the criteria

3.7 Participants

The study was conducted from November 15 to December 5, 2022. Participants were recruited through the communication tool of University of Hyogo. A total of 12 participants (6 males and 6 females) were recruited, and all were first- to fourth-year undergraduate students majoring in social informatics.

The participant who took the shortest time to complete the experiment finished in approximately 45 min while the participant who took the longest time finished in 1 h and 30 min. All 12 participants completed the study and were each paid 1,455 JPY.

4 Results

This section provides a detailed description of the results obtained from the web page evaluation and opinion formation analysis. These analyses were conducted to address the two research questions introduced in Sect. 1.

4.1 Web Page Evaluations Analysis

This section analyzed the types of web pages that were found helpful by the participants. First, the analysis method is described, followed by a detailed description of the results.

Table 3. Types of web pages found helpful by the participants.

	Homework task	Vaccine task	Sum of both tasks
Expertise	2	1	3
Authoritative	0	2	2
Objectivity	4	10	14
Detail	7	6	13
Double-sided presentation	3	1	4
Comprehensibility	3	0	3
Opinion	7	2	9
Example	2	1	3
Viewpoint	4	2	6
Knowledge acquisition	15	6	21
Other	16	5	21
Sum	63	36	99

Approach. To analyze the evaluation of the web pages, an analysis of the free-response statements in the posttask questionnaire regarding the reasons for the evaluation of the web pages viewed by participants was conducted. Specifically, the web pages, where the participants rated "somewhat helpful," "very helpful," or "extremely helpful," were annotated. Table 2 presents the labels and their definitions used in the annotation process. The labels were mainly prepared based on the existing studies [12,13,18] that discussed the credibility of web pages. For example, the label "Expertise" was annotated to the reasons in which the participants felt the author of the page has sufficient knowledge about the topic.

The labeling was performed on a per-web-page basis. Three annotators, one being an author of this study and two being recruits from the institution, annotated the responses collected in Sects. 3.5 and 3.6. The annotators were asked to judge whether the label was appropriate to the response. Multiple labels could be given to one response. Furthermore, the annotation process was performed independently. If one of the annotators assigned a different label to the response, all three annotators will discuss as to what the appropriate label(s) will be. Furthermore, the "knowledge acquisition" label was excluded from analysis as it was considered natural for participants to find web pages that provided information they did not know of previously during their search.

Table 4. Types of opinion formation.

	Homework task	Vaccine task
Damage minimization type	2	0
Merit oriented type	0	3
Demerit oriented type	0	2
Credibility oriented type	2	0
Majority type	1	0
Single page type	1	0
Prior belief type	1	0

Findings. Table 3 presents the labeling results in the web page evaluation. It can be seen that in the homework task, viewpoint was evaluated the highest, followed by objectivity. Detail and double-sided presentation were also evaluated. Participants were then interviewed. When asked why they found that the double-sided presentation of the web page they viewed was helpful, one of the participants responded, "I feel that a person who writes both merits and demerits is considering various things." (ID5) When asked why they found that objectivity of the web page they viewed was helpful, one of the participants responded, "I feel that information based on evidence, such as research, is more credible." (ID3) These results indicate that in the homework task, web pages that contain information and opinions from multiple perspectives and those that contain evidence-based information such as experimental results, are more helpful. In the vaccine task, objectivity was evaluated by most of the participants, followed by detail. Since the topic of vaccines also involves health information, it is likely that the participants referred to web pages that provided evidence-based information, such as research results. When asked why they responded that the objectivity of the web page they viewed was helpful, one of the participants responded, "Media and articles are subjective, so I think that data from research is more reliable." (ID7) These results indicate that in the vaccine task, many people refer to web pages that contain evidence-based information such as experimental results

4.2 Opinion Formation Analysis

This section describes the results of the analysis of how searchers formulate their opinions based on the information they obtain. The type of data that was used, the analysis method, and a detailed description of the analysis results are presented.

Approach. To analyze opinion formation, the free-form responses and interview content obtained from the posttask questionnaires completed by participants were examined. Specifically, the reasons for participants' opinion formation decisions based on the free-form responses and interview content were manually classified into various types through discussion among the research team. A single participant may have multiple types of opinion formation. For example, participant ID1 may present two types of opinion formation, such as "damage minimization" and "prior belief." Table 4 lists the seven types of opinion formation.

Findings. The analysis revealed seven types of opinion formation.

- Damage minimization
- Merit oriented
- Demerit oriented
- Credibility oriented
- Majority
- Single page
- Prior belief

These seven types are described in detail below.

Damage Minimization Type. This type of opinion formation avoids negative consequence as much as possible. One of the participants responded in the posttask questionnaire:

> "I thought that assigning too much homework was not good, but not assigning any homework at all would obstruct academic progress." (ID3)

This type of participant seems to focus more on minimizing losses rather than maximizing gains.

Merit-Oriented Type. This type of opinion formation considers the merits more than the demerits for a given topic. One of the participants responded in the posttask questionnaire:

> "I determined that the symptoms of developing severe illness from getting infected with the novel coronavirus were more severe than any side effects from the novel coronavirus vaccine." (ID9)

This type of participant seems to focus more on the greater advantages while perceiving the disadvantages.

Demerit-Oriented Type. This type of opinion formation considers the demerits more than the merits for a given topic. One of the participants responded in the posttask questionnaire:

> "I was afraid to vaccinate my own children against the novel coronavirus because of the unknown potential long-term side effects." (ID7)

This type of participant seems to formulate opinions by judging that the disadvantages exceeded the advantages.

Credibility-Oriented Type. This type of opinion formation refers to web pages with high credibility. Credibility is defined as "the degree of confidence in the intention of the sender to convey the most reasonable claims" [8]. One of the participants responded in the posttask questionnaire:

> "Many websites expressing opposing views have distorted Professor Cooper's research findings that 'too much homework has many disadvantages' and have claimed that homework should not be assigned."(ID11)

This type of participant seems to focus more on the impartial information of a web page.

Majority Type. This type of opinion formation prioritizes opinions advocated in the majority of viewed web pages. One of the participants responded in the posttask questionnaire:

> "There are many articles that argue homework includes the intention of making study habits, and I agree with this view."(ID10)

This type of participant seems to focus more on the information described in most web pages they viewed.

Single-Page Type. This opinion formation type prioritizes information from the most reliable web page. One of the participants responded in the posttask questionnaire:

> " The study by Professor Harris Cooper, who has conducted research on homework, described the many benefits of doing homework."(ID11)

This type of participant seems to focus more on the most helpful web pages among those viewed.

Prior Belief Type. This type of opinion formation prioritizes prior thoughts about the search task. One of the participants responded in the posttask questionnaire:

> "Since I work as a cram school tutor part-time, I had a personal belief based on my experience that homework is necessary."(ID5)

This type of participant seems to focus more on information in web pages that contain the same opinions as they did prior to conducting the search.

5   Discussion

This section discusses the reflections and implications of the insights obtained from the analysis in the previous section, followed by an examination of the limitations of the analyses conducted in this study.

5.1 Implications

From the web page analysis results evaluation in Sect. 4.1, it is concluded that information and opinions from multiple perspectives were evaluated in the homework task because the topic included various positions involved. The topic "Is homework necessary for elementary school students?" involves interests from various positions, including elementary school students, parents, school teachers, and cram schools. Therefore, it was assumed that information from various viewpoints, rather than just a minority of viewpoints, was evaluated. In the vaccine task, the topic "Should children be vaccinated against the novel coronavirus?" has a property that is closer to health information. Health information is directly related to human life; therefore, information based on solid evidence rather than individual opinions was considered helpful.

Based on the opinion formation analysis in Sect. 4.2, as the topics treated in this study involved both advantages and disadvantages, the opinion formation types that compared both views, such as damage minimization, merit- orientation, and demerit- orientation, were observed.

From the web page analysis evaluation in Sect. 4.1 and the opinion formation analysis in Sect. 4.2, it can be concluded that various opinion formation types exist, and presenting web pages that are relevant to each type can encourage cautious opinion formation by searchers. For example, credibility-oriented searchers tend not to rely heavily on web pages with low credibility. This suggests that if a web page that contains an opposing view has high credibility, the searcher is more likely to adopt that view. In other words, searchers may change their opinions significantly depending on the credibility of the web pages they browse. Therefore, by presenting more high-credibility web pages, searchers can be encouraged to form their own opinions by examining their both advantages and disadvantages. In summary, it is assumed that providing relevant web pages for each searcher type can promote careful opinion formation.

5.2 Limitations

This study has three limitations. First, the participants were recruited from the same information science department as the author; hence there may be bias in the selection. Hölscher et al. found that experienced searchers are better able to create complex queries and find relevant information compared to general searchers [11]. Therefore, it is possible that information science students are skilled searchers and may have obtained more relevant search results than general searchers. Moreover, it is assumed that more detailed data can be obtained by conducting user studies that consider the age of the searchers and their search expertise.

Second, the user study addressed only two topics: "Is homework necessary for elementary school students?" and "Should children receive the COVID-19 vaccine?" However, topics contain a variety of properties. For example, the topic "Should children receive the COVID-19 vaccine?" contains the nature of advantages and disadvantages as well as health information. Since topics have various properties, conducting a user study with an increased number of controversial topics, such as "Should students have to wear school uniforms?" and "Should euthanasia be legal?", may enable the discovery of useful web pages and opinion formation patterns that were not obtained in this study.

Finally, the questionnaire and interview responses of participants are analyzed. However, analyzing the log data of participants' search behavior may enable support from the perspective of search behavior. For example, if participants were not able to input diverse queries, recommending search queries may allow them to obtain more diverse information, thereby supporting opinion formation. Moreover, if participants had viewed many web pages that contain only one side of an argument, then presenting web pages that contain the opposing argument may enable support for exposure to diverse information. In the future, an analysis that focuses on the search behavior of participants will be conducted.

6   Conclusion

This study investigated the types of web pages people refer to regarding controversial topics and how these pages ultimately affect the formation of their own opinions. A user study was conducted involving 12 participants, with data collected from questionnaires and interviews. As for the web page evaluation analysis, the data of web page evaluations answered by the participants was labeled based on previous studies and as discussed among the authors. The labeling results showed that in the homework task, searchers reported that useful web pages included those that contained information and opinions from various perspectives and those that contained evidence-based information such as experimental results. In the vaccine task, many searchers also reported that useful web pages included those that contained evidence-based information, such as the results of an experiment. Furthermore, in the opinion formation analysis, the free descriptions of opinion formation reasons answered by the participants were manually classified into seven types: damage minimization, merit oriented, demerit oriented, credibility oriented, majority, single page, and prior belief. The findings of this study suggest that the usefulness of a search system, which presents easily referenced web pages by considering the opinion formation type of searchers, can be demonstrated when searching for controversial topics.

Acknowledgement. This work was supported in part by JSPS KAKENHI Grant Numbers JP21H03774, JP21H03775, JP22H03905.

References

1. Ajjour, Y., Braslavski, P., Bondarenko, A., Stein, B.: Identifying argumentative questions in web search logs. In: Proceedings of the 45th International ACM SIGIR Conference on Research and Development in Information Retrieval, pp. 2393–2399 (2022)

2. Allam, A., Schulz, P., Nakamoto, K.: The impact of search engine selection and sorting criteria on vaccination beliefs and attitudes: two experiments manipulating google output. J. Med. Internet Res. **16**, e100 (2014)
3. Chelaru, S., Altingovde, I.S., Siersdorfer, S., Nejdl, W.: Analyzing, detecting, and exploiting sentiment in web queries. ACM Trans. Web **8**(1), 1–28 (2013)
4. Chen, S., Khashabi, D., Callison-Burch, C., Roth, D.: Perspectroscope: a window to the world of diverse perspectives. In: Proceedings of the 57th Annual Meeting of the Association for Computational Linguistics, pp. 129–134 (2019)
5. Cuan-Baltazar, J.Y., Muñoz-Perez, M.J., Robledo-Vega, C., Pérez-Zepeda, M.F., Soto-Vega, E.: Misinformation of COVID-19 on the internet: infodemiology study. J. Med. Internet Res. Public Health Surveill. **6**(2), e18444 (2020)
6. Draws, T., Inel, O., Tintarev, N., Baden, C., Timmermans, B.: Comprehensive viewpoint representations for a deeper understanding of user interactions with debated topics. In: Proceedings of the ACM SIGIR Conference on Human Information Interaction and Retrieval, pp. 135–145 (2022)
7. Draws, T., Tintarev, N., Gadiraju, U., Bozzon, A., Timmermans, B.: This is not what we ordered: Exploring why biased search result rankings affect user attitudes on debated topics. In: Proceedings of the 44th International ACM SIGIR Conference on Research and Development in Information Retrieval, pp. 295–305 (2021)
8. Fogg, B.J.: Persuasive Technology: Using Computers to Change What We Think and Do. Morgan Kaufmann, San Francisco (2002)
9. Gezici, G., Lipani, A., Saygin, Y., Yilmaz, E.: Evaluation metrics for measus results. Inf. Retrieval J. **24**, 85–113 (2021)
10. Gyllstrom, K., Moens, M.F.: Clash of the typings: finding controversies and children's topics within queries. In: Proceedings of the Advances in Information Retrieval - 33rd European Conference on IR Research, pp. 80–91 (2011)
11. Hölscher, C., Strube, G.: Web search behavior of internet experts and newbies. Comput. Netw. **33**(1), 337–346 (2000)
12. Kapoun, J.: Teaching undergrads web evaluation: a guide for library instruction. College Res. Lib. News **59**(7), 522–523 (1998)
13. Metzger, M.J., Flanagin, A.J., Zwarun, L.: College student web use, perceptions of information credibility, and verification behavior. Comput. Educ. **41**(3), 271–290 (2003)
14. Moz Inc.: 2020 Google search survey: how much do users trust their search results? https://moz.com/blog/2020-google-search-survey. Accessed 10 Oct 2022
15. Pogacar, F.A., Ghenai, A., Smucker, M.D., Clarke, C.L.: The positive and negative influence of search results on people's decisions about the efficacy of medical treatments. In: Proceedings of the ACM SIGIR International Conference on Theory of Information Retrieval, pp. 209–216 (2017)
16. Pothirattanachaikul, S., Yamamoto, T., Yamamoto, Y., Yoshikawa, M.: Analyzing the effects of document's opinion and credibility on search behaviors and belief dynamics. In: Proceedings of the 28th ACM International Conference on Information and Knowledge Management, pp. 1653–1662 (2019)
17. Stab, C., et al.: Argumentext: searching for arguments in heterogeneous sources. In: Proceedings of the 2018 Conference of the North American chapter of the Association for Computational Linguistics, pp. 21–25 (2018)
18. Sun, Y., Zhang, Y., Gwizdka, J., Trace, C.B.: Consumer evaluation of the quality of online health information: systematic literature review of relevant criteria and indicators. J. Med. Internet Res. **21**(5), e12522 (2019)

19. Tatsumi, H., Mitani, H., Haruki, Y., Ogushi, Y.: Internet medical usage in japan: current situation and issues. J. Med. Internet Res. **3**(1), e12 (2001)
20. White, R.: Beliefs and biases in web search. In: Proceedings of the 36th International ACM SIGIR Conference on Research and Development in Information Retrieval, pp. 3–12 (2013)
21. White, R.W., Drucker, S.M.: Investigating behavioral variability in web search. In: Proceedings of the 16th International Conference on World Wide Web, pp. 21–30 (2007)
22. Yamamoto, T., Yamamoto, Y., Fujita, S.: Exploring people's attitudes and behaviors toward careful information seeking in web search. In: Proceedings of the 27th ACM International Conference on Information and Knowledge Management, pp. 963–972 (2018)

Applying a Vector Search Method in Reference Service Question-Answer Retrieval Systems

Te-Lun Yang[1]([✉])[iD], Guan-Lun Huang[2][iD], and Yuen-Hsien Tseng[1,2][iD]

[1] Graduate Institute of Networking and Multimedia, National Taiwan University, Taipei, Taiwan
d12944007@ntu.edu.tw
[2] Graduate Institute of Library and Information Studies National Taiwan Normal University, Taipei, Taiwan
{60915003E,samtseng}@ntnu.edu.tw

Abstract. We have developed a reference service question-answer retrieval system prototype based on dense vector search technology. When librarians receive reference questions, they can utilize reference service question-answer systems to determine if similar questions have been asked before and how they were resolved. Readers can also search the system to see if their questions have been answered. However, traditional reference service question-answer retrieval systems primarily rely on keyword-based searches, which may not capture questions with different phrasing but identical meaning. Vector search has emerged as a promising approach to address this limitation, and it has been widely researched and applied in various domains. Nevertheless, there is a lack of research on applying vector search in reference service question-answer retrieval systems. Thus, we conducted initial experiments in this area. Leveraging ElasticSearch vector search technology, which can efficiently search through large datasets, we adopted this technology in our study. For building our system, we collected question-answer pairs from the Taipei Public Library's Online Reference Service Platform, one of Taiwan's most prominent online reference services. We report the data set we used and the system architecture.

Keywords: Dense vector search · Reference service · Question-answer system · Full-text search engine · Taipei public library

1 Introduction

Libraries' reference services can benefit from retrieval in question-answer databases, allowing for the reuse of previously answered questions, either directly or with minor adjustments [1]. However, most search engines in reference service

---

These authors contributed equally to this work.
To whom all correspondence should be addressed.

© The Author(s), under exclusive license to Springer Nature Singapore Pte Ltd. 2023
D. H. Goh et al. (Eds.): ICADL 2023, LNCS 14457, pp. 204–209, 2023.
https://doi.org/10.1007/978-981-99-8085-7_18

databases primarily rely on keyword matching, which may not retrieve sentences with different phrasing but the identical meaning. Vector retrieval methods offer an effective solution to this problem. Currently, there is no application of vector search in reference service databases in Taiwan. There are related studies, such as the reference service robot developed by the National Taiwan Normal University [2] and the reference service robot utilizing the reference service blog of the National Taiwan University Library as a knowledge base [4]. These systems typically employ keyword-matching methods to provide answers to readers. However, the target users of the studies above are readers, which differs from our intended goal. Our goal is to develop a case-based reasoning system for librarians' use. Case-based reasoning means using past experiences to understand and solve new problems [5] We aim to provide librarians with our system, allowing them to search for similar past questions when they receive new ones and refer to how similar queries were answered using reference resources, thus saving time and providing more accurate answers. Ultimately, librarians still provide solutions to readers rather than directly by machines. Therefore, in this study, we explore establishing a librarian-oriented case-based reasoning system to enhance the efficiency and effectiveness of library reference services. In the subsequent sections, we describe the dataset and simple data visualization. Next, we present the system implementation including system architecture and relevant methods. The conclusion section summarizes our research work.

2   Data Collection

Previous studies have also used smaller datasets, focusing on university libraries. Therefore, we surveyed the available reference service platforms in Taiwan and obtained past question-answer pairs. We found that the National Central Library launched the Reference Service Zone (參考服務園地) system in March 2002, accumulating 5,745 reader inquiries by the end of 2009 [7]. However, this website has been closed. Currently, the National Central Library provides reference services through the "Academic Knowledge Service Network (學術知識服務網)." However, the number of question-answer pairs is less than a thousand. On the other hand, the Taipei Public Library's Online Reference Service (線上參考服務) Platform has collected over 13,000 question-answer pairs spanning different topics. Consequently, we ultimately decided to use the Taipei Public Library as the source of our question-answer dataset. In this study, a total of 13,635 question-answer pairs were used, categorized into 16 categories: "Shanghai Library Consultation (上海圖書館諮詢)" (5 pairs), "World History (世界史地)" (339 pairs), "Word Transliteration (字詞音譯)" (36 pairs), "Religion (宗教)" (87 pairs), "Applied Science (應用科學)" (745 pairs), "Literature (文學)" (314 pairs), "Domestic Geography (本國地理)" (44 pairs), "Domestic History (本國歷史)" (95 pairs), "Social Science (社會科學)" (827 pairs), "Generalities (總類)" (1,344 pairs), "Natural Science (自然科學)" (2,097 pairs), "Taipei Public Library-related (臺北市立圖書館相關)" (5,141 pairs), "Art (藝術)" (205 pairs), "Language (語言)" (281 pairs), "Uncategorized (未分類資料)" (885 pairs), and

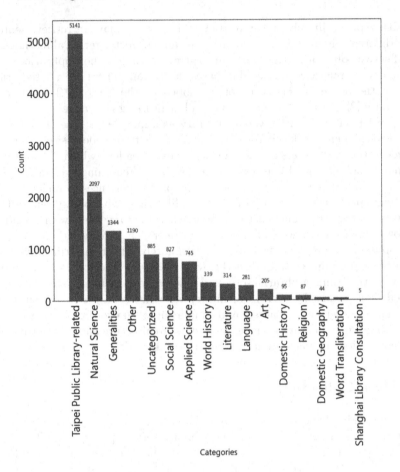

Fig. 1. The quantity of each category.

"Other (其他)" (1,190 pairs). Figure 1 displays the number of question-answer pairs in each category, arranged in descending order based on their quantity. The maximum sentence length (number of words) of the questions is 3984, the minimum is 12, the average sentence length is 413.836, and the standard deviation is 369.656. Figure 2 displays the quantity each category represents based on the spacing of text lengths as questions. The maximum sentence length (number of words) of the answers is 43343, the minimum is 1, the average sentence length is 1673.688, and the standard deviation is 2231.864. Figure 3 is presented similarly to Fig. 2, showing the distribution of answer categories based on text length spacing.

3   System Implementation

3.1   System Architecture

This system differs from traditional information retrieval methods based on statistical measures in terms of similarity calculation during the retrieval process.

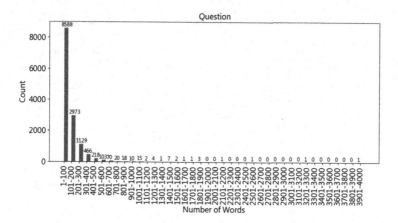

Fig. 2. The quantity based on the sentence lengths of the answer.

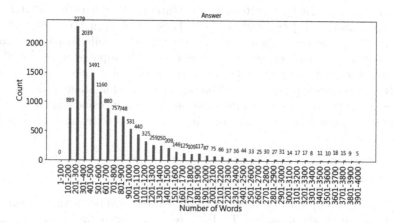

Fig. 3. The quantity based on the sentence lengths of the questions.

Instead of matching based on word frequency or word weights, it utilizes dense vector search. To perform vector search effectively, the system transforms the user's question text into vectors using SBERT and compares them with the indexed data stored in ElasticSearch (ES). The indexed data includes questions, question vectors, and corresponding answers. The system calculates the cosine similarity between the user's question vector and the question vectors in the index, finding the top-k closest results. The results are then ranked in descending order based on their cosine similarity values, which are floating-point numbers ranging from 0 to 1. The system also retrieves the corresponding answer text associated with the question vector from the index for user review (Fig. 4).

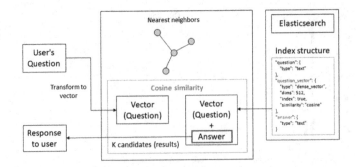

Fig. 4. A system architecture primarily focused on vector search.

3.2 Sentence-BERT (SBERT)

SBERT (Sentence-BERT) by Reimers and Gurevych [6] differs from BERT (Bidirectional Encoder Representations from Transformers) in terms of generating vectors (also known as embeddings) based on words. While BERT incorporates word embeddings considering the context of the entire input sentence [3], SBERT addresses the limitations of BERT in generating embeddings based on sentences. SBERT introduces a pooling operation during the output stage of BERT to create fixed-length sentence embeddings. It also supports cosine similarity calculations between embeddings, enhancing the effectiveness of sentence-level comparisons.

3.3 ElasticSearch (ES)

ES (ElasticSearch) is a full-text search engine that supports various similarity calculation methods, including TF-IDF (term frequency-inverse document frequency), BM25, DFR (divergence from randomness), and DFI (divergence from independence). Starting from version 7.3, ES also supports vector search, allowing customizable similarity matching. In version 8.0 and onwards, ES introduces the support for Approximate Nearest Neighbor (ANN) search, similar to the k-nearest neighbor (kNN) algorithm. While kNN performs well in low-dimensional data structures like KD-trees, it struggles with high-dimensional data such as images and videos. ANN improves the performance of high-dimensional search. In addition to cosine similarity and dot product, ANN offers the calculation of Euclidean distance (l2 norm) for similarity comparison. Figure 5 illustrates the process of vector search.

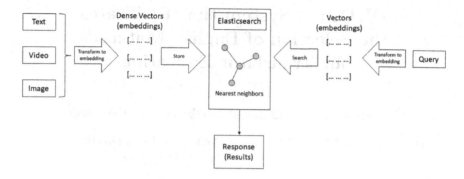

Fig. 5. Process of Vector Search.

4 Conclusion and Future Work

We propose an alternative approach for a reference service question-answer retrieval system using vector search, which other researchers have not attempted. However, we have not yet provided this system to librarians for actual usage and usability evaluation. In future work, we plan to give the system for usability evaluation by reference librarians and investigate whether vector search truly outperforms boolean search in finding similar reference questions.

References

1. Bui, Y.: A hybrid retrieval approach for library reference question/answer databank. Proc. Am. Soc. Inf. Sci. Technol. **46**(1), 1–4 (2009)
2. Chen, Y.: Development and evaluation of a chatbot for reference service in national Taiwan normal university library. National Taiwan Normal University, Taipei (2019)
3. Devlin, J., Chang, M.W., Lee, K., Toutanova, K.: BERT: Pre-training of deep bidirectional transformers for language understanding. arXiv preprint arXiv:1810.04805 (2018)
4. Fan, W.: The implementation and evaluation of chat robot application on virtual reference service of university library. J. Libr. Inf. Sci. **46**(1), 4–31 (2020)
5. Kolodner, J.L.: An introduction to case-based reasoning. Artif. Intell. Rev. **6**, 3–34 (1992). Reza Entezari-Maleki
6. Reimers, N., Gurevych, I.: Sentence-BERT: sentence embeddings using Siamese BERT-networks. arXiv preprint arXiv:1908.10084 (2019)
7. Wang, M., T.F.T.T.: The use study of the digital reference service from the national central library. Nat. Cent. Libr. Bull. **100**(1), 65–98 (2011)

QRDP: A System that Facilitates the Selection of English Materials for Translator Education

Takeshi Abekawa(✉) , Rei Miyata , and Kyo Kageura

The University of Tokyo, 7-3-1 Hongo, Bunkyo-ku, Tokyo 113-0033, Japan
{abekawa,miyata,kyo}@p.u-tokyo.ac.jp

Abstract. We are currently developing a system that facilitates teachers of translation to evaluate and select suitable document segments as materials for translator training. The system needs to satisfy several requirements. Firstly, because translation is an act that deals with documents and not with texts in linguistics, it takes into account *documentational* features. Secondly, it should facilitate teachers to *select* suitable documentational segments that usually consist of several paragraphs, as translation generally requires a long time, especially for trainees. Thirdly, it should facilitate teachers to compare different segments in the same document or from different documents, because teachers often need to use more than one material in a class or use progressively advanced materials in a course. The system should preferably relate documentational features to translation competences. These requirements make the system different from most existing text analysis systems. In the demo, we show the trial version of the system, explaining the core functionalities together with the background design concepts.

Keywords: Document profiling · Translation · Translator education

1 Introduction

In this demonstration, we present QRDP (which stands for QR Document Profiler), a system that facilitates the selection of source document materials for translation in the translation education setup. The system currently focuses on English documents, as the demand for translating English documents into other languages is the highest. As of now, the system is available online for a limited range of users.

There are a number of systems that analyse input texts and output various textual characteristics such as readability scores [5,9,13], vocabulary level [14], and/or basic quantitative textual features [2,22]. Some of the most widely used among such systems are: Automatic Readability Checker [1], CVLA: CEFR-based Vocabulary Level Analyzer [4,23], Lexos [15], TextInspector [20], and Text

Supported by JSPS KAKENHI Grant-in-Aid (S) Grant Number 19H05660.

Analytics with Sketch Engine [21]. The objectives or emphases of these systems vary, e.g. evaluating texts for use in language teaching/learning setup, in lexicographical tasks, etc., but they all regard texts essentially as linguistic entities and analyse texts at the language level.

This fact motivated us to develop the system QRDP that facilitates those who teach translation to choose materials for translation practice, because translation is not about language but about documents [10]. While the information QRDP outputs has much in common with many text evaluation systems, it has features that reflect its mission of facilitating the choice of materials for translation education. Below we first elaborate on the nature of translations and the factors involved in the selection of materials for translation practice, and then give the design concept and an overview of the system QRDP.

2   Background

2.1   Translation as a Documentational Process

Translation deals with documents and not languages [11]. This fact is indeed well reflected in our ordinary use of the word "to translate." Suppose you, as a translator, are asked what you translate. The answer would be something like "I translate patent documents," "I translate novels," "I mostly translate product manuals," etc., and not "I translate sentences," "I translate paragraphs," "I translate words," or "I translate texts." Reflecting this fact, in translation education, language competence is often regarded as a prerequisite. For instance, European Master's in Translation Competence Framework explicitly states that it "takes as a premise that a high level of language competence in at least two working languages (CEFR level C1 and above or an equivalent level in comparable reference systems) should be a prerequisite for access to any EMT master's degree course in translation" [7, p. 6].

Dealing with documentational features and elements constitutes a substantial part of actual translation process. For instance, to translate an excerpt from an international treaty, the translator must identify that the segment is an excerpt from a particular treaty, check whether its official translation in the target language exists or not, and use the corresponding part of the official translation if it exists, unless specific conditions are given. The same expressions that occur as an enumerated item and in a section heading may have to be translated differently, while different occurrences of a term should be translated consistently by using the corresponding target language term that is specified by the domain or by the translation project. The concept that "the crime of aggression" represents must be verified in relation to the date of publication of the document (whether the document the translator is translating was published before or after Kampala Amendments to the Rome Statute in 2010 may critically affect the translation). All these processes are *documentational*, and not addressed in language teaching/learning or in linguistics.

2.2 Selecting Materials for Translation Practice

The mission of translator education is to nurture students' competences required to become professional translators. Courses involved in professional translation training worldwide (mostly at the master's level) adopt a curriculum that balances theory with practice, in which translation practice plays an essential role [18]. In translation practice classes, selecting appropriate materials is essential and often time-consuming. In selecting materials, at least three factors need to be taken into account.

Firstly, while it is theoretically true that translation deals with documents and language-level treatment is a prerequisite, it is not practically possible to assume that all translation learners have a sufficient level of language competences. In translation practice, even if all learners have the required level of language competences, it is often not possible to consolidate documentational processes separately from linguistic processes. Reflecting this reality, nurturing language-level competences constitutes a non-negligible part of translator education [3,6]. In choosing materials for translation practice, therefore, teachers should take into account both linguistic factors and documentational factors. For instance, if students are supposed to learn how to deal with different structural elements of a document in a class, choosing linguistically challenging material can hamper achieving the goal. Alternatively, teachers may want to focus on language-level issues without being concerned with documentational aspects of translations. In any case, in selecting materials for translation practice, teachers take into account both linguistic and documentational factors.

Secondly, materials are often chosen in relation to other materials. Teachers choose different materials as the course progresses or as the focus shifts. In so doing, they may want to choose materials that contain different documentational elements but have approximately the same language level, or may want to choose those that contain the same documentational elements but with different language levels. While there are several criteria for measuring language-level text difficulties, we do not have established criteria for measuring documentational difficulties or status apart from such upper-level categories as register types or genres. Therefore, the selection of materials in this regard tends to depend on individual teachers' experience, knowledge, and/or expertise.

Thirdly, as translation is a time-consuming and laborious process, it is often not possible to select the whole document as an appropriate material. Teachers should choose a small segment of a document that consists only of several paragraphs. Selecting materials for translation practice consists not only of selecting documents but also of selecting suitable parts of them, taking into account the expected time necessary for students to deal with the materials in accordance with the requirements defined in the class.

Considering these factors that are involved in the selection of translation materials, we examined existing text evaluation or analysis systems and found that it would be necessary to develop a new system that focuses on facilitating the selection of translation materials. While these systems provide language-level evaluations to a satisfactory degree, they do not address document-level analysis. They do not facilitate the selection of segments, either.

The discussions so far started from the point at which candidate documents are already chosen, putting aside the process of choosing candidate materials in the first place. Facilitating this process is also essential.

3   Facilitating the Selection of Translation Materials

3.1   Requirements for the System

The observations given in Sect. 2 indicate that the system that facilitates the selection of translation materials should have the following functionalities:

Document Analysis: In addition to analysing given documents in terms of conventional language-level features such as readability, vocabulary level or linguistic complexity of texts, the system should be able to evaluate documentational features. These include document properties (domain, genre, format, etc.), formal elements (tags, meta-data, fonts, etc.), structural elements (titles, itemisations, citations, etc.), and "non-linguistic" content elements (technical terms, named entities, etc.) [16]. Technologies (and to some extent resources) are already available in most of these evaluations for English. Given this situation, the issue here is not to provide as many metrics as possible, but to limit metrics in a suitable manner.

Segment Manipulation: The system should enable users to select a segment of a document and examine its linguistic and documentational characteristics. This requires a suitable interface that is connected to document analysis functions.

Comparative Evaluation: The system should enable users to compare multiple documents, mainly in two scenarios: to select multiple materials with similar features at once, and to select a new material that has the desired difference from reference materials. To provide these functions, it is important to keep a history of document selections for a user and provide easy-to-manipulate interface with intuitive visualisations.

Candidate Document Proposal: The system should preferably propose candidate materials that fit specifications given by the user or are similar to the document given by the user. In order to achieve this, the system should either keep a substantial number of documents as data or be able to launch real-time document retrieval or both.

We have developed basic functionalities for all these aspects.

3.2 QRDP: The System Prototype

The characteristics of QRDP compared to most text analytic systems are mainly two: it analyses not only linguistic features but also documentational features, and it facilitates the selection of document segments. We depict some features of the system in a simplified scenario that emphasises the selection of document segments as translation materials. Here we use two essential linguistic features for selecting translation materials, i.e. Fresch-Kincaid readability score [19] and CEFR vocabulary level [8].

Figure 1 is a screenshot of the system interface at which the user is selecting document candidates from the pool of documents QRDP provides. Currently, QRDP provides news dataset from Common Crawl site for experimental use [17]. It shows that the keyword "COVID-19" is given as a topic (shown on the top-right input window), and the score range 10–13 by Flesch-Kincaid readability score is specified (indicated in the top pull-down menu and the slide bar on its right). The user can specify basic features of the documents. Once a set of desired candidate documents are obtained, the user can select documents for further scrutiny. At this interface, the user can also upload her/his own documents of choice or specify URLs.

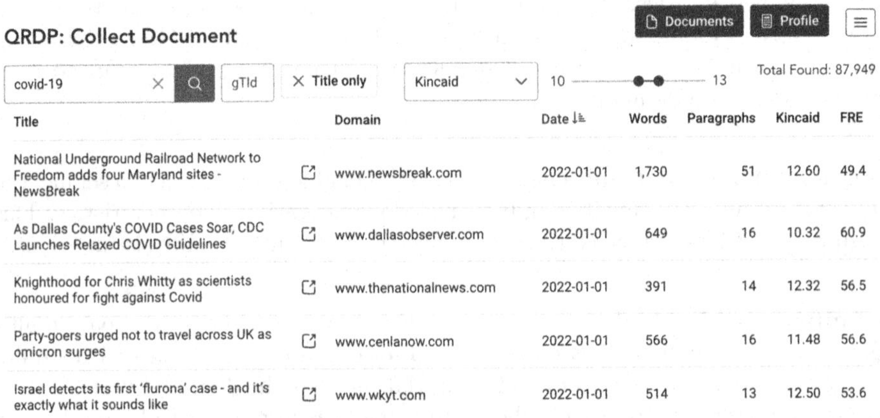

QRDP: Collect Document

Title		Domain	Date ↓↥	Words	Paragraphs	Kincaid	FRE
National Underground Railroad Network to Freedom adds four Maryland sites - NewsBreak	☐	www.newsbreak.com	2022-01-01	1,730	51	12.60	49.4
As Dallas County's COVID Cases Soar, CDC Launches Relaxed COVID Guidelines	☐	www.dallasobserver.com	2022-01-01	649	16	10.32	60.9
Knighthood for Chris Whitty as scientists honoured for fight against Covid	☐	www.thenationalnews.com	2022-01-01	391	14	12.32	56.5
Party-goers urged not to travel across UK as omicron surges	☐	www.cenlanow.com	2022-01-01	566	16	11.48	56.6
Israel detects its first 'flurona' case - and it's exactly what it sounds like	☐	www.wkyt.com	2022-01-01	514	13	12.50	53.6

(covid-19 gTld Title only Kincaid 10 ●—● 13 Total Found: 87,949)

Documents · Profile

Fig. 1. QRDP interface at which the user is selecting document candidates from the system pool, with "covid-19" as a keyword and the Kincaid score between 10 and 13.

Figure 2 is a screenshot of the interface at which the user is observing the distribution of words by their CEFR levels. Different CEFR-level words are indicated by colour in the text and the basic statistics are shown on the right panel. In Fig. 2, the user picked up two consecutive paragraphs that contain some C2-level words. When the user completes the selection, the statistics for the selected segments will be shown. So the user can select segments interactively by referring to relevant features. A range of linguistic and documentational features can be visualised on the left-side panel of the screen.

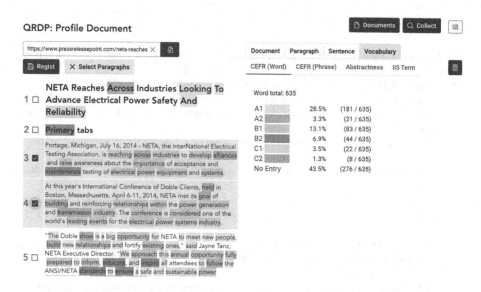

Fig. 2. QRDP interface at which the user is choosing a segment consisting of two consecutive paragraphs that contain some CEFR C2-level words. (The document in this figure is obtained from https://www.pressreleasepoint.com/neta-reaches-across-industries-looking-advance-electrical-power-safety-and-reliability).

4   Conclusions and Outlook

In the demonstration, we will show the functionalities of the system in accordance with several use scenarios, emphasising the interactive process of evaluating documents in terms of their linguistic and documentational features, selecting appropriate segments among documents, comparing the selected segments, and finalising the selection.

The prototype system is currently available to a limited range of experimental users. It will be augmented with enriched comparative evaluation functions that enable users to select new documents based on the past selections, as well as with candidate document proposal functions, which are currently being developed. As of now, the interpretations of linguistic and documentational metrics are left to users, except for well-established qualitative categories such as CEFR level and school/university grade levels. We are separately developing a scheme that provides core competence categories that are connected to basic linguistic and documentational features [12]. Providing estimations of required competences based on the evaluation of linguistic and documentational features will further facilitate usability. The full system will be made public by the end of 2023.

Acknowledgements. This work is partially supported by JSPS KAKENHI Grant-in-Aid (S) Grant Number 19H05660. The authors would like to thank Dr. Atsushi Fujita of National Institute of Information and Communications Technology for constructive discussion.

References

1. Automatic Readability Checker Homepage. https://readabilityformulas.com/free-readability-formula-tests.php. Accessed 7 July 2023
2. Baayen, R.H.: Word Frequency Distributions. Kluwer, Dordrecht (2001)
3. Chodkiewicz, M.: The EMT framework of reference for competences applied to translation: perceptions by professional and student translators. J. Specialised Transl. **17**, 37–54 (2012)
4. CVLA: CEFR-based Vocabulary Level Analyzer (ver. 2.0) Homepage. https://cvla.langedu.jp/. Accessed 7 July 2023
5. Dubay, W.H.: The Principles of Readability. Impact Information, Costa Mesa (2004)
6. Esfandiari, M.R., Shokrpour, N., Rahimi, F.: An evaluation of the EMT: compatibility with the professional translator's needs. Cogent Arts Hum. **6**(1), 1–17 (2019)
7. European Master's in Translation: Competence framework 2022. https://commission.europa.eu/system/files/2022-11/emt_competence_fwk_2022_en.pdf. Accessed 8 July 2023
8. EnglishProfile: The CEFR for English. https://www.englishprofile.org/wordlists/. Accessed 14 July 2023
9. Flesch, R.F.: A new readability yardstick. J. Appl. Psychol. **32**(3), 221–233 (1948)
10. Kageura, K.: The status of documents and related concepts in translation and in library science. In: A-LIEP 2019, pp. 1–13 (2019)
11. Kageura, K.: What do translators translate? AAMT J. **71**, 14–19 (2019). (in Japanese)
12. Kageura, K., Yamamoto, M., Miyata, R.: A typology of basic translation competences: towards diagnosing and assessing acts in core translation processes in terms of competences. In: The 23rd ITRI International Conference (2023)
13. Kincaid, J.P., Fishburne, R.P., Jr., Rogers, R.L., Chissom, B.S.: Derivation of new readability formulas (Automated Readability Index, Fog Count and Flesch Reading Ease Formula) for Navy enlisted personnel. University of Central Florida, Millington, Institute for Simulation and Training (1975)
14. Lewrenz, A.S.: A vocabulary grade placement formula. J. Exp. Educ. **3**(3), 236 (1935)
15. Lexos Homepage. http://lexos.wheatoncollege.edu/statistics. Accessed 7 July 2023
16. Miyata, R., Miyauchi, T.: Metalanguages for source document analysis: properties and elements. In: Miyata, R., Yamada, M., Kageura, K. (eds.) Metalanguages for Dissecting Translation Processes: Theoretical Development and Practical Applications, pp. 63–79. Routledge, London (2022)
17. Nagel, S.: News Dataset Available site (2016). https://commoncrawl.org/2016/10/news-dataset-available/. Accessed 14 July 2023
18. Piao, H., Kageura, K.: A review for the design of a translation education curriculum aiming at the development of translator competence: Towards transferring "knowing how" through "knowing that". Studies in Lifelong Learning Infrastructure Management, vol. 47, pp. 1–17 (2022). (in Japanese)
19. readability 0.3.1. https://pypi.org/project/readability/. Accessed 14 July 2023
20. TextInspector Homepage. https://textinspector.com/. Accessed 7 July 2023
21. Text Analytics with Sketch Engine Homepage. https://www.sketchengine.eu/tools-for-text-analysis/. Accessed 7 July 2023

22. Tuldava, J.: Methods of Quantitative Linguistics. Wissenschaftlicher Verlag Trier, Trier (1995)
23. Uchida, S., Negishi, M.: Assigning CEFR-J levels to English texts based on textual features. In: Proceedings of the 4th Asia Pacific Corpus Linguistics Conference, pp. 463–467 (2018)

A Privacy-Preserving Technique to Identify the Useful Content of Documents Owned by Multiple Institutes

Rina Kagawa[✉] , Akira Imakura , and Masaki Matsubara

University of Tsukuba, Tsukuba, Japan
kagawa-r@md.tsukuba.ac.jp, imakura@cs.tsukuba.ac.jp,
masaki@slis.tsukuba.ac.jp

Abstract. Documents must contain the content needed to ensure effective asynchronous communication among remote users. To identify what should be included in documents, it is useful to centralize and analyze data. However, if complex data combinations can reveal sensitive individual information, data sharing becomes challenging. This study proposes a method that realizes feature selections using multiple regression analyses without sharing the original data by sharing dimensionality-reduced data instead of the original information. The proposed method was demonstrated to select those features that significantly increased the documents' usefulness based on textual feedback documents for amateur musicians. The proposed method estimated almost the same p-values and linear model parameters for almost all features as when the original data was shared. The proposed method contributes widely to studies of digital libraries, in that it can be applied to any data type.

Keywords: Document · Privacy-Preserving Analysis · Musical Education

1 Introduction

1.1 Background

The importance of documents enabling asynchronous information sharing in remote settings was emphasized during the COVID-19 pandemic. To determine the content to be included in the documents [11,13], prior studies relied on expert opinions [1,14], but this may not align with lay-readers' preferences. Recent research integrated various data sources, conducted lay-reader evaluations, applied supervised feature selection, and identified content that significantly enhanced document quality [2,6,9]. However, collecting and analyzing

This study was partially supported by JST-Mirai Program Grant Number JPMJMI19G8, JSPS KAKENHI Grant Number JP19K19347.

data across multiple parties, even when de-identified, can still pose privacy risks by potentially inferring sensitive individual data. This challenge persists despite existing privacy laws and regulations [15], making it difficult to gather distributed data.

Therefore, this study aims to realize feature selection without sharing any original research data owned by many institutions in a distributed manner. The typical technology used to meet the demands is federated learning systems [7,10] or encryption [8]. However, federated learning systems require iterative cross-institutional communication. Encryption requires a huge computational cost.

1.2 Study Objective

This study focused on feature selection using multiple regression and proposes a technique to approximate the model parameters and corresponding statistics such as p-values of multiple regression without sharing the original research data distributed to each local party or iterative computation. Our method allows each local party to identify document content through supervised feature selection without collecting original data on document content and usefulness.

This study adopted the data collaboration framework [4,5], which is a non-model share-type federated learning with small communication costs. The proposed method shares a dimensionality-reduced data representation, *intermediate representation*, instead of the original data, allowing each local party to approximate the linear model parameters and the corresponding statistics. To demonstrate our proposed method, the empirical experiment focuses on identifying useful content in feedback documents of musical performances.

2 Problem Setting

This study aims to enable each involved party to obtain the linear model parameters and corresponding statistics, such as p-values, based on multiple regression analyses without sharing the original data distributed to each party.

Let m and n denote the number of features and training data samples. Let $X = [\boldsymbol{x}_1, \boldsymbol{x}_2, \ldots, \boldsymbol{x}_n]^{\mathrm{T}} \in \mathbb{R}^{n \times m}$ and $\boldsymbol{y} = [y_1, y_2, \ldots, y_n]^{\mathrm{T}} \in \mathbb{R}^n$ be the training dataset and the corresponding ground truth. Here, we assume that data samples are partitioned into $c \geq 2$ parties as follows:

$$X = \begin{bmatrix} X_1 \\ X_2 \\ \vdots \\ X_c \end{bmatrix}, \quad \boldsymbol{y} = \begin{bmatrix} \boldsymbol{y}_1 \\ \boldsymbol{y}_2 \\ \vdots \\ \boldsymbol{y}_c \end{bmatrix}.$$

Then, each the i-th party has the local dataset

$$X_i \in \mathbb{R}^{n_i \times m}, \quad \boldsymbol{y}_i \in \mathbb{R}^{n_i}, \quad n = \sum_{i=1}^{c} n_i,$$

and want to obtain (an approximation of) a linear model parameter $\boldsymbol{w}$ and the corresponding p-value for the centralized datasets, that is,

$$\min_{\boldsymbol{w} \in \mathbb{R}^m} \|\boldsymbol{y} - X\boldsymbol{w}\|_2^2 + R(\boldsymbol{w}),$$

without sharing the local datasets X_i and $\boldsymbol{y}_i$, where $R(\boldsymbol{w})$ is a regularization term.

3   Proposed Method

3.1   Basic Concept

To solve the problem outlined in the previous section, we propose a data collaboration analysis with pseudo-sample generation using a random orthogonal transformation. The basic concepts of the proposed method are as follows:

- The proposed method protects the privacy of X_i based on the data collaboration framework [3], which shares a dimensionality-reduced intermediate representation instead of the original data.
- The proposed method also protects the privacy of $\boldsymbol{y}_i$ based on a new pseudo-sample generation using a random orthogonal matrix $R_i, R_i^{\mathrm{T}} R_i = I$, based on the norm equivalence by orthogonal transformation as

$$\|\boldsymbol{y} - X\boldsymbol{w}\|_2^2 = \sum_{i=1}^c \|\boldsymbol{y}_i - X_i\boldsymbol{w}\|_2^2$$

$$= \sum_{i=1}^c \|R_i(\boldsymbol{y}_i - X_i\boldsymbol{w})\|_2^2.$$

3.2   Proposed Method

The outline of the proposed method is shown in Fig. 1. The proposed privacy-preserving method works on two roles: *worker* and *coordinator*. Workers have the private dataset X_i and $\boldsymbol{y}_i$, which must be analyzed without sharing them. Coordinator supports the collaboration analysis.

First, all workers generate the same anchor data $X^{\mathrm{anc}} \in \mathbb{R}^{r \times m}$, which is shareable, such as a random matrix. Then, each worker constructs intermediate representations with the pseudo-sample based on a random orthogonal transformation in the following three steps:

Step 1 Generate a random orthogonal matrix $R_i \in \mathbb{R}^{n_i \times n_i}$ such that $R_i^{\mathrm{T}} R_i = I$.
Step 2 Generate a dimensionality reduction function $F_i \in \mathbb{R}^{m \times \tilde{m}_i}$ from X_i (and $\boldsymbol{y}_i$), where $\tilde{m}_i < m$. Here, we can use non-supervised and supervised dimensionality reduction methods.

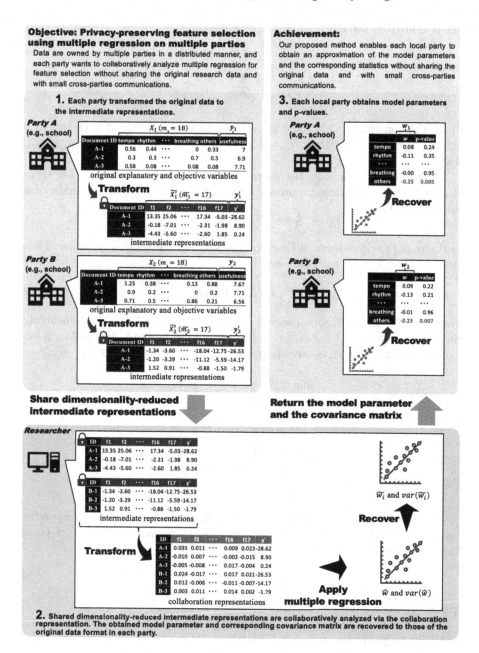

Fig. 1. Outline of the proposed method with $c = 2, n_1 = n_2 = 3$. **Remark:** *Human cannot infer the original explanatory and objective variables from the intermediate representations, and the transformation differs from school to school. Without sharing the original explanatory and objective variables, shared dimensionality-reduced intermediate representations are collaboratively analyzed via the collaboration representation, then, each school can obtain the model parameters and p-values.*

Step 3 Construct the intermediate representations

$$\widetilde{X}'_i = R_i X_i F_i \in \mathbb{R}^{n_i \times \widetilde{m}_i},$$
$$\boldsymbol{y}'_i = R_i \boldsymbol{y}_i \in \mathbb{R}^{n_i},$$
$$\widetilde{X}^{\mathrm{anc}}_i = X^{\mathrm{anc}} F_i \in \mathbb{R}^{r \times \widetilde{m}_i}.$$

Then, the constructed intermediate representations are shared with the coordinator. Here, we note that R_i and F_i depend on i and are not shared with others.

At the coordinator side, the shared intermediate representations are transformed to the collaboration representations $\widehat{X}'_i = \widetilde{X}'_i G_i$ that can be analyzed as one dataset. Let

$$[\widetilde{X}^{\mathrm{anc}}_1, \widetilde{X}^{\mathrm{anc}}_2, \ldots, \widetilde{X}^{\mathrm{anc}}_c] \approx U_{\widehat{m}} \Sigma_{\widehat{m}} V_{\widehat{m}}^{\mathrm{T}} \tag{1}$$

be the rank $\widehat{m}$ approximation based on the singular value decomposition. Then, matrices $G_i \in \mathbb{R}^{\widetilde{m}_i \times \widehat{m}}$ are computed by

$$G_i = (\widetilde{X}^{\mathrm{anc}}_i)^{\dagger} U_{\widehat{m}} C, \tag{2}$$

where $\dagger$ denotes the Moore–Penrose inverse and $C \in \mathbb{R}^{\widehat{m} \times \widehat{m}}$ is a nonsingular matrix, for example, $C = I$ and $C = \Sigma_{\widehat{m}}$ are used in practice. The collaboration representations $\widehat{X}'_i = \widetilde{X}'_i G_i$ are analyzed as a single dataset, that is,

$$\min_{\widehat{\boldsymbol{w}} \in \mathbb{R}^{\widehat{w}}} \| \boldsymbol{y}' - \widehat{X}' \widehat{\boldsymbol{w}} \|_2^2 + R(\widehat{\boldsymbol{w}}),$$

where

$$\widehat{X}' = \begin{bmatrix} \widehat{X}'_1 \\ \widehat{X}'_2 \\ \vdots \\ \widehat{X}'_c \end{bmatrix}, \quad \boldsymbol{y}' = \begin{bmatrix} \boldsymbol{y}'_1 \\ \boldsymbol{y}'_2 \\ \vdots \\ \boldsymbol{y}'_c \end{bmatrix}.$$

The coordinator then obtain the model parameter $\widehat{\boldsymbol{w}}$ and the corresponding covariance matrix $\mathrm{var}(\widehat{\boldsymbol{w}})$ for the collaboration representation. They are transformed for the intermediate representation, that is,

$$\widetilde{\boldsymbol{w}}_i = G_i \widehat{\boldsymbol{w}}, \quad \mathrm{var}(\widetilde{\boldsymbol{w}}_i) = G_i \mathrm{var}(\widehat{\boldsymbol{w}}) G_i^{\mathrm{T}} \tag{3}$$

and are shared to the i-th worker.

Using the local function F_i, each worker obtain the model parameter and the corresponding covariance matrix for the raw dataset as

$$\boldsymbol{w}_i = F_i \widetilde{\boldsymbol{w}}_i, \quad \mathrm{var}(\boldsymbol{w}_i) = F_i \mathrm{var}(\widetilde{\boldsymbol{w}}_i) F_i^{\mathrm{T}}. \tag{4}$$

The algorithm of the proposed method is summarized in Algorithm 1.

Algorithm 1 Proposed method

Input: $X_i \in \mathbb{R}^{n_i \times m}$ and $y_i \in \mathbb{R}^{n_i}$ individually
Output: w_i and $\text{var}(w_i)$ for each i

Worker-side $(i = 1, 2, \ldots, c)$

1: Generate X^{anc} and share to all workers
2: Generate a random orthogonal matrix R_i
3: Generate a dimensionality reduction function F_i
4: Compute $\widetilde{X}_i' = R_i X_i F_i, y_i' = R_i y_i,$
    and $\widetilde{X}_i^{\text{anc}} = X^{\text{anc}} F_i$
5: Share $\widetilde{X}_i', \widetilde{X}_i^{\text{anc}},$ and y_i' to coordinator

Coordinator-side

6: ↘ Obtain $\widetilde{X}_i', \widetilde{X}_i^{\text{anc}},$ and y_i' for all i
7:    Compute G_i from $\widetilde{X}_i^{\text{anc}}$ for all i by (1) and (2)
8:    Compute $\widehat{X}_i' = \widetilde{X}_i' G_i$ for all i
9:    Set $\widehat{X}$ and y'
10:   Analyze $\widehat{X}'$ and y' to obtain $\widehat{w}$ and $\text{var}(\widehat{w})$
11:   Compute $\widetilde{w}_i$ and $\text{var}(\widetilde{w}_i)$ by (3)
12: ↗ Return $\widetilde{w}_i$ and $\text{var}(\widetilde{w}_i)$ to each worker

Worker-side $(i = 1, 2, \ldots, c)$

13: Obtain $\widetilde{w}_i$ and $\text{var}(\widetilde{w}_i)$
14: Compute w_i and $\text{var}(w_i)$ by (4)

Privacy Analysis. The privacy of the data collaboration framework was also analyzed in [3]. The proposed method has the following similar double privacy layer:

- No one can infer the private data X_i and y_i under the protocol;
- Even if F_i and R_i are stolen, the private data X_i is still protected regarding ε-DR privacy [12].

Under the protocol (Algorithm 1), F_i and R_i for the intermediate representation are private and cannot be inferred by others because both the input and output of F_i and R_i are not possessed. Therefore, it is impossible to infer the original data X_i and y_i only from the shared intermediate representation $\widetilde{X}_i'$ and y_i'. In addition, F_i is set to a dimensionality reduction function such that $\widetilde{m}_i < m$. Therefore, it is impossible to obtain the original data X_i from $\widetilde{X}_i' = R_i X_i F_i$ even when using F_i and R_i.

4 Empirical Experiments

The proposed method was demonstrated using feedback documents from various music schools, where professional teachers provided feedback for amateur players. It aimed to select features that significantly improved document usefulness.

4.1   Preprocessing of the Feedback Documents

The published feedback documents about three instruments written in Japanese were used[1]: 144 documents for piano from 24 schools (6 documents per school), 252 documents for guitar from 13 schools (19 or 20 documents per school), and 239 documents for oboe from 12 schools (19 or 20 documents per school). Each document was annotated for both explanatory and objective variables. 18 types of content and how much of it is described in the documents were explanatory variables. The usefulness of each document rated by amateur music players was an objective variable. More details are shown in Supplemental file[2].

4.2   Methods

Using the number of sentences meaning each of the 18 types of features (explanatory variables) and the usefulness (objective variables) of the documents, we identified features that significantly increased the usefulness of the documents based on multiple regression. We compared results from three different methods.

Centralized Analysis. All original explanatory and objective variables distributed to each school were centralized. A multiple regression was applied to the centralized data.

Local Analysis. Multiple regression was performed using only the local dataset. That is, it was performed within each local party without centralizing original research data distributed to each school.

Proposed Method. Our proposed method was used.

4.3   Results

Performance of the Proposed Method. Figure 2 shows (i) p-value and (ii) w of each of the 18 features estimated for each musical instrument by each of the three methods. The following 10 features with small p-values (≤ 0.05) were obtained using the proposed method (Fig. 2(i)): **Piano:** *fingering*; **Guitar:** *note value, playing method,* and *others*; **Oboe:** *tempo, dynamics, note value, playing method, tone,* and *breathing.*

All of these 10 features had small p-values (≤ 0.05) by the Centralized analysis (Fig. 2(i)). On the other hand, the Local analysis failed to estimate small p-values (≤ 0.05) for these 10 features. Moreover, the proposed method estimated correctly yielded small p-values (≤ 0.05) for all essential features with small p-values (≤ 0.05) calculated by the Centralized analysis except *fingering* of oboe.

---

[1] **piano:** https://zenodo.org/record/7753365, **guitar:** https://zenodo.org/record/7778923, and **oboe:** https://zenodo.org/record/4964997.

[2] https://zenodo.org/record/8354923.

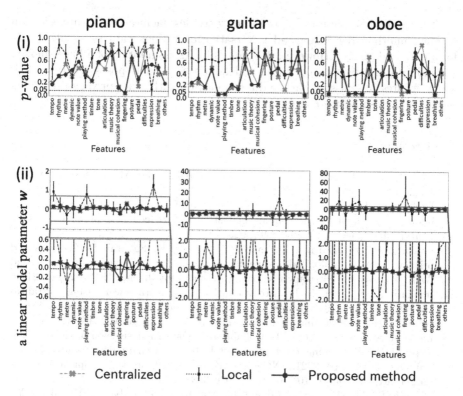

Fig. 2. Results of (i) *p*-value and (ii) ***w***. **Remark:** *The proposed method (blue) esti-mated almost the same p-values and **w** values for almost all features as the Centralized analysis (orange), while the Local analysis (black) did not.*

As shown in Fig. 2(ii), the proposed method estimated almost the same ***w*** values for all features as the Centralized analysis, while the Local analysis did not. It ensured consistent positive and negative values of ***w*** as the Centralized analysis for all features, while the Local analysis did not.

From these results, we confirmed that the proposed method successfully works on the privacy-preserving feature selection of distributed data without iterative cross-institutional communications.

5 Discussion and Conclusion

To achieve supervised feature selection while preserving privacy and avoiding cross-institutional data sharing or iterations, this study introduced a method that integrates transformed data rather than the original. The method identified the significance of *note value* and *playing method* sentences in feedback documents for oboe and guitar students. Notably, this is the first application of the non-model share-type federated learning framework to document formalization.

The method is useful for digital library studies, facilitating feature selection through multiple regression and is versatile for various data types like waveform data and images. However, it's limited by its assumption of a linear model. Extending it to generalized linear and nonlinear models poses a future challenge. Addressing missing data and a comparison with other privacy-preserving methods are also a future study.

References

1. Day, R.A., et al.: The origins of the scientific paper: the IMRAD format. J. Am. Med. Writers Assoc. **4**(2), 16–18 (1989)
2. Derham, C., Balloo, K., Winstone, N.: The focus, function and framing of feedback information: linguistic and content analysis of in-text feedback comments. Assess. Eval. High. Educ. **47**(6), 896–909 (2022)
3. Imakura, A., Bogdanova, A., Yamazoe, T., Omote, K., Sakurai, T.: Accuracy and privacy evaluations of collaborative data analysis. In: Proceedings of The Second AAAI Workshop on Privacy-Preserving Artificial Intelligence (PPAI-21) (2021)
4. Imakura, A., Sakurai, T.: Data collaboration analysis framework using centralization of individual intermediate representations for distributed data sets. ASCE-ASME J. Risk Uncertainty Eng. Syst. Part A: Civ. Eng. **6**, 04020018 (2020)
5. Imakura, A., Ye, X., Sakurai, T.: Collaborative Data Analysis: Non-model Sharing-Type Machine Learning for Distributed Data. In: Uehara, H., Yamaguchi, T., Bai, Q. (eds.) PKAW 2021. LNCS (LNAI), vol. 12280, pp. 14–29. Springer, Cham (2021). https://doi.org/10.1007/978-3-030-69886-7_2
6. Kagawa, R., Matsubara, M., Miyata, R., Matsuzaki, T., Baba, Y., Yamakata, Y.: An experimental framework for designing document structure for users' decision making-an empirical study of recipes. arXiv preprint arXiv:2305.01359 (2023)
7. Konečnỳ, J., McMahan, H.B., Yu, F.X., Richtarik, P., Suresh, A.T., Bacon, D.: Federated learning: strategies for improving communication efficiency. In: NIPS Workshop on Private Multi-Party Machine Learning (2016)
8. Li, X., Dowsley, R., De Cock, M.: Privacy-preserving feature selection with secure multiparty computation. In: International Conference on Machine Learning, pp. 6326–6336. PMLR (2021)
9. Matsubara, M., Kagawa, R., Hirano, T., Tsuji, I.: Analysis of the usefulness of critique documents on musical performance: toward a better instructional document format. In: Ke, H.-R., Lee, C.S., Sugiyama, K. (eds.) ICADL 2021. LNCS, vol. 13133, pp. 344–353. Springer, Cham (2021). https://doi.org/10.1007/978-3-030-91669-5_27
10. McMahan, H.B., Moore, E., Ramage, D., Hampson, S., et al.: Communication-efficient learning of deep networks from decentralized data. arXiv preprint, pp. arXiv:1602.05629 (2016)
11. Miyata, R.: Controlled Document Authoring in a Machine Translation Age. Taylor & Francis (2021)
12. Nguyen, H., Zhuang, D., Wu, P.Y., Chang, M.: AutoGAN-based dimension reduction for privacy preservation. Neurocomputing **384**, 94–103 (2020)

13. Reiter, E.,D.R.: Building Natural Language Generation Systems. Cambridge: Cambridge University Press (2000)
14. Weed, L.L.: Medical records, medical education, and patient care: the problem-oriented record as a basic tool. (No Title) (1971)
15. Wu, Z., Zheng, C., Xiejian, J., Zhou, Z., Xu, G., Chen, E.: An approach for the protection of users' book browsing preference privacy in a digital library. Electron. Libr. **36**(6), 1154–1166 (2018)

Information Seeking and Use

An Empirical Analysis of Newcomers' Contributions to Software-Engineering Conferences

Rand Alchokr[1]([✉]) [iD], Jacob Krüger[2] [iD], Yusra Shakeel[1,3] [iD], Gunter Saake[1] [iD], and Thomas Leich[4] [iD]

[1] Otto-von-Guericke University, Magdeburg, Germany
{rand.alchokr,shakeel,saake}@ovgu.de
[2] Eindhoven University of Technology, Eindhoven, The Netherlands
j.kruger@tue.nl
[3] Karlsruhe Institute of Technology, Karlsruhe, Germany
[4] Harz University and Metop GmbH, Wernigerode and Magdeburg, Germany
tleich@hs-harz.de

Abstract. Newcomer researchers play a key role in advancing research: They introduce new ideas and perspectives, have a high motivation, and can positively impact the performance of long-lasting teams. However, newcomers face obstacles when engaging in research—some of which they can overcome based on learning and mentoring (e.g., using research methods, scientific writing), but also potential biases of other researchers or unfair barriers (e.g., gate keeping, perceived expertise). In this paper, we report a study on newcomers' contributions to three major software-engineering conferences, and what these contributions may indicate regarding potential obstacles. Precisely, we investigated to what extent newcomers contributed to the main tracks of the highly reputable software-engineering conferences ASE, ESEC/FSE, and ICSE, analyzing a total of 4,620 papers and 7,337 authors. Furthermore, we investigated whether the reviewing model impacted the extent of newcomers' contributions, since all three conferences recently switched from single-blind to double-blind reviewing. The results indicate a decline in newcomer researchers contributing to the conferences, a trend that somewhat stabilized in recent years at a fortunately high level (i.e., more than 50% of authors for all conferences). Furthermore, for ICSE, we found an indicator that the changed reviewing model mitigated the declining trend, but this was not visible for the other conferences, and that more newcomers are involved in high-reputation papers.

Keywords: Software engineering · Newcomers · Peer review

1 Introduction

Newcomers are those researchers of a venue who got their first paper at that specific venue accepted (they may have papers at other venues before). They can initiate transitions within a research community since they can be the key drivers for novel research and modernization in that community. Newcomers

D. H. Goh et al. (Eds.): ICADL 2023, LNCS 14457, pp. 231–247, 2023.
https://doi.org/10.1007/978-981-99-8085-7_21

usually start with a high motivation that may inspire their peers, potentially broadening their knowledge and perspectives. For such and other reasons, it is essential to understand newcomers' involvement in the research community, analyze their contributions (i.e., papers), and try to reveal hidden obstacles regarding their involvement. Some previous studies found such obstacles [9,21], for instance, bias of experienced researchers against newcomers during single-blind peer reviewing. Identifying such obstacles in different research communities is highly important to derive appropriate countermeasures, and thus improve the quality of as well as fairness in research. Moreover, the obtained insights can be transferred to other communities, if required.

In this paper, we report a multi-case study in which we analyzed the contributions of newcomers to three major software-engineering conferences. Our idea is to study historical changes that may be caused by obstacles newcomers face, particularly with respect to bias during peer reviewing (all three conferences recently switched from single-blind to double-blind reviewing). Unfortunately, we can only study the contributions (i.e., accepted papers), since detailed submission data (i.e., author data of rejected papers) is not available. Still, we investigated a factor that has been rarely studied, but can bias a reviewer's decision [17]: the *reputation* in terms of papers published at these conferences and the academic age of the author (in terms of years the author published at any venue and not restricted to those we are studying). Studying these factors allows us to understand whether it has become more challenging for newcomers to publish papers on their own (i.e., without previous experience or established co-authors). Based on our data, we analyze whether there are any pattern changes in the contributions of newcomers, particularly after the switch to double-blind reviewing. For this purpose, we extracted all paper (4,620) and author (7,337 distinct) data for the main tracks until 2020 of the: 1) International Conference on Automated Software Engineering (ASE); 2) Joint European Software Engineering Conference and Symposium on the Foundations of Software Engineering (ESEC/FSE); and 3) International Conference on Software Engineering (ICSE). These conferences have a high reputation, which is why researchers of any academic age and reputation aim to publish there. The recent switches to double-blind reviewing (ASE 2016; ESEC/FSE 2017; ICSE 2018) make them ideal subjects to analyze the differences between experienced researchers and newcomers with respect to the reviewing model. We publish all of our data in an open-access repository.[1]

Since it is impossible to study rejected papers, we use proxy measures and must be careful with interpreting our results. Still, our findings reveal important insights concerning the contributions of newcomers at major software-engineering venues. For instance, the findings show a changing trend for at least one of the three conferences (i.e., ICSE) towards more opportunities for newcomers after adopting double-blind reviewing. We hope that our results motivate the software-engineering as well as other communities to investigate the obstacles for different groups of researchers in more detail and that they help implement appropriate countermeasures.

---

[1] https://doi.org/10.5281/zenodo.8369616.

2   Background and Related Work

Newcomers are new members of a research community. Specifically, they are new to a certain venue, for instance, authors who publish their first paper at a certain conference [23]. Typically, such newcomers have a high motivation that can inspire others, improve the work atmosphere, and introduce innovative ideas. So, it is essential to understand how they are involved in the research community. For instance, one experiment revealed the existence of explicit bias in the peer-reviewing process towards newcomers (or novices) by comparing the outcome of a review when the paper is written by a prominent author (a Nobel laureate) or by a relatively unknown author [13]. Furthermore, we identified a list of publishing impediments that hinder newcomers and juniors [2]. These indicate that new researchers may face challenges in contributing to a community, with studies like ours helping to reveal and tackle such challenges.

At software-engineering conferences, the program committees carry the responsibility of performing peer reviews, while also dealing with the rapid development of science, higher submission numbers, and the demand for increasing quality [28]. So, many program committees have evolved in recent years (e.g., becoming broader and larger), which directly impacts how new contributions are selected at established conferences. A peer review should be above all fair, meaning that any paper is "judged on the merit of one's ideas, not on the basis of academic rank, gender, place of work, publication record, and so on" [17]. Researchers in different communities are debating the pros and cons of reviewing models with respect to such properties, aiming to further improve the quality and fairness of reviews [4, 8, 10, 12, 25, 32]. To this end, the blinding of papers is an important and regularly discussed property of the reviewing models. Namely, some models reveal author and reviewer information to varying degrees to each other and the chairs [19, 27]. Typically, a review can be 1) un-blinded, which means that the reviewers and authors know each other; 2) single-blinded, which means that the reviewers know the authors, but not vice versa; or 3) double-blinded, which means that reviewers and authors are completely concealed [22, 24]. Other forms of blinding (e.g., triple-blind) enforce even stricter rules, but these three forms are the most relevant ones [11]. Researchers have found that various biases may occur within different reviewing models, particularly single-blind reviewing. This violates the overarching goal of an unbiased and fair review [14]. For instance, interviews with experts on the pros and cons of implementing double-blind reviewing at software-engineering venues showed that the challenges involved are mostly logistical, and are outnumbered by the benefits in terms of fairness for authors and their scientific progress [4]. More precisely, reviewers will judge a contribution more objectively based on its scientific value if the authors' names are concealed. Similarly, reports of different software-engineering conferences on introducing double-blind reviewing (e.g., ICSE'18 [6]), indicate the same perception among their reviewers. However, these insights are based on the personal perceptions of involved researchers, not actual data. In contrast, a study shows a significant increase in the acceptance rate of female first-authors in the Behavioral Ecology Journal after introducing double-blind reviewing [5]. Two studies to determine the acceptance rates under double-blind reviewing, particularly for junior researchers within the ACM SIGMOD community, show no differences between the acceptance rates under double-blind and double-blind reviewing for the first study [15]. However, the second study dug into more details and found that double-blind reviewing benefits the fairness towards newcomers [29].

Lastly, author characteristics that have the potential to influence reviewers' judgment have been collected [4,14]. We are concerned with three of the 17 characteristics mentioned: 1) reputation within the community, 2) number of prior publications, and 3) the number of (co-)authors. Such characteristics can be primary sources of bias during single-blind reviewing. Building on the aforementioned studies, we investigate these three characteristics and connect them to the academic age of researchers at three software-engineering conferences. So, we aim to elicit novel and complementary insights into how these characteristics and introducing double-blind reviewing impact newcomers.

3   Methodology

Next, we describe the goal and conduct of our multi-case study.

3.1   Goal and Research Questions

In this paper, we focus on potential reputation biases, implying that reviewers favor papers (under single-blind or un-blinded reviewing) with highly prestigious authors. Related studies indicate that authors, for instance, from prestigious affiliations, with high publication records, or more overall visibility receive less critical reviews, more grant funding, and are cited more often [14,17,18,26]. This implies that newcomers who do not have a high reputation may be negatively impacted if they do not collaborate with the right co-authors. With our multi-case study, we aim to understand how the contributions of newcomers at three major software-engineering conferences have evolved. The results of such an analysis can hint at certain biases and provide a good overall impression of newcomers' situation, even though proving actual biases is hardly possible, due to the anonymity implemented in most peer-reviewing models used (e.g., we cannot obtain data for rejected paper or the involved reviewers). Concretely, we defined two research questions (RQs) to guide our multi-case study:

RQ1 *How has the proportion of newcomers at the conferences evolved over time?*
RQ2 *Has adopting double-blind reviewing impacted newcomers?*

3.2   Data Collection

We display an overview of our entire data collection process in Fig. 1. Next, we explain the individual steps we employed.

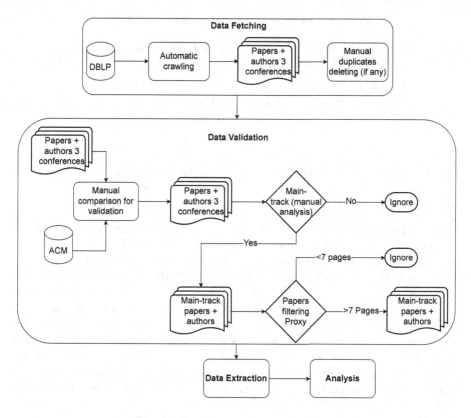

Fig. 1. Flowchart of our methodology.

Subject Conferences. We studied conferences since computer-science (and particularly software-engineering) research is generally more focused on those instead of journals compared to other communities [7,16,28]. Therefore, we analyzed the main tracks of three major software-engineering conferences (i.e., cases of our study): ASE, ESEC/FSE, and ICSE. We selected these conferences because they have a high reputation, indicating that newcomers and established researchers submit high-quality papers; and they recently introduced double-blind reviewing for their main tracks (ASE 2016; ESEC/FSE 2017; ICSE 2018). For our analysis, we considered all papers published since the first edition of each conference (ASE 1991; ESEC/FSE 1987; ICSE 1976) until 2020, the most recent year for which all data was available when we started our study.

Data Fetching. To collect our data, we automatically crawled *dblp*,[2] which provides bibliographic data structured (among others) by publication venues. We chose dblp because it covers all three conferences completely, is open-access, and has high data quality (e.g., distinguishing authors with the same names). Regarding ambiguities of author names, each author listed in dblp has a web-

---
[2] https://dblp.uni-trier.de/.

Table 1. Overview of the data in our final dataset.

Conference	Period	# Papers	# Authors	# Distinct Authors
ASE	1991–2020	1,068	3,737	2,482
ESEC/FSE	1987–2020	1,252	4,312	2,614
ICSE	1976–2020	2,300	7,434	4,380
Total		4,620	15,483	7,337

site that serves as an identifier to distinguish them from others with the same name. Even though this is likely not perfect, this property of dblp increases the robustness and reliability of our data.

Data Validation. To improve the comparability and quality of our data, we studied only main-track papers of all three conferences. For this purpose, we checked the extracted data manually and flagged each main-track paper (1 = main track, 0 = not main track). Then, we manually compared the labels to official information in the ACM Digital Library[3] to identify mislabeled papers; and matched the numbers of accepted papers to official statistics in the ACM Digital library (if available). We experienced that, particularly for older editions of the conferences, main-track papers are not clearly labeled across dblp and ACM. For this reason, we decided to enforce one more proxy criterion if the above validation was not conclusive: if we could not clearly label a paper as belonging to the main track, we excluded it if it comprised fewer than seven pages. Overall, our validation helped us to identify 4,620 main-track papers out of 11,106 papers in our initial dataset.

Data Extraction. For each paper, we extracted standard bibliographic data, namely its title, DOI, authors, publishing year, and page count. We used this data to validate the quality of our dataset and to investigate our research questions. For each author, we extracted their name, the identifier for their dblp website, as well as the first and last year they actively published at any venue (not only the three conferences we studied). We used a combination of paper (i.e., conference, year), author (i.e., start and end year), and combined (i.e., papers of an author) data to measure reputation and academic age (explained shortly). In Table 1, we summarize the properties of our final dataset. We extracted a total of 4,620 main-track papers that have been written by 15,483 authors. Note that this column (# Authors) includes authors multiple times if they wrote more than one paper. In contrast, we display the number of distinct authors who published at each conference's main track in the last column (7,337).

3.3 Data Analysis

Newcomers. Newcomers are researchers who are *new to a specific venue* [23]. So, for our study, we refer to a newcomer if the researcher did not publish a

---

[3] https://dl.acm.org/proceedings.

main-track paper before at that specific conference. We employ no restrictions on the academic age, meaning that a newcomer can be at any academic age. To get the number of newcomers at the main track of a conference (c) in a specific year (y), we used an SQL query that is reflected by the following relation:

$$Newcomer_{y,c} \notin Authors_{year<y,c} \tag{1}$$

This relation fetches all authors in a specific year and conference who have not previously published at that conference.

Academic Age. The academic age is the time span for which a researcher has actively published [3]. We used this property to calculate an author's reputation. Consequently, we calculated the academic age individually for each author and published paper ($Year_{paper}$) based on the authors' first publication ($Year_{firstPaper}$) as follows:

$$Age_{academic} = Year_{paper} - Year_{firstPaper} + 1 \tag{2}$$

To exemplify our calculation, consider an author who published their first paper in 2010 and another one in 2012, thus the author's academic age when publishing this particular paper was three years.

Author Reputation. For each author in our dataset, we measured the reputation for a respective time and paper. There could be various formulations to measure an author's reputation. Some could include the author's own characteristics and related bibliometrics, such as the h-index or citation count. However, as we fetch the data from dblp, which lacks these metrics, and as we concentrate on newcomers of the three conferences, we consider the following equation to assess the reputation of an author on a specific paper:

$$Reputation_{author} = MT * Age_{academic}/Max(Age_{academic}) \tag{3}$$

MT is the number of main-track papers the author has so far. Note that an author can have different reputation values for individual papers, depending on the academic age and previous productivity. We computed reputation based on the number of main-track papers an author published at *all three conferences* at that point in time. For comparability, we normalized the academic age based on the highest one in our dataset (54 years).

Paper Reputation. As paper reputation we refer to the sum of all reputations of its respective authors. We choose this measure to capture the co-authorships effect on newcomers and to investigate the level of collaboration newcomers have with other authors who have different reputation levels, resulting in high, average, or low reputation papers. In the previous Eq. 3, we calculate one author's reputation. Now, we judge all authors as a whole rather than by picking one isolated authors. We calculate each paper's reputation separately by accumulating its authors' reputations as follows:

$$Reputation_{paper} = \sum_{author=1}^{N} Reputation_{author} \tag{4}$$

So, the result of Eq. 3 reflects the reputation of a paper.

4   Results and Discussion

In the following, we report and discuss the results of our analysis structured based on our research questions. We managed and analyzed our data using the R statistics environment using different libraries [20]. Note that in most areas we focus on describing our actual data and observations instead of statistical tests, which can be misinterpreted and misleading [30, 31].

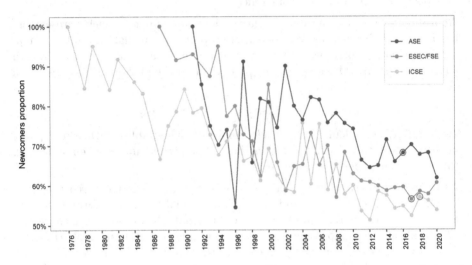

Fig. 2. Proportion of newcomers accepted each year at the three conferences.

4.1   RQ$_1$: Proportion of Newcomers

Measurements. To understand the extent of newcomers' involvement in the conferences over time (RQ$_1$), we measured for each conference individually the ratio of newcomers. We used Eq. 1 to compute each conference's newcomers. Note that we look at newcomers by considering the number of papers they are involved in regardless of their position on the paper. This measurement provides an intuition as to what degree a conference's community involves and accepts newcomers, even though we cannot consider the submission data.

Results. In Fig. 2, we display the proportion of authors who published their first main-track paper at each of the three conferences separately (i.e., newcomers). The red circles mark the years in which each conference adopted double-blind reviewing. As we would expect, the proportion of newcomers starts high and gets lower over time, somewhat stabilizing around 2010 for all three conferences. The high variance particularly in the earlier years may be caused by various reasons, such as the conference's locations, policy changes, or gained reputation. Interestingly, the proportion of newcomers never dropped below 50% for any conference. Note that the empty data points for the early phases of ICSE (no regular/annual editions) and ESEC/FSE (ESEC started 1987 bi-yearly before FSE in 1993) are not missing, but the conferences did not happen.

We support these observations with statistical analyses to illustrate the stability of newcomers' proportions after 2010 at the three conferences combined. To this end, we calculated the standard deviation and variance to capture how far from the normal and how spread out these proportions are:

1) First, we calculated the mean: we summed up all proportions of newcomers at the three conferences in all years and divided that by the number of conference occurrences (102), resulting in a mean of 70.76%.
2) Second, we calculated the standard deviation of 12.03%.

Table 2. Overview of the proportion of newcomers each year across the three conferences combined.

	Co(1999 & older)	Co(2000–2009)	Co(2010–2020)
+1STD (94.82%)			
STD1⇐	16	3	0
+2STD (82.79%)			
STD2⇐	15	11	2
Mean 70.76%			
STD3⇐	8	13	20
-1STD (58.69%)			
STD4⇐	1	3	11
-2STD (46.69%)			

Co = Number of conferences accruing at that period of time, STD = Standard Deviation

For the standard deviation, we used:

$$Standard\_Deviation = \sqrt{\frac{1}{N-1}\sum_{i=1}^{N}(x_i - \bar{x})^2} \tag{5}$$

with N being the total number of conference occurrences (102) and x the newcomers' proportions for each occurrence. Our results show which proportions are within one standard deviation of the mean, enabling us to establish a notion of what is typical, what is more than the typical proportion, and what is less. We illustrate the results in Table 2.

Observations. From Fig. 2 and Table 2, we can observe:

O_1 The overall trend is a decline in the proportion of newcomers.

O_2 Except for outliers, and particularly since around 2010, older conferences have a lower ratio of newcomers with accepted papers.

O_3 In contrast, the age of a conference apparently does not cause the proportions of newcomers to stabilize (i.e., they stabilize around 2010 for all conferences).

O_4 The introduction of double-blind reviewing seems to have a slight impact on the proportion of newcomers.

Discussion. Considering O_1, it is obvious that all conferences start with a 100% proportion of newcomers that then decreases. However, it is positive that more than 50% of the authors in each year published their first main-track paper at the corresponding conference. While the ongoing decline is concerning, combining this observation with the fact that more authors publish at the conference every year indicates that the absolute number of newcomers involved in each conference also increases, but more and more work seems to be driven by collaborations between experienced researchers [1, 33]. O_2 supports this finding, indicating that a conference's growing community naturally decreases the proportion of newcomers. Therefore, we would argue that over time it becomes harder for newcomers to get their papers accepted, which may be caused by higher quality standards or a shift in what is perceived as valuable research at each conference. Thus, newcomers first have to learn how to perform research on the expected quality. However, it may also be the result of gatekeeping and biases towards newcomers, since they lack a high reputation. Interestingly, these observations somewhat contradict O_3, which indicates that the proportions of newcomers stabilized at the same time for all conferences. Our results (cf. Table 2) show that most conferences held in the years from 2010 to 2020 had a proportion of newcomers that falls mostly within one standard deviation (12.07%) of the mean (20 conferences), whereas older conferences had more distributed or spread out proportions. This may indicate that the software-engineering community became more collaborative and international overall, or that the borders between its sub-communities and their conferences started to vanish (e.g., in terms of topics or perceived reputation). It may also indicate that the reputation and quality of the conferences could have a negative impact on the proportion of newcomers, since they may be discouraged to submit to highly selective venues. Still, we cannot explain this phenomenon in detail with our analysis, but argue that it deserves further research.

Finally, O_4 may indicate that introducing double-blind reviewing did only have a slight improvement on the proportion of newcomers. We can see that for ICSE and ASE the proportions of newcomers immediately increased; however, the proportion dropped low in 2020 for ASE (we shortly analyze this situation in more detail). Considering our previous observations, we actually argue that such stable or slightly increased proportions are already a success, since it means that the total number of newcomers increases.

4.2   RQ$_2$: Double-Blind Reviewing

Since our analysis, for now, was on an abstract level and did not consider other factors (e.g., the reputation of coauthors), we continue with a detailed analysis of the time period around the introduction of double-blind reviewing. More precisely, we analyze the period with the stabilized proportions (2010–2020) as well as the same number of years before and after introducing double-blind reviewing at each conference (2011–2020 for ASE, 2013–2020 for ESEC/FSE, 2015–2020 for ICSE). So, we aim to obtain a better understanding of the impact of double-blind reviewing. Therefore, we explore the conjecture that when the identity of the authors is revealed, their evaluation will be affected by the previous productivity.

Measurements. We measured for each conference

- the proportion of newcomers at the main tracks in an equal period of time before and after double-blind reviewing has been adopted; and
- the proportion of newcomers involved in papers with a specific overall reputation (i.e., considering the reputation of coauthors);

For the first measurement, we calculated the number of newcomers using Eq. 1 at each conference during the specified period of time and compared it to the number of all authors at the same period. Then, we measured the percent change and whether its an increase or decrease by comparing the old percentage value to the new value using Eq. 6 (*Val*: value, *abs*: absolute value):

$$Perc\_Change = (second\_Val - first\_Val)/abs(first\_Val) * 100\% \quad (6)$$

A positive percent change indicates an increase in the proportion of newcomers, whereas a negative change represents a decrease.

For the second measurement, we used Eq. 4 to elicit the reputation of each paper. We exported the results into separate spreadsheets to manually calculate the top and bottom 25% of papers in terms of their authors' reputation. Also, we elicited the proportion of newcomers each year within these two sub-groups of papers.

Results. In Fig. 3, we present an overview of the proportion of newcomers at each conference before and after double-blind reviewing has been adopted. We collected the data of each conference for a time span of 10, 8, and 6 years for ASE, ESEC/FSE, and ICSE, respectively. The three plots in Fig. 3 show the proportion of newcomers in main-track papers. We distinguish two categories: **a)** the distinct number of authors in the main tracks; and **b)** the number of author's papers (since an author can have more than one paper). We perform this detailed analysis to gain more knowledge on the proportion of papers by newcomers compared to the overall research community. The results indicate a slight increase in the proportion of newcomers after switching to double-blind reviewing. To investigate the reasons behind this in more detail, we checked the **paper's reputation** based on coauthors' **academic age**. First, using Eq. 4, we

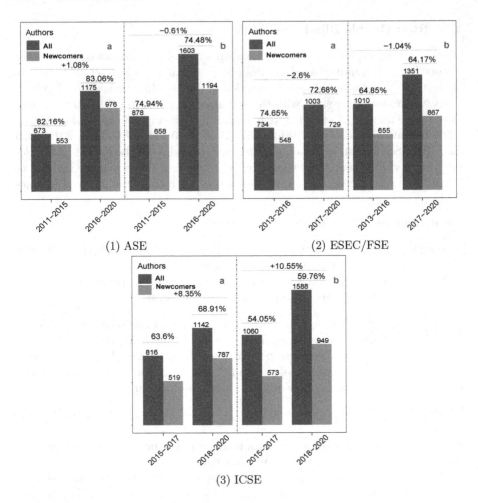

Fig. 3. Authors' contributions before and after double-blind reviewing has been introduced, distinguished by (a) the number of distinct authors and (b) number of paper contributions in the main tracks.

calculated each paper's reputation to study the bottom and top 25% of papers. Then, we analyzed the number of newcomers in each of these categories (top 25%, bottom 25%) to understand their involvement. We display the corresponding results in Fig. 4. As we can see, the proportion of newcomers involved in high-reputation papers increased after double-blind reviewing was introduced until a certain point, at which it declined again. Interestingly, newcomers seem to be underrepresented at the bottom and even more in high-reputation papers, but for ESEC/FSE and ICSE both groups became more similar after introducing double-blind reviewing.

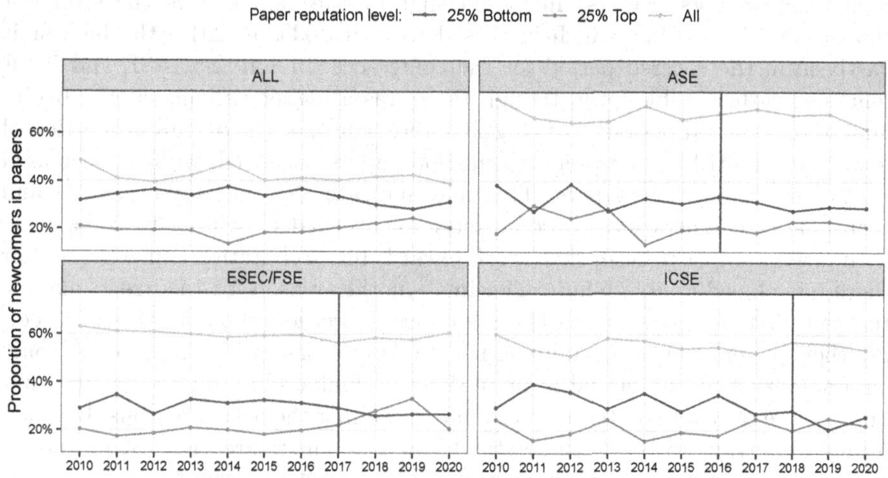

Fig. 4. Proportion of newcomers compared to papers' reputation.

Observations. From Fig. 3 and Fig. 4, we observe:

O_6 The proportion of newcomers after adopting double-blind reviewing at ICSE increased, whereas it remained stable at ASE, and decreased at ESEC/FSE.

O_7 More newcomers are involved in high-reputation papers after adopting double-blind reviewing.

Discussion. As we can see in Fig. 3 (O_6), the proportions of newcomers contributing to the conferences vary. Namely, ICSE exhibits the lowest proportion of newcomers contributing in either of the two time periods (before and after double-blind reviewing) compared to ESEC/FSE and ASE. Still, considering the percentage change of newcomers in the considered time periods, surprisingly, ICSE has the highest increase. Notably, ASE has a remarkably high proportion of newcomers, but it still exhibits a slight increase in the proportion of newcomers after introducing double-blind reviewing. Interestingly, the proportion dropped slightly for ESEC/FSE, which indicates that newcomers got fewer papers accepted under double-blind reviewing. These different trends may have various root causes that are subject to future work. For instance, the results for ICSE could indicate that it was particularly challenging for newcomers to publish there, but apparently only while author identities were revealed. This may be caused by potential biases towards newcomers, due to their missing reputation, or because of gatekeeping. In contrast, the ASE community apparently was always more inclusive, and thus the effect was smaller. However, we cannot explain the actual root causes for these trends, which require more analysis. To initiate research in that direction, we concentrated on investigating the potential impact of the academic age and reputation of coauthors. Regarding O_7, we can see in Fig. 4 that the number of newcomers in top publications (high reputation authors' papers) increased slightly. We can observe the strongest change for ESEC/FSE, which increased to up to 33% in 2019, the highest it has been in the covered period for the conference. In contrast, ASE and ICSE remained rather stable, even though there was a higher variance at the beginning of the covered periods. It is highly interesting that the overall proportion of newcomers contributing to high-reputation papers increased, while it decreased for bottom-reputation papers. This may indicate that more experienced and reputable researchers have become more encouraged or willing to collaborate with newcomers or to push their work towards high-reputation conferences after these introduced double-blind reviewing. Another reason for this trend may be the fact that newcomer researchers are less concerned about reviewers rejecting their papers simply for missing reputable authors—which may be not only an assumption but an actual positive effect of double-blind reviewing. Still, our findings are only a first step towards understanding the actual reasons. It is definitely important to better understand how newcomers are involved in papers, and whether potential biases of reviewers may transfer to coauthors.

5   Threats to Validity

Peer reviewing is a confidential process for outsiders who are not involved, meaning that we have no data on the number of submitted papers and their authors. Consequently, we can only use data from accepted papers, making our study vulnerable to survivorship bias. This also means that we cannot account properly for years with a lot of submissions of newcomers or with overall low acceptance rates, challenging our ability to derive insights on actual biases towards newcomers. To tackle such problems, we make the following reasonable assumption (considering the speed and growth of software-engineering research): If there is no bias towards newcomers, their prevalence in the accepted papers should stay stable to some degree from a certain point in time onwards. Building on this assumption, we derived measurements to reflect on the contributions of newcomers at the three conferences. Another threat to validity could be the metrics we used to compute the academic age and reputation, as these may be calculated differently by other researchers depending mainly on their perspective. Additionally, some parts of our data may be incorrect. As we described, we extracted our data from dblp, which is a reliable data source. However, throughout the conferences' editions, the labeling of sessions and papers changed and during our validation, we found several mismatches between dblp and the ACM Digital Library. Since we focus most of our study on a more recent period, we argue that this threat is marginal for our actual findings—seeing that the data quality for more recent years is considerably better and more consistent.

Lastly, we focused our analysis on three software-engineering conferences. However, there are numerous other venues that researchers submit to, and that can impact a researcher's reputation the same way as these three conferences. So, our findings may be skewed toward a certain part of the software-engineering community. Still, we involved a large dataset in our analysis and derived several measurements to investigate our research objectives in a reliable way. Since other researchers may derive different findings, we make our dataset and analysis scripts publicly available.

6   Conclusion

In this paper, we reported a multi-case study on the involvement of newcomers in software-engineering research. For this purpose, we studied their contributions to three of the most prestigious software-engineering conferences, ICSE, ESEC/FSE, and ASE. Through analyzing the data of 4,620 main-track papers and their 7,337 authors, we were able to measure the involvement of newcomers, who have not previously published papers at the conferences' main tracks. From our data, we observed a decline in newcomers' overall proportion as authors at the conferences. Moreover, we analyzed the impact of double-blind reviewing, which was recently adopted by these venues, on newcomers. Even though only slightly, double-blind reviewing appears to have a positive impact on newcomers, mitigating or even reversing the observed decline to some extent. More precisely, our results indicate an increase in the proportion of newcomers at ESEC/FSE and ICSE, particularly in high-reputation papers after introducing double-blind reviewing.

As discussed before, our findings are only a first step in a comprehensive research topic concerning newcomer researchers. Further studies are required to explain our findings in more detail, potentially confirming or refuting some of them. A particular problem is the complexity of peer reviewing and potential biases that may occur in the process, involving numerous human factors that may be hard to impossible to study. So, for future research, we already started to expand our study with a more comprehensive dataset including additional years, mainly 2021, 2022, and later 2023. We believe this will provide a clearer look into double-blind reviewing and its impact. Furthermore, we plan to investigate other obstacles newcomers face and concentrate on different review models in more detail. Ideally, we could use actual submission data. Finally, approaching community members via survey research and experiments to corroborate our interpretations of the data with community perceptions, concerns, and experiences is an important direction to shed light on the research community.

References

1. Alchokr, R., Krüger, J., Shakeel, Y., Saake, G., Leich, T.: A closer look into collaborative publishing at software-engineering conferences. In: Silvello, G., et al. (eds.) TPDL 2022. LNCS, vol. 13541. Springer, Cham (2022). https://doi.org/10.1007/978-3-031-16802-4_38
2. Alchokr, R., Krüger, J., Shakeel, Y., Saake, G., Leich, T.: Peer-reviewing and submission dynamics around top software-engineering venues: a juniors' perspective. In: International Conference on Evaluation and Assessment in Software Engineering (EASE). ACM (2022)

3. Alchokr, R., Krüger, J., Shakeel, Y., Saake, G., Leich, T.: On academic age aspect and discovering the golden age in software engineering. In: International Conference on Cooperative and Human Aspects of Software Engineering (CHASE). ACM/IEEE (2022)

4. Bacchelli, A., Beller, M.: Double-Blind review in software engineering venues: the community's perspective. In: International Conference on Software Engineering (ICSE). IEEE (2017)

5. Budden, A.E., Tregenza, T., Aarssen, L.W., Koricheva, J., Leimu, R., Lortie, C.J.: Double-blind review favours increased representation of female authors. Trends Ecol. Evol. **23**(1), 4–6 (2008)

6. Chechik, M., Harman, M., Zimmerman, T., Crnkovic, I.: ICSE 2018 PC Chairs Report (2018)

7. Chen, J., Konstan, J.A.: Conference paper selectivity and impact. Commun. ACM **53**(6), 79–83 (2010)

8. Cox, A.R., Montgomerie, R.: The cases for and against double-blind reviews. PeerJ **7**, e6702 (2019)

9. Diem, A., Wolter, S.: The use of bibliometrics to measure research performance in education sciences. Res. High. Educ. **54**(1), 86–114 (2013)

10. Fox, C.W., Paine, C.E.T.: Gender differences in peer review outcomes and manuscript impact at six journals of ecology and evolution. Ecol. Evol. **9**(6), 3599–3619 (2019)

11. Görögh, E., Ross-Hellauer, T.: Guidelines for open peer review implementation (2019)

12. Helmer, M., Schottdorf, M., Neef, A., Battaglia, D.: Gender bias in scholarly peer review. eLife **6**, e21718 (2017)

13. Huber, J., Inoua, S., Kerschbamer, R., König-Kersting, C., Palan, S., Smith, V.L.: Nobel and novice: author prominence affects peer review. Proc. Natl. Acad. Sci. **119**(41) (2022)

14. Lee, C.J., Sugimoto, C.R., Zhang, G., Cronin, B.: Bias in peer review. J. Am. Soc. Inf. Sci. Technol. **64**(1), 2–17 (2012)

15. Madden, S., DeWitt, D.: Impact of double-blind reviewing on SIGMOD publication rates. SIGMOD Rec. **35**, 29–32 (2006)

16. Meyer, B., Choppy, C., Staunstrup, J., van Leeuwen, J.: Viewpoint research evaluation for computer science. ACM **52**(4), 31–34 (2009)

17. Peters, D.P., Ceci, S.J.: Peer-Review practices of psychological journals: the fate of published articles, submitted again. Behav. Brain Sci. **5**(2), 187–195 (1982)

18. Petersen, A.M., et al.: Reputation and impact in academic careers. Proc. Natl. Acad. Sci. **111**(43), 15316–15321 (2014)

19. Prechelt, L., Graziotin, D., Fernández, D.M.: A community's perspective on the status and future of peer review in software engineering. information and software technology. J. Comput. Graph. Stat. **95**, 75–85 (2018)

20. R Core Team: R: A Language and Environment for Statistical Computing (2018). https://www.R-project.org

21. Rørstad, K., Aksnes, D.: Publication rate expressed by age, gender and academic position - a large-scale analysis of Norwegian academic staff. J. Informetr. **9**(2), 317–333 (2015)

22. Saini, J.R., Sonthalia, N.R., Dodiya, K.A.: Identification of author and reviewer from single and double blind paper. Int. J. Comput. Inf. Eng. **8**(2), 442–446 (2014)

23. Seeber, M., Bacchelli, A.: Does single blind peer review hinder newcomers? Scientometrics **113**(1), 567–585 (2017). https://doi.org/10.1007/s11192-017-2264-7

24. Snodgrass, R.: Single-versus double-blind reviewing: an analysis of the literature. ACM Sigmod Rec. **35**(3), 8–21 (2006)
25. Soldani, J., Kuhrmann, M., Pfahl, D.: Pains and gains of peer-reviewing in software engineering. ACM SIGSOFT Softw. Eng. Notes **45**, 12–13 (2020)
26. Tahamtan, I., Safipour Afshar, A., Ahamdzadeh, K.: Factors affecting number of citations: a comprehensive review of the literature. Scientometrics **107**(3), 1195–1225 (2016). https://doi.org/10.1007/s11192-016-1889-2
27. Tomkins, A., Zhang, M., Heavlin, W.D.: Reviewer bias in single-versus double-blind peer review. Proc. Natl. Acad. Sci. **114**, 12708–12713 (2017)
28. Tran, H., Cabanac, G., Hubert, G.: Expert suggestion for conference program committees. In: 2017 11th International Conference on Research Challenges in Information Science (RCIS) (2017)
29. Tung, A.K.H.: Impact of double blind reviewing on SIGMOD publication: a more detail analysis. SIGMOD Rec. **35**, 6–7 (2006)
30. Wasserstein, R.L., Lazar, N.A.: The ASA statement on p-Values: context, process, and purpose. Am. Stat. **70**, 129–133 (2016)
31. Wasserstein, R.L., Schirm, A.L., Lazar, N.A.: Moving to a world beyond "p < 0.05". Am. Stat. **73**, 1–19 (2019)
32. Weller, A.C.: Editorial peer review for electronic journals: current issues and emerging models. J. Am. Soc. Inf. Sci. **51**, 1328–1333 (2000)
33. Wren, J.D., Kozak, K.Z., Johnson, K.R., Deakyne, S.J., Schilling, L.M., Dellavalle, R.P.: The write position. EMBO Rep. **8**(11) (2007)

Examining Digital Humanities Tools Used by Taiwanese Historians with the Digital Visitors and Residents Framework

Tien-I. Tsai[✉] iD

National Taiwan University, Taipei 10617, Taiwan
titsai@ntu.edu.tw

Abstract. This poster examines digital humanities tools used by historians in research contexts based on existing literature, and examines five top-used tools with the digital visitors and residents framework that helps describe digital tools in two dimensions—visitor/resident and personal/institutional. Through delineating literature on humanities scholars' information practices throughout the decades, changes in historians' information behavior were identified. Top-five digital cultural heritage collections and tools used by historians were selected for case analysis based on the tools used in papers presented at a renowned digital humanities conference in Taiwan—the DADH. The digital visitors and residents framework was then used to examine the tools used by historians. The findings indicate that all three types of tools were institutional-level tools. Among which, primary source databases either encourage users to be visitors or residents; GIS/map systems tend to be a tool for visitors, and text analysis platforms tend to be a tool for residents. The poster concludes with implications for information professionals who support humanities scholars in research contexts.

Keywords: Digital Humanities · Historians · Humanities Scholars · Digital Visitors and Residents

1 Introduction

The field of humanities as a discipline is broad and diverse by nature. Among humanities scholars, historians rely on a wide variety of sources of information during their research processes. Examining digital humanities tools that support historians can help better understand how information professionals and database providers could support humanities research.

1.1 Information Use Behavior of Humanities Scholars

The information practices of humanities scholars may change as technology develops. Although humanities scholars seem to share some similar information behavior characteristics, such as relying on books, personal collections, and primary cultural heritage collections to contribute to knowledge construction [1–3], existing literature throughout decades identified changes in humanities scholars' preferences for using digital tools. Research in the 1990s tended to emphasize the important role of library print materials, including primary sources, and discuss scholars may not be capable of utilizing databases or may not believe databases meet their needs [4] other studies focus on issues regarding the use of print versus digital sources [2].

In the first decade of the 2000s, digital cultural heritage collections have been playing an important role in humanities scholars' information practices in research contexts [5]. While historians continue to value information discovered through reading book reviews, browsing for comprehensive searches, and print materials, some changes in the advent of electronic resources have increased historians' use of catalogs and indexes in their efforts to identify appropriate primary and secondary sources of information [6]. In the latter half of the 2000s, research tended to focus even more on how humanities scholars use databases and digital resources [7–11].

In the last decade (the 2010s), research continued discussing digital tools and resources used by humanities scholars from different perspectives. For instance, Given and Willison found humanities scholars use a wide variety of digital tools in their digital research practices such as databases, repositories, search engines, software, and online services (e.g., communication tools, online storage services, text analysis tools, digital content creation tools, digital organization tools) [12]. Chen found that while books were still an important source, electronic resources also played an important role throughout the process of research [13].

While most research in different decades discussed how humanities scholars use digital databases or other technological tools, research in the 1990s tended to highlight the role of the library and library instruction as well as discuss why scholars tend not to utilize digital resources. Although research after the 2000s still emphasized how humanities scholars value print materials and primary sources, the research tended to depict how humanities scholars accept new tools at the same time. This phenomenon implies that it is worthwhile to further examine how digital resources and digital humanities tools may help scholars engage with the digital information environment.

1.2 The Framework of Digital Visitors and Residents

White and Le Cornu use the metaphor of digital visitors and residents to depict users who use an online tool without building profiles online versus users who see online tools as a place to leave traces and interact with others [14]. The framework of digital visitors and residents (V & R) was further developed by the University of Oxford, OCLC (Online Computer Library Center) Research, and the University of North Carolina, Charlotte; the framework was used to study learners at different stages, including secondary school students, undergraduate students, graduate students, and scholars and was later developed and expanded to study learners in various contexts [15]. This framework was developed as an operationalized visual elicitation approach and an online application to study how individuals engage with the digital information environment. The findings also provide practical implications [16].

While this framework was originally designed to prompt participants to position the digital tools they used in specific contexts onto a two-dimensional space—a continuum of modes in terms of visitor/resident and personal/institutional, since it provides two spectrums to depict information sources and tools used by individuals, we can apply the framework to discuss any digital tool based on given information without eliciting specific personal accounts. Various applications and modifications can be found in the literature [17–19].

As Engelsmann et al. stated, it could be difficult to map all the behaviors to the framework, but the framework provides a solid foundation for in-depth discussions [19]. The main purpose of this poster is to discuss how digital humanities tools may help scholars organize information in their digital humanities research. Instead of eliciting humanities scholars' first-person accounts, this poster examines digital humanities tools used by scholars, as identified in the literature, with the digital visitors and residents framework.

2   Case Selection Procedure

The International Conference of Digital Archives and Digital Humanities (DADH) is a renowned digital humanities conference that has been held in Taiwan annually since 2009. In order to discuss commonly used digital cultural heritage collections and tools used by historians in Taiwan, the tools used multiple times in DADH papers presented by authors with affiliation at a department of history at a university or research institute were selected. According to the lists generated by the research centers for humanities at National Taiwan University and the Center for Digital Cultures at Academia Sinica, there are more than 50 digital tools. However, after excluding tools that no longer exist or can be accessed, only five tools were used multiple times by historians in the DADH proceedings.

The five digital humanities tools that have been identified for the case analysis include Taiwan History Digital Library (THDL), National History Database of Academia Historica, Taiwan Centurial Historical Map, Digital Humanities Research Platform, and Docusky Collaboration Platform. Information about the tools was gathered and consolidated from the official websites of these tools, the research centers for digital humanities and digital cultures, as well as the Humanities and Social Science Databases Catalog (HUSSCat). The main functions and features are presented in Table 1. The digital visitors and residents framework was then used to analyze the above tools. In the current context, digital humanities tools are all institutional tools, so the following discussions will focus on the visitors and residents continuum.

3   Findings and Discussion

3.1   Examining Digital Humanities Tools with Digital Visitors and Residents Framework

The above five tools used by historians in Taiwan reflect most of the digital humanities tools. Based on the nature of the digital humanities tools, we can identify three major types: (1) primary source databases such as THDL and National History Database, (2) GIS/map systems such as Taiwan Centurial Historical Map, and (3) text analysis platforms such as Digital Humanities Research Platform and Docusky Collaboration Platform.

Table 1. Features of digital humanities tools.

Tool	Creator (Institution)	Browse	Search	Text Analysis	Data Visualization	GIS	Collaboration	Visitor (V)/ Resident (R)
Taiwan History Digital Library (THDL)	National Taiwan University	v	v		v			R
National History Database of Academia Historica	Academia Historica	v	v					V/R
Taiwan Centurial Historical Map	Center for GIS, Academia Sinica	v	v		v	v		V
Digital Humanities Research Platform	Center for Digital Cultures (ASCDC), Academia Sinica	v	v	v	v	v	v	R
Docusky Collaboration Platform	National Taiwan University	v	v	v	v	v	v	V/R

Note: V means the user can only use the tool as a visitor; R means only as a resident; V/R means the users can use it either way

Figure 1 presents the digital humanities tools in the two-dimensional space based on the framework of digital visitors and residents. Regardless of the types of digital humanities tools, almost all digital humanities tools inherit a highly research-oriented purpose, and thus are mostly institutional on the y-axis of the spectrum in the framework of digital visitors and residents. Therefore, all three major types of digital humanities tools appear below the x-axis of the framework.

When further examining the top-used tools along with the tools listed on the Research Center for Digital Humanities at National Taiwan University and the Center for Digital Cultures at Academia Sinica, we learn that most are primary source databases. Among the three major types, primary source databases consist of a wide variety of materials. Therefore, the database design differs from not providing functions that help users become residents to those providing logins and collaboration to support users becoming a resident. The users may be able to choose whether they prefer to use the tool as a visitor or a resident.

While some of the text analysis platforms may provide options for users to try the platform with sample texts so that they do not need to leave too many traces on the platform, if scholars use the tool for research purposes, it is very likely that the user has to be a resident to upload the texts and do analysis. On the other hand, the GIS/map system in the current poster does not provide logins, and the users can only search for

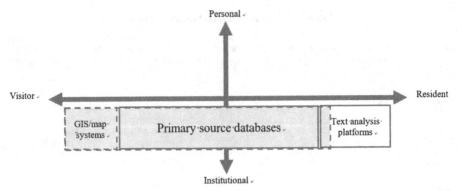

Fig. 1. Mapping Digital Humanities Tools with Digital Visitors and Residents Framework. Note: The shaded GIS/map system area represents the general GIS/map systems. The smaller GIS/Map systems on the left represent the tool introduced in this poster.

the maps. Although the system also provides external GIS tools, the GIS/map system itself tends to let users remain visitors.

Overall, GIS/map systems are typically designed for visitors to browse and use historical maps; text analysis platforms are typically designed for residents to save data and leave personal information. Primary source databases provide different functions with diverse purposes, and thus, can be designed either for visitors or residents.

3.2 The Current Use of the Digital Visitors and Residents Framework and Its Implications

Instead of using the digital visitors and residents framework to explore users' behavior, this poster attempts to apply the digital visitors and residents framework in a different way. Instead of eliciting first-account personal experiences from historians, the poster uses the digital visitors and residents framework at a meta-level by analyzing the tools used by historians from the researcher's perspective rather than from historians' personal accounts. While this meta-level discussion provides a different perspective on understanding information practices, this type of discussion cannot replace first-person accounts. Users' first-person accounts and meta-level discussions about the tools used by users are both important. That is to say, the framework of digital visitors and residents may not only help us understand scholars who use the tools but also help us contemplate the design of the tools.

Additionally, it is essential to develop digital humanities tools that accommodate different needs in terms of fulfilling both digital visitors and residents. There have already been a wide variety of primary-source databases developed in Taiwan. It is important to learn whether or not scholars need a wider variety of GIS/map systems and sophisticated text analysis platforms for different purposes. Maintaining primary source databases is not an easy task. The Research Center for Digital Humanities at National Taiwan University and the Center for Digital Cultures at Academia Sinica have been taking great responsibility for fulfilling sustainable development goals for the databases and have been developing new digital humanities tools. Building and sharing best practices in maintaining established tools and developing new tools are critical to the field of digital humanities.

4 Conclusion

Information behavior changes as technology develops, especially when it comes to digital humanities-related contexts. Through reviewing relevant literature, we can see the changes. While most characteristics of humanities scholars exhibited in their information seeking behavior remain true, humanities scholars have become more aware and use various digital tools.

This poster examines the digital humanities tools used by historians at the DADH conference using the digital visitors and residents framework. Three major types of digital humanities have been identified, including (1) primary source databases such as THDL and National History Database, (2) GIS/map systems such as Taiwan Centurial Historical Map, and (3) text analysis platforms such as Digital Humanities Research Platform and Docusky Collaboration Platform. While primary source databases tend to either encourage users to be visitors or residents, GIS/map systems tend to be a tool for visitors. Text analysis platforms tend to be a tool for residents.

Future research may use the digital visitors and residents framework to explore the information practices of historians and other humanities scholars beyond Taiwanese contexts. Based on the current discussion, a survey and follow-up interviews based on the framework can be used to solicit first-person accounts from scholars.

In order to achieve a sustainable future of digital humanities, it is important to keep track of the changing practices in the field through learning the information practices of scholars and the tools they use through longitudinal research. This poster starts the dialogue and foresees that future endeavors from different stakeholders can continue collaborating to maintain sustainability in digital humanities research through understanding the changing patterns of humanities scholars and the tools they use.

Acknowledgment. This work was supported by the Ministry of Education of Taiwan (112L9A001). The author would like to thank Drs. Ying-Hsang Liu and Koraljka Golub for providing comments for an earlier version of this manuscript.

References

1. Watson-Boone, R.: The information needs and habits of humanities scholars. Ref. Q. **34**(2), 203–215 (1994)
2. Chang, S.-J.L.: Digital libraries for humanities scholars: an empirical study of users' information behaviors. J. Libr. Inf. Stud. **14**, 33–48 (1999)
3. Al Shboul, M.K., Abrizah, A.: Information needs: developing personas of humanities scholars. J. Acad. Librariansh. **40**(5), 500–509 (2014)
4. Cheng, L.-M.: Information-seeking behavior of the humanists. J. Educ. Media Libr. Sci. **29**(4), 388–410 (1992)
5. Wu, M.-D., Huang, W.-C., Chen, S.-C.: Humanities scholars and databases for ancient Chinese books. J. Libr. Inf. Stud. **4**, 1–15 (2006)

6. Dalton, M.S., Charnigo, L.: Historians and their information sources. Coll. Res. Libr. **65**(5), 400–425 (2004)
7. Baruchson-Arbib, S., Bronstein, J.: Humanists as information users in the digital age: the case of Jewish studies scholars in Israel. J. Am. Soc. Inform. Sci. Technol. **58**(14), 2269–2279 (2007)
8. Buchanan, G., Cunningham, S.J., Blandford, A., Rimmer, J., Warwick, C.: Information seeking by humanities scholars. In: Rauber, A., Stavros Christodoulakis, A., Tjoa, M. (eds.) ECDL 2005. LNCS, vol. 3652, pp. 218–229. Springer, Heidelberg (2005). https://doi.org/10.1007/11551362_20
9. Rimmer, J., Warwick, C., Blandford, A., Gow, J., Buchanan, G.: An examination of the physical and the digital qualities of humanities research. Inf. Process. Manage. **44**(3), 1374–1392 (2008)
10. Sukovic, S.: Convergent flows: Humanities scholars and their interactions with electronic texts. Libr. Q. **78**(3), 263–284 (2008)
11. Williams, P., Stevenson, I., Nicholas, D., Watkinson, A., Rowlands, I.: The role and future of the monograph in arts and humanities research. ASLIB Proc. **61**(1), 67–82 (2009)
12. Given, L.M., Willson, R.: Information technology and the humanities scholar: documenting digital research practices. J. Am. Soc. Inf. Sci. **69**(6), 807–819 (2018)
13. Chen, S.C.: Exploring the use of electronic resources by humanities scholars during the research process. Electron. Libr. **37**(2), 240–254 (2019)
14. White, D. S., Cornu, A. L.: Visitors and residents: a new typology for online engagement. First Monday **16**(9) (2011)
15. OCLC Research: Digital Visitors and Residents: What Motivates Engagement with the Digital Information Environment. https://www.oclc.org/research/areas/user-studies/vandr.html
16. Connaway, L.S., Kitzie, V., Hood, E.M., Harvey, W.: The many faces of digital visitors & residents: Facets of online engagement. OH: OCLC Research (2017)
17. Wright, F., White, D., Hirst, T., Cann, A.: Visitors and residents: mapping student attitudes to academic use of social networks. Learn. Media Technol. **39**(1), 126–141 (2014)
18. Jones, D., Albion, P.R., Heffernan, A.: Mapping the digital practices of teacher educators: implications for teacher education in changing digital landscapes. In: Chamblee, G., Langub, L. (eds.) Proceedings of Society for Information Technology & Teacher Education International Conference, pp. 2878–2886 (2016)
19. Engelsmann, H.C., Greifeneder, E., Lauridsen, N.D., Nielsen, A.G.: Validation of the visitor and resident framework in an e-book setting. Inf. Res. **19**(2) (2014). http://InformationR.net/ir/19-2/paper623.html

Gen Z Transitions to University: A Preliminary Study on Everyday Information-Seeking Practices

Chei Sian Lee[1(✉)], Rachel Qing Yu Yeo[1], Shutian Zhang[2], Dion Hoe-Lian Goh[1], Rebecca P. Ang[3], and Betsy Ng[3]

[1] Wee Kim Wee School of Communication and Information,
Nanyang Technological University, Singapore, Singapore
{leecs,ashlgoh}@ntu.edu.sg, YEOQ0010@e.ntu.edu.sg
[2] Wuhan University, Wuhan, China
shutianzh@whu.edu.cn
[3] National Institute of Education, Nanyang Technological University, Singapore, Singapore
{rebecca.ang,betsy.ng}@nie.edu.sg

Abstract. Generation Zs (Gen Zs), characterized as digital natives, approach their university journey with distinct information practices shaped by their reliance on everyday digital technologies. Yet, studies on how Gen Zs navigate the transition to university remain scant. This exploratory study aims to understand how everyday information-seeking practices help Gen Zs during this transition. We conducted focus group discussions with 42 Gen Z undergraduates from both STEM (Science, Technology, Engineering, and Mathematics) and non-STEM academic disciplines to understand the challenges they faced and everyday information-seeking practices they adopted when transitioning to university. Our results reveal that participants utilized information searching-as-learning and serendipitous searching on platforms such as YouTube, Reddit, and Telegram during the transitional phase. Implications of our work are discussed.

Keywords: Transition · Everyday Information-Seeking Practices · Digital Technologies · Generation Z

1 Introduction

The generation known as Generation Z (Gen Z), born between 1995 to 2012, are currently embarking on their university journey [1]. As digital natives, Gen Zs' information behaviors and practices are distinct due to their daily access to and use of digital and social media [2] which we refer to as everyday digital technologies. Gen Zs leverage these technologies as a central part of their everyday life [3]. As such, their associated everyday information practices will differ from the earlier generations (e.g., millennials and Gen X). Everyday information practices refer to a composition of specific information actions such as recognizing information sources during information seeking and evaluating accuracy and quality during information use [4]. Specifically, despite the importance of everyday information-seeking practices [5], research on its roles during the transition to university is still limited.

© The Author(s), under exclusive license to Springer Nature Singapore Pte Ltd. 2023
D. H. Goh et al. (Eds.): ICADL 2023, LNCS 14457, pp. 255–262, 2023.
https://doi.org/10.1007/978-981-99-8085-7_23

Transition is a passage from one life phase to another [6] and occurs in all stages of life. Among all the life transitions, students' transition to university has garnered more attention because a successful transition into higher education is critical as it is a predictor of positive outcomes (e.g., learning success, and better well-being) [7, 8]. Notably, it is also one of the most challenging phases and the challenges include academic pressure, environmental changes, socializing anxiety, financial difficulties, and mental health issues [9–13]. Students in transition are likely to have specific information needs hand require the ability to navigate the vast amount of information on various digital technological platforms.

Research has indicated that the information environment plays a key mediating role in transitions [14, 15]. Several studies have reported that individuals strengthen their information literacy through various information practices, thereby better adapting to the new environment and its discourse [16, 17]. On the other hand, the lack of information or associated information practices can exacerbate transition challenges and make it more difficult for students to integrate into their new environments [18].

The COVID-19 pandemic has also brought new challenges to Gen Zs, disrupting their social and academic lives [19, 20] and increasing their reliance on digital and social media. Unsurprisingly, their learning and information needs as well as information-seeking practices are also impacted [21]. Thus, research must shed light on the everyday information-seeking practices of the digital technologies Gen Zs use during their transition to university.

While research has been conducted on transitions in higher education, prior studies have focused primarily on learning processes [22], students' emotions and identity development in transition [7] or antecedents to a successful transition [23]. Studies on how Gen Zs navigate the transition to university focusing on everyday information-seeking practices remain scant.

This exploratory research addresses this gap and aims to understand the roles played by everyday seeking information practices when Gen Zs transition to the university. Guided by the notion of everyday information- practices [4], focus group discussions (FGDs) were conducted to understand Gen Z's transition challenges, their everyday information practices, and the everyday digital technologies and the information sources used during the transition to university. Furthermore, the information-seeking practices are likely to differ across disciplines. Hence, differentiating the information-seeking practices required for STEM (Science, Technology, Engineering and Mathematics) versus non-STEM majors during the transition will be needed. This research poses the following research questions (RQ): *What are the information-seeking practices students employ on digital media to aid their transition to university? What are the differences between STEM students versus non-STEM students?*

2   Methodology

A total of 42 Gen Z undergraduates were recruited from a large local university in Singapore. Of these, 43% of participants were male (n = 18) and 57% (n = 24) were female. Thirty participants were from Year 1 and Year 2 in their respective Bachelor's programs while the rest were in Year 3 and 4 (n = 12). Participants' ages ranged from 21 to 26 years. The participants were paid SGD$10 for their participation. Table 1 shows the demographic profiles of participants.

Eight FGDS were conducted, with 5 to 6 participants per session. Each FGD lasted approximately 45 to 60 min. Questions in the FGDs included feelings about transitioning to university, the specific challenges that participants faced during the transition process, how they overcame their challenges using online and offline resources, and how this experience has impacted their subsequent transitions. Thematic analysis was conducted on the data collected. The study was approved by the first author's Institutional Review Board.

Table 1. Demographic of participants

Demographic Profiles	Count (Percentages)
Gender	
Male	18 (42.86)
Female	24 (57.14)
Year of Study	
Year 1 & 2	30 (71.42)
Year 3 & 4	12 (38.57)
Academic Discipline	
STEM Degree	17 (40.48)
Non-STEM Degree	25 (59.52)
Total	42

3 Results and Discussion

Our results show that terms such as "exciting" yet "stressful", "overwhelming", and "confusing" were used to describe transitions to university, indicating the mixed emotions experienced (see Figs. 1 and 2). Participants from non-STEM courses reportedly felt the transition process to be more "stressful" and "unpredictable" as compared to their peers in STEM-related courses indicating subtle differences in the emotions experienced by students from different disciplines. Participants also employed a wide range of digital platforms to cope with their transition challenges (e.g., Reddit, Google, YouTube, Telegram). Some participants also revealed that they relied on their social networks (family, friends) to obtain social support indicating the relevance of social networking and messaging services during this transitional phase.

Two major themes emerged in our thematic analysis as everyday information seeking practices. They were **information searching-as-learning**, referring to information seeking as a learning process [24] and **serendipitous searching**, referring to the unintentional discovery of information while engaged in an information activity [25]. Further, two main

Fig. 1. Terms Used by STEM Students

Fig. 2. Terms Used by non-STEM students.

transition issues were identified, and they are **academic** and **non-academic** in nature. Specifically, academic issues pertain to the transition challenges that relate to learning in the university (e.g. coursework) while the non-academic issues are other transition challenges including social networks and financial matters.

Information searching-as-learning was found to be more commonly utilized by students facing **academic issues** during the transition. Specifically, we found that their searches usually involved clarifying theoretical understanding or acquiring complementary learning materials and resources. Interestingly, our results showed that STEM students relied on the YouTube platform as part of the information searching-as-learning strategies. For instance, a Year 2 Male Aerospace Engineering student remarked "*I found like a lot of YouTube channels that go through the content, just like engineering YouTube channels are like aligned very similarly with the syllabus.*"

Non-STEM students on the other hand utilized Reddit as a platform to search for credible content. For instance, a Year 2, Male, Business student shared, "*I'll look through the comments to see the ones..that make the most sense most. Reddit also has this function where you can upvote or downvote, so the most upvoted one generally is more credible.*" Our results indicated information searching-as-learning was useful for academic-related matters as participants explained that search outcomes generated useful new ideas to complement formal learning [24, 26].

We did not find any differences between the STEM and non-STEM students in the information-seeking practices for **non-academic transition issues**. Here searching without a planned goal was more commonly observed, aligning with **serendipitous searching**. They employed serendipitous searching to see what they might possibly find online. Reddit, as well as Telegram were more commonly used platforms for such tasks.

Notably, the participants exhibited a "fear of missing out (FOMO)" mindset, expressing concerns about potentially missing any valuable information. This led to serendipitous searching. For instance, a female, English Linguistics student shared that "*I will look at everything on the Reddit [University] page, as there might be things that I didn't think of but might be useful for me*". In addition to serving as an information source, Reddit was also recognized as a platform that provided emotional connection and support during the university transition. Another Year 3 student elaborated, "*I actually went on Reddit to see if there were others who felt the same. When I read other's experiences, I felt like, oh, I kind of relate to them even though they are anonymous. So, it feels like I was not going through my troubles alone*". Our observations revealed that many students encountered difficulties in both academic and non-academic matters (e.g. loneliness) during the COVID-19 pandemic when they were in transition. In particular, the ability to search for emotional information and seek support played a vital role in contributing to their overall well-being.

Non-academic problems faced by participants can be widely attributed to a change in learning and physical environment (new campus), changing social identity (student status), and other disruptive factors (e.g. COVID-19 pandemic). In particular, amongst students who transitioned to the university during the COVID-19 pandemic, the difficulty of making long-lasting and meaningful friendships with their classmates or course mates was a commonly faced problem. In response, the students searched for online social connections and extensively used messaging platforms such as Telegram to join new groups and make friends within the community, often uncovering new information they did not expect to find. A Year 3 student explained, "*For my batch, we made a telegram group and I think in the first few weeks, everyone spammed with questions ....all those kind of stuff. So I thought that was pretty helpful.*" Another Year 2 student agreed, "*I think it's quite hard to make friends on Reddit, so most of the time, it's just Telegram.*" Hence, the **serendipitous searching strategy** for non-academic concerns can also be associated with social connection maintenance as students realize the importance of having continuous connections with their peers to prepare for future life transitions.

4   Conclusion

This preliminary study uncovered information searching-as-learning and serendipitous searching as everyday information-seeking practices of Gen Zs during the transition to university. We found that YouTube and Reddit were cited as platforms that Gen Zs regularly used for searching and learning to address academic concerns during university transition. We also found that STEM and non-STEM students had different information-seeking practices. STEM students rely on digital sources (e.g., YouTube) to search for learning content to complement formal learning. Non-STEM students, however, tend to search on Reddit by filtering and verifying the content. Furthermore, Telegram was found to be a viable platform for building personal and professional connections in school and beyond, addressing non-academic concerns during the transition to university. Notably, there were no significant differences between the information-seeking practices of STEM and non-STEM students for addressing non-academic challenges during the transition to university.

Aligned with prior research on transitions, this study confirmed that information plays a crucial role in the university transition process for Gen Zs [14]. Our investigation has important research implications. In particular, the insights gained from our findings will serve as a foundational understanding to anticipate future transition challenges of Gen Zs (e.g., workplace transition). Furthermore, a more nuanced analysis of a specific information practice or combination of practices that Gen Zs employ and their effects on a specific transition challenge (e.g., academic-related) or other life transitions could be studied to contextualize everyday information practices in future research.

In terms of practical implications, the insights uncovered are helpful to higher education institutions and educators in developing transition programs or toolkits for Gen Zs. Additionally, by differentiating the STEM and non-STEM students, this study delved deeper into the information needs and the required information resources for students in different disciplines during the transition. Consequently, the findings have significant implications for the advancement of digital libraries, aiming to cater to diverse academic fields and offer tailored support [27].

We acknowledge that the relatively small number of participants is a limitation in the generalizability of this research. Furthermore, most of our participants underwent the university transition amidst the COVID-19 pandemic, which added complexity to the process [21, 28]. Future work may want to explore the effects of individual differences among Gen Zs in managing the transition to higher education [29]. Nevertheless, the present study enhances our understanding of Gen Z's information-seeking practices during their transitions to university. Notably, the sample size is consistent with prior research, and hence the qualitative results can serve as a useful starting point to shed light on the everyday information practices of Gen Zs in navigating the transition to higher education.

Acknowledgment. This work was supported by NTU College of Humanities, Arts, and Social Sciences Research Grant #022351–00001.

References

1. Pichler, S., Kohli, C., Granitz, N.: DITTO for Gen Z: a framework for leveraging the uniqueness of the new generation. Bus. Horiz. **64**, 599–610 (2021). https://doi.org/10.1016/j.bushor.2021.02.021
2. Blocksidge, K., Primeau, H.: Adapting and evolving: generation Z's information beliefs. J. Acad. Librariansh. **49**, 102686 (2023). https://doi.org/10.1016/j.acalib.2023.102686
3. Anderson, M.: Teens, social media and technology (2018). https://www.pewresearch.org/internet/2018/05/31/teens-social-media-technology-2018/. Accessed 13 Sep 2023
4. Savolainen, R., Thomson, L.: Assessing the theoretical potential of an expanded model for everyday information practices. J. Am. Soc. Inf. Sci. **73**, 511–527 (2022). https://doi.org/10.1002/asi.24589
5. Savolainen, R.: Everyday Information Practices: A Social Phenomenological Perspective. The Scarecrow Press, Lanham, MD (2008)
6. Chick, N., Meleis, A.I.: Transitions: a nursing concern. In: Nursing Research Methodology, pp. 237–257. CO: Aspen Publication, Boulder (1986)

7. Coertjens, L., Brahm, T., Trautwein, C., Lindblom-Ylänne, S.: Students' transition into higher education from an international perspective. High. Educ. **73**, 357–369 (2017). https://doi.org/10.1007/s10734-016-0092-y

8. Thomas, L., Vines, J., Briggs, P.: Exploring digital support for the student transition to university through questionable concepts. Pers. Ubiquit. Comput. **26**, 79–92 (2022). https://doi.org/10.1007/s00779-021-01570-z

9. Briggs, A.R.J., Clark, J., Hall, I.: Building bridges: understanding student transition to university. Qual. High. Educ. **18**, 3–21 (2012). https://doi.org/10.1080/13538322.2011.614468

10. Piel, M.H.: Challenges in the transition to higher education for foster care youth. New Dir. Commun. Coll. **2018**, 21–28 (2018). https://doi.org/10.1002/cc.20288

11. Nelavai, N., Ramesh, S.: An insight into the challenges faced by first year engineering students: poor foundational knowledge. Procedia Comput. Sci. **172**, 823–830 (2020). https://doi.org/10.1016/j.procs.2020.05.118

12. Cage, E., Jones, E., Ryan, G., Hughes, G., Spanner, L.: Student mental health and transitions into, through and out of university: student and staff perspectives. J. Furth. High. Educ. **45**, 1076–1089 (2021). https://doi.org/10.1080/0309877X.2021.1875203

13. Gosai, S.S., Tuibeqa, A.T., Prasad, A.: Exploring the transition challenges of first-year college of business students in Fiji. Int. J. Educ. Res. **117**, 102131 (2023). https://doi.org/10.1016/j.ijer.2022.102131

14. Schumacher, K.L., Meleis, A.I.: Transitions: a central concept in nursing. Image J. Nurs. Sch. **26**, 119–127 (1994). https://doi.org/10.1111/j.1547-5069.1994.tb00929.x

15. Willson, R.: Transitions theory and liminality in information behaviour research: applying new theories to examine the transition to early career academic. J. Documentation **75**, 838–856 (2019). https://doi.org/10.1108/JD-12-2018-0207

16. Lloyd, A.: Learning to put out the red stuff: becoming information literate through discursive practice. Libr. Q. Inf. Commun. Policy **77**, 181–198 (2007). https://doi.org/10.1086/517844

17. Lloyd, A.: Informing practice: information experiences of ambulance officers in training and on-road practice. J. Documentation **65**, 396–419 (2009). https://doi.org/10.1108/00220410910952401

18. Bronstein, J.: A transitional approach to the study of the information behavior of domestic migrant workers: a narrative inquiry. J. Documentation **75**, 314–333 (2018). https://doi.org/10.1108/JD-07-2018-0112

19. Shirish, A., Chandra, S., Srivastava, S.C.: Switching to online learning during COVID-19: theorizing the role of IT mindfulness and techno eustress for facilitating productivity and creativity in student learning. Int. J. Inf. Manage. **61**, 102394 (2021). https://doi.org/10.1016/j.ijinfomgt.2021.102394

20. Sharaievska, I., et al.: "Messy transitions": students' perspectives on the impacts of the COVID-19 pandemic on higher education. High. Educ. (Dordr). 1–18 (2022)https://doi.org/10.1007/s10734-022-00843-7

21. Ma, L., Lee, C.S.: A motivational design approach to integrate MOOCs in traditional classrooms. In: Ishita, E., Pang, N.L.S., Zhou, L. (eds.) Digital Libraries at Times of Massive Societal Transition: 22nd International Conference on Asia-Pacific Digital Libraries, ICADL 2020, Kyoto, Japan, November 30 – December 1, 2020, Proceedings, pp. 187–195. Springer, Cham (2020). https://doi.org/10.1007/978-3-030-64452-9_16

22. Gale, T., Parker, S.: Navigating change: a typology of student transition in higher education. Stud. High. Educ. **39**(5), 734–753 (2014). https://doi.org/10.1080/03075079.2012.721351

23. Ramos, A., Venneman, S., Donche, V., Verschueren, K.: Factors facilitating and hindering the transition to higher education for high-ability students. J. Coll. Stud. Dev. **63**, 315–332 (2022). https://doi.org/10.1353/csd.2022.0026

24. Rieh, S.Y., Collins-Thompson, K., Hansen, P., Lee, H.-J.: Towards searching as a learning process: a review of current perspectives and future directions. J. Inf. Sci. **42**, 19–34 (2016). https://doi.org/10.1177/0165551515615841

25. Conrad, L.Y., Moeller, P.D.: Search, serendipity, and the researcher experience. Ser. Libr. **72**, 190–193 (2017). https://doi.org/10.1080/0361526X.2017.1292744

26. Lee, C.S., Osop, H., Goh, D.H.-L., Kelni, G.: Making sense of comments on YouTube educational videos: a self-directed learning perspective. Online Inf. Rev. **41**, 611–625 (2017). https://doi.org/10.1108/OIR-09-2016-0274

27. Wu, Q., Lee, C.S., Goh, D.H.-L.: Understanding user-generated questions in social Q&A: a goal-framing approach. J. Am. Soc. Inf. Sci. **74**, 990–1009 (2023). https://doi.org/10.1002/asi.24770

28. Lim, K.K., Lee, C.S.: Investigating learner's online learning behavioral changes during the COVID-19 pandemic. Proc Assoc Inf Sci Technol. **58**, 777–779 (2021). https://doi.org/10.1002/pra2.559

29. Lee, C.S., Goh, D.H.-L., Chua, A.Y.K., Luyt, B.: Choosing communication portfolios to accomplish tasks: the effects of individual differences. Comput. Educ. **53**, 1167–1176 (2009). https://doi.org/10.1016/j.compedu.2009.05.024

Review of In-App Nudges Towards User Decision Behavior: A Topic Modeling Approach

Kok Khiang Lim[✉] and Chei Sian Lee

Wee Kim Wee School of Communication and Information, Nanyang Technological University, Singapore, Singapore
w200004@e.ntu.edu.sg, leecs@ntu.edu.sg

Abstract. The prevalence of mobile applications meant that individuals made more decisions online in their daily lives for a wide range of activities, and sometimes poor decisions were made. This study aims to characterize user decision behavior from the influence of in-app nudges to make positive decisions within the digital environment. We extracted 1,368,941 user online reviews from two major online mobile application stores, Apple App Store and Google Play Store, using a Python script. Topic modeling analysis was conducted. Our analysis uncovered nine latent topics that represented user decision behavior. The results show that five topics indicated positive user decision behavior and had higher ratings. In comparison, the remaining four topics were related to poorer app functionality and implementation that could not effectively support decision-making, leading to lower ratings. These findings emphasize the significance of nudge research in a digital environment and highlight the broad applicability of in-app nudges across various contexts. Moreover, the design and implementation of nudges play a crucial role in determining their effectiveness.

Keywords: Nudge · Decision Behavior · Topic Modeling

1 Introduction

The increasing digitization of our environment means that more decisions are made online when individuals visit websites or use mobile applications (or apps) for private and professional daily activities [1]. These decisions (e.g., purchase or lifestyle decisions), be it easy or difficult, essential or unimportant, sometimes turn out to be wrong calls [2]. Studies have attributed poor decision-making to irrational behavior that contradicts user intentions, even knowing that the consequences were likely detrimental [2]. The decision-making process is affected by various cognitive biases and heuristics [3], resulting in suboptimal decision-making and costly errors [4]. For example, deciding whether to avoid a dieting routine or adhere to the plan [5].

The concept of nudging, specifically digital nudges, has increasingly gained relevance and has been introduced in the digital environment (e.g., online web, apps, and wearable devices) as in-app nudges that subtly influence user decision behavior in a non-intrusive nor coercive manner towards desirable outcomes [6, 7]. Nudge techniques, such

D. H. Goh et al. (Eds.): ICADL 2023, LNCS 14457, pp. 263–269, 2023.
https://doi.org/10.1007/978-981-99-8085-7_24

as visual cues, default options, or reminders, are some commonly used tools to support decision-making within a digital environment while at the same time preserving the freedom of choice, have demonstrated their effectiveness in intervening decision behavior [2, 8]. For instance, a mobile app that nudges students of upcoming deadlines has demonstrated its effectiveness in reducing missed assignments [9]. Many past studies were conducted to understand the effects and factors of apps on users' behaviors and engagement e.g., [10, 11], or to review how nudges had influenced users' behaviors e.g., [12, 13]. However, few studies have examined users' perspectives and responses to these in-app nudges, given that their purposes were to affect and support users in their everyday activities. With the growing significance of nudging in the digital landscape [7], it becomes crucial to comprehend the users' perspective to advance our understanding of designing nudge-based applications. Hence, this study aims to address the gap by analyzing user online reviews posted on two major online app stores (Apple App Store and Google Play Store) to characterize user decision behavior from the influence of in-app nudging. Structural Topic Modeling (STM), a variation of topic modeling that has the advantage of incorporating metadata (e.g., date and ratings) as covariates in the analysis of the dataset [14], is used to perform the analysis.

2 Methods and Results

The analysis of user decision behavior was conducted in three steps, (1) search for relevant apps, (2) collect user online reviews from the identified apps, and (3) perform topic modeling analysis. First, search terms related to or reflected nudge techniques, such as "reminder", "notification", "schedule", "plan", "manage", "task", "to do", "goal", and "motivate" were developed to search in the app stores. A total of 341 unique apps were found, and their names, descriptions, and metadata, such as ratings, published date, genre, and app hyperlink, were downloaded automatically using a Python script. The downloaded data was manually validated for inclusion in the second step if the app's (1) title, description, and/or screenshots were related and developed with nudge techniques; (2) was available in the English language; and (3) was available for download in the U.S. app stores. In contrast, the app was excluded if (1) it was not relevant to this study, such as fitness trainer, transactional activities (e.g., financial investment), or health monitoring (e.g., heart rate monitoring); (2) no user review in the apps store; or (3) the number of reviews was less than 5. The validation concluded 207 apps for inclusion in the analysis (134 apps were excluded due to 31 not being relevant to this study, 49 had no reviews, and 54 had reviews less than 5).

Second, user online reviews were collected based on the identified apps in step one with a second Python script. A total of 1,368,941 reviews from eleven genres between 2019 and 2022 were compiled and pre-processed for analysis by removing duplications, stopwords, numbers and punctuations, and lemmatizing the remaining words. The pre-processing further filtered down the dataset to 987,779 reviews, in which the genre, for example, *Productivity*, had the highest number of reviews ($n = 693,116$), followed by *Health & Fitness* ($n = 209,334$), *Tools* ($n = 35,286$) and *Personalization* ($n = 10,112$). The last step, STM on R script, was performed on the user reviews with app ratings as the covariates. The STM analysis determined that nine topics were optimal to represent the dataset based on the three metrics assessment: held-out likelihood estimation, semantic coherence, and residuals measure [15, 16]. Further, the STM was fine-tuned to obtain the best model fit using the exclusivity and semantic coherence measures [15, 16]. The authors manually assigned the uncovered topics from STM with succinct phrases to describe and summarize the theme of the topic's keywords and associated reviews.

Table 1 shows the nine topics and their associated keywords and topic proportions. Five out of nine topics (4, 5, 6, 7, and 8, with a total topic proportion of 58.9%) show user behaviors were positively affected by the in-app nudges, with topic 7 having the highest topic proportion (12.8%) on nudging decision-making. The users generally rated these five topics higher (see Fig. 1), indicating positive user decision behavior. In contrast, the remaining 41.1% of the four topics were related to poor app functionality (topics 1, 2, and 9) and paid apps (topic 3). These topics were rated lower by the users (see Fig. 1).

Table 1. Results and extracted reviews from STM analysis.

Topic	Topic Label	Topic Proportion	Top ten keywords	Example of extracted reviews
1	Unreliable app	0.128	update, phone, can't, now, try, new, back, sync, get, doesn't	"App will not open. I enter my login info… still does not work…"
2	Cumbersome app	0.095	task, add, calendar, event, date, widget, feature, show, create, able	"Very inconvenient… why would anyone want that feature?…"
3	Non freemium app	0.091	free, pay, use, version, premium, now, year, feature, get, money	"They mentioned absolutely nothing to me about the app costing…"
4	Keeping track of behavior	0.096	keep, track, food, calorie, help, daily, lose, weight, goal, eat	"Great program for tracking caloric intake, caloric output, exercises and daily activity…"
5	Supporting daily tasks	0.103	note, list, need, like, opinion, make, color, save, different, perfect	"Excellent. Able to set reminder on my note… My to go when I need to remember thing or write a list of any sort…"

(continued)

Table 1. (*continued*)

Topic	Topic Label	Topic Proportion	Top ten keywords	Example of extracted reviews
6	Essential part of daily activity	0.091	work, thank, reminder, nice, notification, amaze, star, give, alarm	"good app for set reminder. If you have problem you forget that your work have slip out of your mind set a reminder…"
7	User-friendly app	0.187	good, use, love, great, easy, simple, useful, helpful, year, far	"Easy to use, straightforward, and helpful for remind me to do little thing that I may not otherwise think about…"
8	Affecting changes in habits	0.115	much, really, help, get, make, recommend, lot, like, habit, life	"this app really helps me focus in class and when I am studying/doing homework! …"
9	Ambivalence towards the app	0.097	time, day, thing, want, like, see, set, every, need, start	"I like that it reminds me but I don't like that it expects me to drink 12 oz of water in one sitting…"

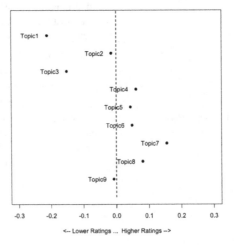

Fig. 1. Topical contrast between lower and higher ratings.

3   Discussion and Conclusion

This study is one of the recent studies investigating user decision behavior arising from the influence of in-app nudging from the perspective of user online reviews. Overall, the topic modeling approach uncovered nine latent topics from eleven genres of mobile apps to represent the themes in the user online reviews dataset. The results (58.9% from five topics) show strong evidence that users were receptive to in-app nudging and benefitted from the influence to change their behaviors. These positive outcomes could be attributed to the apps' ability to deliver the intended nudges (such as tracking and reminding) and the ease of app usage, which is aligned with the concept of nudges, such that appropriate change or design of the environment could affect positive influence on user decision-making accordingly.

In contrast, topics 1, 2, 3, and 9 revealed that a poorly designed digital environment, badly implemented apps, or even getting users to pay for the apps could negatively affect user behavior and their attainment of desired outcomes. Poor app functionality impedes the delivery of nudges and provokes user frustration and rejection of apps (topics 1 and 2). Similarly, paid app (topic 3) was also rated lower, and invoking users' resentment. Besides, unnecessary repeated or overused nudges (topic 9) could backfire or even reverse the intended behavior if the apps do not appropriately consider the context of their application, even if the apps were designed as intended [17]. In conclusion, this study furthers the nudge research from the perspective of user decision behavior, such that their interaction with the digital environment plays a critical role in determining the extent of nudge effectiveness, as well as the use of in-app nudges to guide decision-making is applicable in many contexts.

The findings of this study should be read with consideration of two key limitations. First, the apps included in this study were limited to the U.S. Apple App Store and Google Play Store. This could have excluded apps that were only published in specific app store regions like Asia Pacific or Europe. As such, the findings could not be generalized across other cultural, societal norms and populations, especially when nudge effectiveness depends on the situational context [18]. Nonetheless, it provided a snapshot of a dynamic app market and a preliminary insight that could sufficiently represent the validity of in-app nudging influence on user decision behaviors. Future studies may elucidate apps from other regional stores to compare their differences. Second, the full in-app nudging functionality and quality should have been evaluated in detail, as suggested in past literature reviews [19, 20]. Instead, this study investigated the app using topic modeling analysis on users' online reviews collected through data mining. Past studies have shown that online reviews, a form of user-generated content that was reflective of users' experiences, were deemed credible evaluation data points as they were contributed voluntarily by users in a non-intrusive and unrestrictive manner to share their thoughts, opinions, and consumption experiences [21, 22]. Nonetheless, we plan to investigate the nudging functionality in-depth to provide granular insights into user behavior and habitual changes.

References

1. Mirsch, T., Lehrer, C., Jung, R.: Digital nudging: altering user behavior in digital environments. In: der 13 Internationalen Tagung Wirtschaftsinformatik (WI 2017), pp. 634–648, St. Gallen, Switzerland (2017)
2. Thaler, R.H., Sunstein, C.R.: Nudge: Improving Decisions about Health, Wealth, and Happiness. Yale University Press (2008)
3. Tversky, A., Kahneman, D.: Judgment under uncertainty: heuristics and biases. Science **185**, 1124–1131 (1974). https://doi.org/10.1126/science.185.4157.1124
4. Milkman, K.L., Chugh, D., Bazerman, M.H.: How can decision making be improved? Perspect. Psychol. Sci. **4**, 379–383 (2009). https://doi.org/10.1111/j.1745-6924.2009.01142.x
5. Li, R., et al.: The nudge strategies for weight loss in adults with obesity and overweight: a systematic review and meta-analysis. Health Policy **125**, 1527–1535 (2021). https://doi.org/10.1016/j.healthpol.2021.10.010
6. Okeke, F., Sobolev, M., Estrin, D.: Towards a framework for mobile behavior change research. In: Proceedings of the Technology, Mind, and Society, pp. 27. Association for Computing Machinery, Washington, DC, USA (2018)
7. Weinmann, M., Schneider, C., vom Brocke, J.: Digital nudging. Bus. Inf. Syst. Eng. **58**, 433–436 (2016). https://doi.org/10.2139/ssrn.2708250
8. Schneider, C., Weinmann, M., vom Brocke, J.: Digital nudging: guiding online user choices through interface design. Commun. ACM **61**, 67–73 (2018). https://doi.org/10.1145/3213765
9. Motz, B., Mallon, M., Quick, J.: Automated educative nudges to reduce missed assignments in college. IEEE Trans. Learn. Technol. **14**, 189–200 (2021). https://doi.org/10.1109/TLT.2021.3064613
10. Auf, H., Dagman, J., Renström, S., Chaplin, J.: Gamification and nudging techniques for improving user engagement in mental health and well-being apps. Proc. Des. Soc. **1**, 1647–1656 (2021). https://doi.org/10.1017/pds.2021.426
11. Valle, C.G., Nezami, B.T., Tate, D.F.: Designing in-app messages to nudge behavior change: lessons learned from a weight management app for young adults. Organ. Behav. Hum. Decis. Process. **161**, 95–101 (2020). https://doi.org/10.1016/j.obhdp.2020.10.004
12. Lim, K.K., Lee, C.S.: Nudging learning behaviour: a systematic review. Proc. Assoc. Inf. Sci. Technol. **59**, 744–746 (2022). https://doi.org/10.1002/pra2.712
13. Forberger, S., Reisch, L., Kampfmann, T., Zeeb, H.: Nudging to move: a scoping review of the use of choice architecture interventions to promote physical activity in the general population. Int. J. Behav. Nutr. Phys. Act. **16**, 1–14 (2019). https://doi.org/10.1186/s12966-019-0844-z
14. Lim, K.K., Lee, C.S.: Sharing is learning: using topic modelling to understand online comments shared by learners. In: Stephanidis, C., Antona, M., Ntoa, S. (eds.) HCII 2021. CCIS, vol. 1421, pp. 91–101. Springer, Cham (2021). https://doi.org/10.1007/978-3-030-78645-8_12
15. Naab, T.K., Sehl, A.: Studies of user-generated content: a systematic review. Journalism **18**, 1256–1273 (2016). https://doi.org/10.1177/1464884916673557
16. Roberts, M.E., Stewart, B.M., Tingley, D., Airoldi, E.M.: The structural topic model and applied social science. In: Neural Information Processing Society (2013)
17. Hummel, D., Maedche, A.: How effective is nudging? a quantitative review on the effect sizes and limits of empirical nudging studies. J. Behav. Exp. Econ. **80**, 47–58 (2019). https://doi.org/10.1016/j.socec.2019.03.005
18. Kosters, M., Van der Heijden, J.: From mechanism to virtue: evaluating nudge theory. Evaluation **21**, 276–291 (2015). https://doi.org/10.1177/1356389015590218
19. Stoyanov, S.R., Hides, L., Kavanagh, D.J., Zelenko, O., Tjondronegoro, D., Mani, M.: Mobile app rating scale: a new tool for assessing the quality of health mobile apps. JMIR mHealth uHealth **3**, e27 (2015). https://doi.org/10.2196/mhealth.3422

20. Terhorst, Y., et al.: Validation of the mobile application rating scale (MARS). PLoS ONE **15**, e0241480 (2020). https://doi.org/10.1371/journal.pone.0241480
21. Yoo, K.H., Gretzel, U.: What motivates consumers to write online travel reviews? Inf. Technol. Tourism **10**, 283–295 (2008). https://doi.org/10.3727/109830508788403114
22. Tong, Y., Wang, X., Tan, C.H., Teo, H.H.: An empirical study of information contribution to online feedback systems: a motivation perspective. Inf. Manage. **50**, 562–570 (2013). https://doi.org/10.1016/j.im.2013.02.009

Author Index

Printed in the United States
by Baker & Taylor Publisher Services